2014

Praise for the Book

'Sanjay Jha's *2014: The Great Unravelling* is a gripping book that captures the drama of the 2014 general election and the politics that preceded and followed. A party spokesman's first-hand account gives it an unusual authenticity. An insightful and interesting read.'

—S.Y. Quraishi

'From the Teflon quality of Prime Minister Modi's politics to the Congress's failure to provide a counter-narrative, Sanjay Jha's book is an insider's account at the great churn in how elections are fought, won and lost. If you are interested in politics, do read this book. Agree or disagree, but read it as a student and observer of the contemporary India.'

—Barkha Dutt

'Sanjay Jha takes an incisive look at a decisive period in the country's polity. He may have been apolitical "insider" but spares no one in his thoughtful and objective analysis of contemporary politics.'

—Rajdeep Sardesai

'From such books as *The Great Unravelling* rise the call for action, for change. Read it. It will make you think about where we are heading. And it's not a pretty place.'

—Pritish Nandy

'Jha's introspective, readable and well-intentioned book should be made compulsory reading in the Congress party.'

—Pavan K. Varma

'Most of the coverage that [Sanjay] Jha's *The Great Unravelling* has received has focussed solely on Sanjay's criticisms of the Congress. But there is also an excellent dissection of the state of today's India and the current regime. It's a very good book. A must-read.'

—Vir Sanghvi

'A masterpiece on contemporary politics of India written by someone who is the master of his craft.'

—*Greater Kashmir*

'As a helpless witness to Congress's second crushing defeat at the hands of the BJP, Jha painstakingly chronicles the journey of the saffron party from its failures to becoming a champion of muscular nationalism.'

—*Deccan Herald*

'Jha's book effectively puts to rest that he could be in league with the grand old party's bitter political rival, the BJP.'

—*The Hindu*

'It is a devastating insider's account of the party that should be doing so much more.'

—*The Telegraph*

'Will *The Great Unravelling* help the Congress regain its lost vision and emit a ray of hope for Jha and several Indians for the revival of Mahatma Gandhi's India? If not, permanent blindness shall be the only outcome for the Congress Party with no modern Sanjaya by its side, unlike Mahabharata's King Dhritarashtra.'

—*Free Press Journal*

'Jha structures his narrative like a seasoned batsman would pace a good inning. *The Great Unravelling* is an earnest treatise from a former Congress party member asking questions that remain unanswered.'

—*The New Indian Express*

2014

THE GREAT UNRAVELLING

SANJAY JHA

HarperCollins *Publishers* India

First published in 2020

This edition published by HarperCollins *Publishers* 2024
4th Floor, Tower A, Building No. 10, DLF Cyber City,
DLF Phase II, Gurugram, Haryana – 122002
www.harpercollins.co.in

2 4 6 8 10 9 7 5 3 1

P-ISBN: 978-93-5699-762-2
E-ISBN: 978-93-5699-775-2

Typeset in 11/14.7 Sabon LT Std at
Manipal Technologies Limited, Manipal

Printed and bound at
Nutech Print Services - India

This book is printed on FSC® certified paper
which ensures responsible forest management.

This book is dedicated to my mom and dad from whom I learnt, and never forgot, that all it takes is unconditional love

'No one is born hating another person because of the colour of his skin, or his background, or his religion. People must learn to hate, and if they can learn to hate, they can be taught to love, for love comes more naturally to the human heart than its opposite.'

—Nelson Mandela

The detailed notes pertaining to this book are available on the HarperCollins website. Scan this QR code to access the same.

CONTENTS

Introduction

January 1986. I was all spruced up in a dapper suit tailored by Tatanagar's[1] finest scissor-hands. My heart pounding, I waited to be ushered in for my last round of interviews with Grindlays Bank plc—an old British colossus since acquired by Standard Chartered. At the XLRI business school campus, it was among the most coveted jobs, as Grindlays was known to provide luxurious accommodation, foreign postings, comprehensive training and muscular compensation. The joke went that after working there for a month, one developed a British accent and a stiff upper lip. I was nervous, even though I had prepared sharply, with boilerplate answers on a range of possible queries. The interview went really well, but I was completely unprepared for the last question. 'If you could have dinner with anyone you liked, living or dead, who would be your preferred guest?' asked a poker-faced interviewer, looking at me intently. I barely missed a beat: 'Mahatma Gandhi.' The job was mine.

Mahatma Gandhi was assassinated by Nathuram Godse of the Hindu Mahasabha on 30 January 1948, back when India was a five-month-old newly free nation. Godse had earlier been a member of the Rashtriya Swayamsevak Sangh (RSS), the mothership of the Sangh Parivar, or the Sangh family. A heartbroken nation was plunged into mourning. In one of life's great ironies, the man who championed non-violence even against the oppressive British rule he was fighting, died at the hands of a rabid, right-wing fundamentalist, a fellow Indian. 'Hey Ram' were Gandhi's last words.

As we leap forward seventy-three years, India is a transformed country, almost like a parallel universe to the one ushered in on 15 August 1947. The Bharatiya Janata Party's (BJP) Lok Sabha candidate from Bhopal, the capital of Madhya Pradesh, Pragya Singh Thakur, declared, 'Nathuram Godse was a patriot, is a patriot and will remain a patriot. People calling him a terrorist should look within. Such people will be given a befitting reply in these elections.'[2] This was her response to actor Kamal Haasan's comment, 'The first terrorist post-Independence was Nathuram Godse, a Hindu. It started from there. He killed Mahatma Gandhi.'

Thakur, a Lok Sabha aspirant, was, in effect, calling the Father of the Nation an anti-national, justifying his assassination.[3] There are some moments you wish would remain in the realm of nightmares, to be shaken off the next morning. There is no waking up from reality though.

Thakur herself is accused of masterminding a terror attack that killed six persons in Malegaon, Maharashtra, in 2008. Currently out on bail, she has been lionised by the BJP as an apostle of Hindutva. Prime Minister Narendra Modi spent considerable time defending her innocence, even as the special court that was hearing the case talked about the 'prima facie evidence' against her and lambasted the Central government-controlled National Investigation Agency (NIA) for its shoddy investigation.[4]

The BJP pretended that Thakur's outrageous comment had only been her own. However, India has seen this charade before: BJP Member of Parliament (MP) Sakshi Maharaj too had praised Godse as a patriot, but there was no action against him. Evidently, the animus towards Mahatma Gandhi is no mere electoral ploy; it runs deep, an ideological abhorrence of the principles of secularism, religious tolerance and inclusiveness that he stood for. Besides, it serves a purpose: the foot soldiers of Hindutva get adrenalised by invectives poured on Jawaharlal Nehru and Gandhi. This time too, other BJP leaders joined in, one of them caustically calling Gandhi the Father of Pakistan.[5] Prime Minister Modi reluctantly condemned Thakur's comments. With the last round of voting due on 19 May 2019, he needed to douse the blowback it had elicited. As it turned out, his weak protest was all that was needed, if it was needed at all.

On 23 May 2019, as the results started pouring in, all eyes were on Bhopal, where Thakur was in a high-profile contest against Congress veteran Digvijaya Singh, twice chief minister of Madhya Pradesh. I confess to having been positive she would lose—surely Bhopal would not vote in someone who had disparaged Gandhi and also boasted about laying a curse on the valiant martyr Hemant Karkare. Karkare, the former Anti-Terror Squad chief of Maharashtra, was gunned down by Pakistani terrorists on 26 November 2008 in Mumbai. His resolute investigations were what had led to Thakur's arrest.

Pragya Singh Thakur won the Lok Sabha election by a huge margin, approximately 3.64 lakh votes, in the famous city of lakes. It was the beginning of an intensifying of the hate project—one that had started before India's independence, gathered strength through the 1990s and found fruition in 2014.

Amidst all the toxicity, it was hard to remember that we were once Exhibit A of multicultural diversity and a secular democracy. That era was only two election cycles ago, when a battered, bruised and beleaguered Congress was dumped by a frustrated nation. By the year 2020, the socio-political landscape of the country was radically altered: the state of Jammu and Kashmir (J&K) stood quarantined, the Supreme Court of India seemed disinterested in the pending and urgent habeas corpus petitions, Operation Lotus was focused on the horse-trading of politicians and thirty-eight-year-old Dr Kafeel Khan was in jail for violating the National Security Act because he had spoken up against India's controversial citizenship law.[6] India's economy was nearing a collapse, and its neighbourhood foreign policy was in disarray. But if one watched a cable news channel, it would appear that the country was leading a fightback against the pandemic that was threatening to devour the world.

They say there are two sides to every story. I could not believe that so many were blindsided by Prime Minister Modi's outrageous claims that they voted him in a second time in May 2019. His first term was unequivocally disastrous on several fronts. Yet, I asked myself the question that others were asking of me: was it possible that I (committed to the Congress ideology) and many like me were so blinded by our disdain for the BJP and its divisive politics that we were turning a blind eye to the regime's accomplishments? Had it not successfully engineered the last-mile delivery of government subsidies to the poor in the form of LPG cylinders, rural roads, electricity connections, cash transfers to farmers, health insurance and low-cost housing? What about the unprecedented tit-for-tat military retribution approach with Pakistan, not deterred by the fear of a nuclear retaliation? The Goods and Services Tax (GST) was indeed sloppily administered, but along with the Insolvency and Bankruptcy Code (IBC), had it not created a much-needed legal infrastructure for recoveries of bad debts? Although Modi's neighbourhood foreign policy was an embarrassing failure, with several countries inching closer to arch-rival China, the prime minister had indeed pushed India centre stage in global politics and made it an attractive magnet for foreign capital, had he not? And who could deny that the BJP had amassed huge financial resources (mostly through the allegedly duplicitous means of electoral bonds) that made it a frontrunner in every election it fought? Its competitors were dwarfed by comparison. Also, Modi was still seen by many as an incorruptible big-thinking administrator, a high-stakes gambler (with moves like demonetisation) working to transform India. Had not the man who called himself an 'outsider' to Delhi's entrenched Lutyens elite rearranged the political chessboard? Ultimately, the BJP's competitors, particularly the Congress, were unable to counter the arresting legend of an ordinary chaiwala who had risen from the relative obscurity of a small town in Gujarat to become India's prime minister, were they not?

It was a message from a dear friend—we had studied together at Fergusson College, Pune, several decades ago, and she is now an outstanding voice of the oppressed and the marginalised—that prompted me to write this book. I wrote a tweet of reassurance to the many who were shell-shocked by the outcome of the seventeenth Lok Sabha elections: 'You know what, yes, we have lost. But it feels great to be fighting for the right side.' As darkness spread through Delhi's skies, I prepared to return to Mumbai on the day of the counting: 23 May 2019, earlier than I had planned. My friend's reply to the tweet hit me like a ton of bricks: 'Not good enough, Sanjay. I will have to look for PR [Permanent Residency] Visas outside India because Congress let me down.' I read her message over and over; the 'Congress let me down' was gut-wrenching. I felt responsible. I had let her down. I had failed.

And what about the others, where would they go? The family of Pehlu Khan, the Rajasthani cattle-trader who had been lynched to death; Radhika Vemula, the mother of Rohith Vemula, the Dalit scholar who committed suicide in what was an institutional murder; the relatives of murdered rationalist Govind Pansare, who were still fighting for justice—as were several activists and environmentalists, as was Kanhaiya Kumar, former president of the Jawaharlal Nehru University (JNU) students' union. What about the four Dalit boys chained to a jeep and publicly lashed in Una, Gujarat? What about millions of Kashmiris, incarcerated in their homes, cut off from communication, long before 138 crore Indians went into quarantine? There is no overseas golden visa for most of them.

Was Mahatma Gandhi's party in an irreversible terminal decline that could be deleterious for Indian democracy? What had led to the calamitous defeat of the Congress and the entire opposition in 2019? Did the Congress underestimate the burgeoning Hindutva disposition of large swathes of society? Was India really the world's fastest-growing economy, or was the data airbrushed to please foreign investors? Would India become a constitutionally mandated religious theocracy by 2025, the hundredth anniversary of the RSS? Would Nathuram Godse be looked upon as a troubled, tragic hero of Indian nationalism, with temples constructed in his honour? Does the economy really matter when it comes to choosing Lok Sabha candidates? Is the BJP's 'New India' inward-looking and religion-centric but free-market friendly enough to keep everyone happy? There are so many questions about so many issues that nag us daily.

There is no silver bullet for India's hydra-headed problems. We have reconciled to treating political party manifestos and poll promises like a trailer for a bad Bollywood movie—the best two minutes of 180 minutes of excruciating torture. It is only a sales pitch after all. Yet, this lack of accountability could mean a perilous decade in the lives of about 1,400 million people. It could change their destiny forever. The last few years suggest that something is gravely broken. India is indeed unravelling.

Prologue

'The Idea of India is dead. RIP. Or Rest in Pieces.'
—WhatsApp message I received,
23 May 2019, 3.42 p.m.

'*Kaun jitega?*' (Who will win?) I asked Sanjay, my driver, as he navigated the chaotic traffic outside Delhi's T3 international airport. It was a muggy day, the sun was beating down relentlessly and I was hyper-aware of the nervousness that had gripped me. Sanjay had been my regular man at the wheel in India's capital city for several years. I had discovered over many casual conversations that he had sharp political instincts. In less than twenty-four hours, the world's largest democracy would vote in a new government in its seventeenth general elections since 1947.

'Modi,' said Sanjay monosyllabically, as expansive an answer as any. The response was no surprise. All the major exit polls, from the most reliable to the downright dubious, had agreed that the BJP would win an absolute majority for the second time in the Lok Sabha. As a national spokesperson of the Indian National Congress, India's grand old party founded in 1885, I had a busy day ahead. When you lose, Indian television is a merciless interrogator. When you win, they genuflect with wild abandon. Five years ago, on 16 May 2014, I had experienced the Congress's worst electoral rout, as it garnered a mere forty-four seats. Even the worst doomsayers had not budgeted for such an abysmal show.

Would the 2019 results offer up some miraculous surprise that all the mathematical models had suppressed—that silent voter, or the marginalised sections who deliberately lied to pollsters, perhaps a skewed sample size with an urban bias? A sliver of hope survived; it is the human condition. What if all the exit polls were wrong? They had been wrong before, several times. In 2004. In 2009. In 2014, too, they did not predict the gigantic wave gradually building into what came to be known as TsuNaMo (NaMo, as Prime Minister Narendra Modi is referred to by his supporters). India was always throwing up surprises. As a politician, I have found that the most essential ingredient for survival is optimism—even more so if one is part of an opposition party. So, when I entered the hotel that evening, although we had prepared for the worst, I was still hoping for a massive upset the next day.

I slept fitfully, and it had nothing to do with the butter chicken that I invariably order when in Delhi. The world could be a different place in only a few hours. And here I was, a small part of that epic narrative, my tension mounting. There was also a creeping sense of déjà vu.

I woke up to check the time; it was 4.30 a.m., an unearthly hour for me. I forced myself back to sleep. By the time I next awoke, the sun was out, and even from within the air-conditioned comfort of the Taj Man Singh hotel, I could sense that it was a surly day outside my window on 23 May 2019. Delhi was slumbering almost, the streets deserted, barring an odd car at the roundabouts that the storied Lutyens quarter is known for. I could see an endless stretch of treetops, their green monopoly invaded by a lone architectural mutation, perhaps a tall government office. Far below were the sprawling gardens of the official bungalows of political party leaders. Being a

Mumbai man, conditioned to seeing the privileged live in large skyscrapers, I was always a touch scandalised at this colossal waste of precious real estate. And surely public servants needed to live a more frugal existence? For all the chest-thumping against British rule, colonial ways of doing things had been quietly and conveniently assimilated into India's political culture.

But I had other things to think about just then. In a few hours, the counting would commence, and by evening, all the world would be speculating about India's political destiny. The size of India's voting population is staggering: 900 million. These elections would influence the future of the planet, and quite directly, a sizeable 16 per cent of it.

Honestly, I don't like Delhi. On dark, wintry evenings, its eerie silence is unnerving, especially on these wide roads lined with elegant bungalows on either side, guarded by surreptitious snipers and a posse of security vehicles. In Delhi, VIP security is a status symbol, laughingly referred to as the laal-batti (red beacon-light) culture. The city's men-in-white, its politicians, need protection. Big SUVs zoom around, their tail-lights flashing ominously, tailed by alert SPG (Special Protection Group: black cat commandos) in jeeps—and who can blame them? This nation has lost two prime ministers and the Father of the Nation himself to brutal assassinations. I was in Delhi on that dreadful night when former prime minister Rajiv Gandhi was killed by Liberation Tigers of Tamil Eelam (LTTE) suicide bombers in Sriperumbudur, Tamil Nadu. I can never totally defenestrate that night of 21 May 1991 from my Delhi experience.

All the same, I dressed and prepared to meet the city. In the hotel lobby, I saw a small group huddled together, all wearing ill-fitting three-piece suits. Was that a retired bureaucrat advising a prospective property developer on how to grease the gravy train? I felt like a misfit there, even if I was that most apposite of things: a politician, the visible face of the ecosystem as a national spokesperson of the Congress. In India, as a politician, you can say goodbye to any pretensions of purity. I knew I could never contest an election to the Lok Sabha myself, given the rumours (and reality) of the deployment of large bundles of unaccounted-for cash.[7] Every political party blatantly crossed expenditure rules. Yet Indian democracy had survived seven decades of every sort of venality and contradiction. Another test awaited it today. I expected everyone to be as tightly wound as I was, but for the world at large, it seemed to be business as usual. Clearly, not everyone is a politics junkie. Some don't even vote.

As I went down to the coffee shop for a quick breakfast, the hostess smiled and said: 'Good luck!' I needed that, as did my party. I knew deep down that, barring a magical benediction from the gods, the BJP was a sure-shot winner, and Narendra Modi would hold his seat until 2024.

Modi was the Hindu Hriday Samrat (emperor of the Hindu heart, as the right-wing zealots lovingly referred to him) and India's Pradhan Sevak (principal servant of the country, as he styled himself). Within days of Modi assuming office in 2014, on 4 June, a young IT professional named Mohsin Mohammad Shaikh was lynched in Pune. He was murdered by an extremist fringe group for posting an allegedly provocative post on Facebook. It did not cause the furore it should have. The accused were subsequently acquitted as several witnesses turned hostile.[8] Many thought Shaikh's killing was a one-off incident. Many were still mesmerised by '*Sabka Saath Sabka Vikas*' (all together, prosper together), Modi's election pitch. He was the new messiah in town.

Apart from social schisms, the other legacy of Modi's premiership is yawning economic disparity. An Oxfam report of 2017–18 says that 1 per cent of Indians own 73 per cent of its wealth. India's well-off now aspire to a 54" QLED TV with 3-D glasses and bigger sedans, while the vast majority worry about food inflation, daily wages and malaria. While obscene bonuses are paid to corporate high-fliers already on a millionaires list, there is intense dialogue in Malabar Hill homes over giving domestic workers a 20 per cent salary hike. Inequality has always been India's biggest quandary, and it has aggravated since 2014.[9]

India's unemployment rates are now the highest that they have been since the 1970s,[10] a recipe for social anarchy. A new job description mushroomed early in Modi's reign: cow vigilantes. Bands of aggressive youth began patrolling transport of cattle on highways to prevent trafficking, sale and consumption of beef. Several states in India have banned beef, and these vigilantes now run a parallel cow-police force. These gangs soon proved to be above the law as they wantonly slaughtered innocent people on mere suspicion of transgression. On 28 September 2015, Mohammad Akhlaq was lynched by a mob in Dadri, Uttar Pradesh, because they believed that there was beef in the house. It was a lie, as laboratory results showed. His son, who works with the Indian Air Force, continues to fight for justice. The murder brought back to public memory the butchery of Australian missionary Graham Staines and his family by Hindutva zealots in Odisha in 1999.

At a nearby table, someone was watching live television on his mobile phone. The truth is that Indian democracy is a near hostage to the daunting power of the media; it has had an increasingly corrosive impact. 'Politainment' is what one watches, a hybrid of scurvy politics and mindless melodrama that would embarrass even a Netflix soap opera. The elections of 2019 saw a bizarre hard sell of Modi; there was a Bollywood biopic that released along with a dedicated NaMoTV channel. There was also a full-length web series on the prime minister on a popular streaming app. Modi made himself available for a full-length interview to Bollywood superstar Akshay Kumar, who appeared starry-eyed and fanboy-like. They discussed the prime minister's taste for mangoes, and other such frivolous claptrap.

Anti-Congress films were made by right wing-leaning producers with clear political agendas. One of them, *The Accidental Prime Minister*, had Bollywood veteran Anupam Kher playing Dr Manmohan Singh as a lame-duck remote-controlled (by Congress President Sonia Gandhi) chief executive. The movie, based on a book by Singh's former press advisor, Sanjaya Baru, an accomplished journalist, was a dreadful embarrassment to the Congress on the eve of the elections. Kher, of course, is well known as a card-carrying BJP follower.

It was 7.30 a.m. I ordered tea and the *Indian Express* newspaper. Stock markets boomed even while the capital city reported starvation deaths, creating not a flutter. Meanwhile, another story had not-so-quietly taken over: anti-minorityism. The phenomenon has spread all over the country, particularly in northern India and the BJP-ruled states, and I saw evidence of it in the paper that day, as I do every day now. Religious polarisation has resulted in a fractured society living on the edge. The 180 million Muslims of India are expressly told that they are second-class citizens. In the papers that day, there was fervent discussion on how the business lobby would be bullish following the BJP's triumph; there was not enough conversation about how a very sizeable minority in India would shrivel up, dehydrated by hate.

The newspaper was riddled with the contradictions that make up India. Some years ago, in November 2013, the Archaeological Survey of India had begun digging for 1,000 tonnes of gold under a temple in Unnao, Uttar Pradesh, in response to a priest's premonitions, even as 16,000 of India's outstanding engineers successfully launched the Mangalyaan to Mars, putting India in the elite Western country club that is space research. That gold would have been enough to solve the country's paralysing current account deficit—if it had existed. Many were outraged that India spent Rs 460 crores on the Mars trip; an irony, given that the corporate giant Sahara India had recently bought an Indian Premier League (IPL) team for nearly four times the value of the Mars Mission, at Rs 1,500 crores. Similarly, five-star hotels proliferate at a galloping pace even as several hundred million Indians defecate in the open every single morning, despite a nationwide toilets programme. The country is self-sufficient in foodgrains production, yet 42 per cent of its children under the age of five suffer from serious malnourishment.[11] Amongst the many critics of the state's subsidy for the poor are members of swanky air-conditioned gyms trudging purposefully on treadmills to fight obesity.

Dogged superstition and massive advances in science coexist here. Even as the Modi government is busy promoting Digital India, BJP leaders talk about how the internet existed in the Mahabharata era. The prime minister himself proudly proclaimed that Lord Ganesha is proof of the existence of plastic surgery in India's hoary past. The scientific temper that Article 51A(h) of the Indian Constitution requires citizens to develop[12] appears to have been lost. What greater contradiction than that when the Khans (Shah Rukh, Aamir and Salman) rule Indian hearts, but the actor Emran Hashmi struggles to get an apartment in Mumbai because he is Muslim. Free-market fundamentalists condemned the Food Security Act for 800 million people, but are agitated by even a minute's disruption of power supply to their plush apartments overlooking the Arabian Sea. Some of the latter include business barons who have absconded to one of the world's most expensive cities, London, and live there in opulent luxury.

I was still reading the paper and fretting when a gentleman seated at a table nearby came over to say hello. 'Why did the Congress keep attacking Modi? You should have focused on the economy which is in terrible shape,' he said. He was convinced that the Congress was headed for decimation. As in 2014, Modi had held centre stage throughout the campaign phase, focusing on low blows during the most sulphurous election campaign in Indian election history. Modi alleged that the Congress was in cahoots with elements in Pakistan—absurd, laughable tosh born of a deep, malevolent hate for India's grand old party.[13] An enervated Congress struggled to respond to such inanities. Religious schisms remained the BJP's core strategy, with Uttar Pradesh Chief Minister Yogi Adityanath and BJP President Amit Shah leading the charge. Modi's pathological hostility towards the Gandhi family surfaced intermittently. He launched distasteful attacks on the late prime minister Rajiv Gandhi, punches actually aimed at his son, Rahul Gandhi.

Modi delivered speech after speech, and a craven media obligingly amplified his vituperative barrage, never challenging the most obvious contradictions. There is only spin in the speeches, and the coverage of them; neither has any truck with fact. For instance, even as he lambasts dynasty politics in the Congress party, Modi happily accommodates two Gandhi family dynasts—Maneka Gandhi and Varun Gandhi—in his own party. The BJP has as many dynastic leaders as the Congress, although the latter has the most famous one.[14]

At a private club in Mumbai, a Stanford university postgraduate with a smattering of salt-and-pepper in his enviable hair, had once told me that his biggest fear was that the Muslim population would overtake the majority Hindus in a few decades. I told him that was just a mathematical fantasy meant for WhatsApp forwards.[15] But the conversation made clear to me that the BJP's social media fake-news factory had devoured unguarded minds, even among the most educated of citizens. India's democracy is on creaking legs, and rampant digital manipulation is a big contributor to this decline. Popular social media platforms, like Facebook, Twitter and WhatsApp, have led to the dissemination of morphed images and twisted facts. People are snacking on sound bites, and Modi has monopolised that space by keeping it suitably lubricated with phrases like '*Namdar-Kamdar*' (title owner vs worker) and '*Khandani Chor*' (hereditary thief). He caused enormous damage to the Congress party, which, true to its character, avoided rhetoric (other than '*Chowkidar Chor Hai*') and played it safe. Soon, one would know which political game plan had worked.

In 2019, Modi made no pretence of being a free-market reformer, the chicanery that had befooled many in 2014 (and probably still does). 'It's the economy, stupid' was once a successful campaign for the Democrats in the US. The BJP turned it on its head: a distressing agrarian crisis, record unemployment, collapsed small businesses, plateaued private investment and a questionable gross domestic product (GDP), none of this seemed to matter as people queued up at the Electronic Voting Machines (EVMs).

I was unable to understand this phenomenon. How was Modi able to dominate the daily story, the narrative, even as India's economy was headed south, with macroeconomic fundamentals (factors such as employment, GDP growth, exports and manufacturing) indicating an imminent slowdown? Then again, narrative-setting is easy for someone who has effected a media capture. A kowtowing mainstream media, carrying out psychological brainwash using a saffron detergent, both subverts democracy and allows for a pretence of it. Thus it was that Modi hypnotised the nation with the Balakot counter-airstrike in response to the dastardly Pulwama attack. He positioned himself as the sole guardian of India's territorial boundaries. The prime minister's innumerable lies, alleged Rafale corruption, institutional destruction and broken governance were all forgotten. Modi was on the verge of getting a second term, and that would mean a decade of BJP leadership controlling the futures of 138 crore Indians. I sincerely hoped not, but I was just a solitary voter, and I had a political bias.

It was nearing 8.30 a.m. now. The counting of postal ballots would have already started. In a short while, the early voting trends would appear. It was time to face the truth, whatever it was. I gulped my tea down and headed for my room. The elevator attendant said: 'Good luck, sir!' I thanked him.

I switched on the television set in my room. Every channel was a colourful collage, with psychedelic numbers popping from the left, right and centre. Anchors screamed their lungs out, even as Breaking News interrupted them every thirty seconds and a new voting trend came in. From the beginning, there was one constant: BJP+ leads. As I flipped channels, one thing was clear; the exit polls would be proven right. My worst fears were coming true. The Congress would be trounced again. It was turning out to be even worse than expected. Rahul Gandhi was trailing BJP's popular face Smriti Irani in Amethi, where he had a hat-trick of wins. The party was aflutter. One television channel that had the Congress-led United Progressive Alliance (UPA) at eighty-nine leads suddenly dropped it to forty-two. That was an Olympian somersault. I fervently flipped channels, looking for one that showed a more comforting average. But none complied. By 9.30 a.m., it was time to call the election; the BJP was winning hands down.

By the time I reached the All India Congress Committee (AICC) office at 24, Akbar Road, to do what spokespersons do, the writing was on the wall. The mood was not just sombre, like in 2014, but also sadder. My colleagues were struggling to justify the party's decimation. We had all done our own number-crunching and every one of us had expected the Congress to cross 100, and be in the range of 115 to 125. The alliances that we stitched together would then have ensured that Modi did not reach the halfway mark of 272. A UPA-led coalition arrangement would take office. We were mentally conjecturing UPA-3 with outside support. By late afternoon, we heard that Gandhi was trailing by a sizeable and unbridgeable margin. It was 2.30 p.m. in the afternoon, but all I could see was a dark canopy envelop the skies. Five years had been wasted. Five difficult years lay ahead for a party that had, from 1951 to 1977, won every single election.

I was devastated. As the BJP clocked over 300 seats, and the Congress plateaued at around fifty, the numbers seemed unreal, untrue. In the states where we had recently triumphed (Madhya Pradesh, Rajasthan and Chhattisgarh), a mere five months ago, we were being routed.

A historic mandate, screamed one channel; an unprecedented landslide, shouted another. For once, their hyperbole was not misplaced. Prime Minister Narendra Modi had made a triumphant return, bettering his 2014 performance of 282 seats. I say Modi's victory—and not that of the BJP or of the National Democratic Alliance (NDA), which he represents—because the general elections of 2019 had become, similar to 2014, like a US presidential contest. It was a personality-centric pitch that overwhelmed compelling issues that ought to have been the determining factors in voter sentiment. There were reports that many voters did not even know the name of the BJP Lok Sabha candidate they were voting for; they just pressed the button next to the lotus symbol on the EVM. Modi had not lost a single election since the Gujarat assembly elections of 2002. It was no different this time.

As I braced for the predictable onslaught of scrutiny and sarcasm, I had to ponder a larger question: was the Congress party now in terminal decline? Did NYAY (the minimum income guarantee scheme), supposed to be the party's game-changer, fail to percolate down to the last mile? Was the campaign strategy itself flawed? Was the Congress unable to set the record straight on Modi's raucous accusations of how it had always been soft on terror? Had the Gandhis lost their political capital? Was Rahul Gandhi the right man to lead the party after two successive defeats? I think all of our party spokespersons bravely squared up to the challenge. Some TV anchors could barely conceal their schadenfreude when mocking Rahul Gandhi's leadership. It was a nightmare. We had seen it before in 2014, but this one hurt a lot more.

The traditional template of political contestations stood completely upended when the victor was formally announced. The final tally read as follows—BJP: 303, NDA: 352, Congress: 52, UPA: 91, Others: 99. So where does the Congress party go from not aggregating even 100 Lok Sabha seats in two consecutive elections? But first, we need to understand what really happened.

The Modi–Shah duo had recognised the clear and present danger signalled by Congress wins in the state elections of December 2018. The Congress–Janata Dal (Secular) combine dealt them a sledgehammer blow in Karnataka when it formed the government by checkmating Shah, the BJP's Chanakya. In the Gujarat elections of 2017, the Congress had run the BJP close, bearding the twin lions of Modi and Shah in their own den. Since assuming charge of the Congress in December 2017, Rahul Gandhi had been seeing a positive electoral hit rate. He was also gaining traction on social media, and his relentless assault on Modi on the Rafale corruption scandal had popularised the slogan '*Chowkidar Chor Hai*'. He interacted frequently and freely with different sections of people and held impromptu press conferences, which helped erase the 'Pappu' image that the BJP IT cell had crafted. Gandhi sounded like a refreshingly honest politician who talked compassionate politics. A toxic BJP was nonplussed. Despite an overwhelmingly pro-Modi media, the perception battle had now become a competitive one. And the prime minister was feeling the cracks. Most opinion polls still gave the BJP a clear head start, but the gap was narrowing. With good reason.

The agrarian crisis had grown to enormous proportions. While the government dilly-dallied on minimum support prices (MSPs), farmers were facing diminishing incomes due to falling procurement and lower prices. Farmer suicides were so high, and yet the BJP government denied that any farmers had died by suicide ever since it took over the reigns of government in 2014. India's 'demographic dividend' had become an onerous liability. The BJP's 2014 manifesto had promised two crore jobs per annum, which had not materialised by a long mile. Modi's frying-pakodas business solution for joblessness had invited much ridicule. Young jobless voters, who were whiling away their afternoons and nights watching Varun Dhawan's dancing chops on YouTube and rehearsing to perform on TikTok, were expected to express their frustrations at the EVM.

Demonetisation (in which high-denomination currency notes were rendered useless overnight, ostensibly to fight black money) had been shown up as atrocious hocus-pocus economics. It stalled growth, then slowed it. The clumsy execution of the Goods and Services Tax (GST) had destroyed the informal economy, pauperising millions in its wake. The manufacturing sector was in rigor mortis. Stressed assets in the banking sector were kissing some dark clouds. The sum and substance of it all: a rejuvenated and resolute Rahul Gandhi and Congress party, a faltering economy, corruption charges against Modi himself, all this had the BJP worried.[16] While the BJP still looked in pole position, the lead was likely to diminish as the opposition campaign gathered velocity. Then Pulwama happened.

On 14 February 2019, a suicide bomber (a local Kashmiri recruited for the purpose) rammed his jeep into a truck convoy carrying paramilitary forces of the Central Reserve Police Force (CRPF), killing forty-five of them. It was a dastardly attack, and an angry nation demanded immediate retribution. Masood Azhar, who headed the banned terror organisation Jaish-e-Mohammad (JeM), promptly claimed credit. Television channels declared war, seeking bloodthirsty revenge. Radheshyam Yadav, my garrulous driver of twenty-two years, from Faizabad in Uttar Pradesh, was seething with fury: 'Badla is the only option.' Revenge. The mood of the country had altered dramatically.

Modi dumped his flaky past promises—two crore jobs per annum, the obliteration of black money, doubling of farm incomes and creation of smart cities, among others. He had found his 2019 trump card: muscular nationalism. Balakot became for him what the Kargil war was for former prime minister Atal Bihari Vajpayee. Modi seized on the heart-stopping capture of Wing Commander Abhinandan Varthaman and his subsequent release by Pakistan as proof that his own superman-like prowess had intimidated Islamabad. '*Ghar mein ghus ghus ke maroonga*' (I will enter each and every home and kill them all)—thundering pomposity that sought to resurrect his 56" machismo. People whistled and clapped as if they were watching Amitabh Bachchan bash up goons in the 1970s classic *Deewaar*.

In country after country, the new global leader is an elected autocrat who presides over an illiberal democracy. For these strongmen, the most marketable weapon is fear; Islamophobia is popular political currency. An enemy at the border is usually enough. Modi found one at home too. His speech at Wardha, Maharashtra, lambasted Rahul Gandhi for contesting from Wayanad in Kerala because it was a Hindu-minority parliamentary constituency. A prime minister swears an oath on the Constitution of India to embody its sacred principles in his impartial political conduct. In the elevation of Hindus above all other communities in India, he had cast his oath aside. As he did when he played dog-whistle politics. As counting closed on 23 May, however, it was clear that Modi's stratagem had worked. And how.

In 2014, there were large billboards on Marine Drive, Mumbai, that promoted Modi as Hindu Hriday Samrat. This time, the BJP chose another Hindutva icon to project instead, Sadhvi Pragya Singh Thakur. The political messaging was unambiguous: a terror-accused candidate, allegedly responsible for a bomb blast that had killed six persons in Malegaon and injured several from the minority community, was kosher. In proposing to give Thakur a seat in Parliament, Modi was legitimising the Malegaon attack—an abject low even by the BJP's vulgar polarising standards. Her electoral victory from Bhopal is perhaps the defining moment of the 2019 election and of the reshaping of India.

But it was not the overwhelming majority of seats that the BJP had won that was the real story of these elections; it was the party's vote share. In 2014, BJP's vote share had climbed to a staggering 31 per cent from a mere 18 per cent, seemingly on the back of Modi's dodgy Gujarat model of development. But what explained the considerable jump to 38.5 per cent in 2019, when all talk of development had been given the short shrift? The only reasonable conclusion is that Indians approved of the prime minister's theatrical oratory, majoritarian nationalism and muscular Hindutva, and were, presumably, willing to sacrifice jobs and future prospects for these. The hard populist push also managed to shatter traditional caste and community barriers. Modi has changed India, one must reluctantly concede. India has moved further towards the far right of the political spectrum. On 23 May 2019, Mahatma Gandhi was killed all over again. The party that encapsulates India's constitutional ethos and democratic culture seemed incapacitated.

Yet, hope is all one has in these darkest of times. The Congress must rise again. The party's topmost priority is to aggressively defend the Indian Constitution, which is being systematically challenged and its credibility eroded. BJP leaders have openly declared that the words 'secularism' and 'socialism' must be dropped from it. This is an ideological war in which the BJP's Hindutva enterprise, cleverly disguised as cultural nationalism, is getting fresh purchase. The BJP first trivialised the issue of communal harmony by creating the term 'pseudo-secular', and now every liberal is labelled an Urban Naxal.

For many, the heartbreaking image of Mohammed Naeem, his shirt blood-soaked, pleading for his life as a savage crowd thrashed him in Jharkhand in 2017, would be the haunting legacy of five years of Modi as prime minister. Just as the tear-stained eyes of Qutubuddin Ansari became the tragic and unforgettable face of the Gujarat riots of 2002 when he was chief minister. Or the billowing smoke rising above burning homes in Delhi symbolised the Sikh killings of 1984 under the Congress's watch.

The first step, no doubt, is to recognise what the Congress is up against. The BJP is no ordinary opponent. And the Saffron Project, which has been in operation since before Independence, takes the long view on strategy. It aims, for instance, to gradually infiltrate institutions and catch impressionable youngsters in schools and colleges. The RSS, which is the ideological head of this project, has mastered the art of altering the school syllabus to push its agenda of religious chauvinism.

The Congress is up against a determined adversary that has altered the rules of the game. The BJP's propaganda machine is formidable; its social media troll army is incessant, and its WhatsApp fake news manufacturing capabilities are tremendous. Playing within the BJP's comfort zone is like trying to defeat Rafael Nadal on red clay at the French Open. There is only one option; force your opponent to a surface where the ball skids faster and the grass is green. The Congress needs to reinvent the political discourse while simultaneously maximising its enormous human talent, currently performing at low productivity on account of the bureaucratic cholesterol in its organisational structure.

Internal disorganisation is costing the party dearly—Rahul Gandhi said as much when he was party president. Today, the lumbering Congress looks amateurish when compared to the well-oiled propaganda machine that the BJP has transformed into. The BJP's governance has been shockingly mediocre, if not altogether subpar, but its election machine is tough as Teflon. The Congress needs a renewal. There is too much at stake, and the battle must be won. There is tremendous energy within the party that needs to be liberated for the great struggle ahead. It is time to take bold, pragmatic risks, be unpredictable, and practise political plasticity. Rahul Gandhi correctly said that the 2019 elections were a battle for India's soul. That soul is today smashed to smithereens. But it can be put back again. All is not lost yet.

Late in the afternoon, on 23 May 2019, the Congress formally conceded defeat. The AICC office looked forlorn. People stood in small groups, trying to make sense of the annihilation. 'It is a damn carnage,' said a young Congress leader, a firebrand lawyer, distraught and sullen. Elsewhere in the now deserted AICC lawns, some TV reporters sympathised with us, looking as stunned as we were feeling. 'Sorry,' they said. With only fifty-two seats, the party had faced a complete rout.

As someone who had once memorised India's first prime minister Jawaharlal Nehru's 'at the stroke of the midnight hour' speech, I was distraught by how far India had moved from that dream.

I had always thought that the Idea of India was not just an elitist, intellectual abstraction but the very soul of India, imperishable. I believed in the liberal, tolerant, progressive, inclusive and secular India that Mahatma Gandhi, Jawaharlal Nehru, Sardar Vallabhbhai Patel, Dr Bhimrao Ambedkar and other stalwarts had envisaged when the country became independent on 15 August 1947. For the first time, I was not so sure that the survival of an idea could be taken for granted. But I was sure of one thing: the battle to salvage it, whether in whole or in part, had to be fought.

It was time to return home. A TV crew standing nearby asked for a comment on the election results. I was exhausted. Devastated. But as the lights came on and the transmission went live, I put on a brave face, feigned a smile and began talking. 'Firstly, I would like to congratulate the BJP and Prime Minister Modi for—'

1

HINDUTVA

The Real Agenda

It had been a long day. I had woken up early to catch the first flight out to Delhi and another red eye beckoned (I am the same-day-return-to-home type). By the time the airplane was airborne, I had dozed off. A short-lived reprieve, because the flight attendant gently reminded me that I had the onus of ordering a snack and a drink on my corporate ticket. There was a young man seated next to me who appeared equally dysfunctional when asked to choose between a sandwich, a wrap and chocolate cookies. We exchanged smiles, perhaps conveying our mutual dismay at this exemplary professionalism. Some more sleep would have done wonders for our spiritual constitution.

'Are you the same Sanjay Jha we see on TV?' he asked, looking doubtful.

'Yes,' I said. 'The same. Congress spokesperson.'

His face suddenly brightened. He could not have known this, but his happiness was infectious. In politics, nothing enthuses you more than voluntary public support. My neighbour turned out to be a twenty-seven-year-old chemical engineer who worked with a corporate firm in downtown

Mumbai. He was the very manifestation of India's much-talked-about demographic dividend, the aspirational middle-class seeking greener pastures. In the past, I had often had long conversations with people while travelling, but exchanged formal introductions only at the very end. I had since made a behavioural correction—it is never too late to learn how to win friends and influence people.

'What's your name?' I asked him.

'Javed Khan [name changed],' he said.

'Sir, I want to ask you a question. Will the Congress party win the 2019 elections?' He looked anxious.

'I think so,' I said.

'I hope so,' said Khan, his nervousness evident.

'Are you very worried?' I asked. A superfluous question. I knew he was disturbed—anyone with a Muslim name would be.

'Sir, I have already started applying for jobs overseas. It seems strange to say this, but I am feeling insecure in our own country. My mother anxiously devours the news all evening and looks permanently worried these days. Then she narrates to me the ferocious fights that happen on TV.'

I was saddened, even if it was a reality I knew only too well, confronted as I was with it every day in the television debates I participated in. The anti-Muslim fusillade had been getting shriller, more vicious, with manufactured talking points like 'Love Jihad', 'Ghar Wapsi' and beef bans, in particular, dominating the discourse. India's horrific lynching epidemic had been condemned internationally, and even compelled the Supreme Court to publicly castigate the government and instruct it to frame an anti-lynching law. Javed was the personification of that fear. The fear of one's life—that is the burden of a Muslim name in India today.[17]

When a cabinet minister poses for a photo-op with murderers convicted of a lynching and the prime minister maintains a resounding silence, an unambiguous message of State complicity goes out to the country's minorities. The justification for Rakbar Khan's barbaric killing by a BJP leader was a new low even for this 'new India'.[18] That's why Javed Khan wanted to leave the country.

A day after I met Javed, I encountered a familiar face at a social gathering, an affluent stockbroker who lives in a plush South Mumbai residential tower.

'India has just one problem, and that is its population. We solve that and everything else will be fine,' he pontificated.

'Among other things, yes,' I gingerly cautioned him. 'We are a fractured society, and the recent lynchings are a gruesome reflection of that. We need to fix our society first.'

The Dalal Street bull remained unconvinced. 'I don't think so. Population only. We need tough steps. Sanjay Gandhi was thinking right.'

Exasperated but keen to avoid a spat, I asked, 'The lynching don't offend your sensibilities? Aren't you disgusted by the sickening horror in our own backyard? These are our brothers who are being butchered in broad daylight, for heaven's sake.'

'No,' he said with a straight face. 'It's no big deal.'

'Are you serious? Can I use this in my book without mentioning your name?' I ask, too appalled to attempt a comeback.

'Yes,' he said. 'Why not? It's been happening for years. Hasn't the Congress encouraged minority appeasement? This backlash was expected. I am not saying it's right. But it happens.'

The truth is that it had not been happening for years. But he had no interest in Rakbar Khan or Alimuddin Ansari. As long as the glistening pink papers he read showed that the Sensex had hit another high, he was transfixed.

As Javed Khan and I said goodbye at around midnight a day earlier, I had told him, 'Tell your mother not to worry. You will not have to leave our country.' He looked cheerful for the first time since we had begun chatting.

But it was not me or the Congress that Javed needed in his corner. The country he was born in had a moral obligation to protect him, to make him feel safe. It was his fundamental right guaranteed under India's Constitution. But that country had changed, and some basic assurances were no longer available.[19]

The precise location of that change is May 2014, when Narendra Modi rode a euphoric wave to 7, Race Course Road amidst frenzied BJP supporters, media calisthenics and mind-boggling promises of 'Achhe Din' (happy days). At least temporarily, he had revived national hope and expectations. In the last few months of UPA-2, the mood in the country was indeed downbeat. Modi lit the fireworks of aspirations and rode to power, after which he remained in permanent campaign mode, keeping Indians mesmerised day after day. He dominated the narrative in the months that followed his victory, a man in a hurry, with several deadlines to meet. The Congress, after its utter rout, had been stunned into inaction. The gap between the BJP and the Congress widened with every passing quarter.

The RSS was formally folded into the political mainstream. Within months of Modi assuming his post, RSS Chief Mohan Bhagwat was allowed to broadcast his Hindutva philosophy on the State-run national TV channel, Doordarshan.[20] Modi promptly tweeted his earnest endorsement of Bhagwat's speech. Expectedly, what followed were colourful outbursts of pro-Hindutva dialogues from the likes of Sakshi Maharaj,[21] Yogi Adityanath[22] and Giriraj Singh,[23] among others. Hate-spewing voices like Sadhvi Niranjan Jyoti[24] and Sadhvi Prachi[25] gained prominence. 'Ghar Wapsi' and 'Love Jihad' overwhelmed the political discourse. Meanwhile, the RSS quietly penetrated various crucial institutions, especially education.[26]

Modi found that his political stratagem of running with the hares and hunting with the hounds generally worked well. Despite mounting woes, his popularity remained on the upswing. The TINA (there is no alternative) factor was further cemented. Church attacks continued unabated, prompting ex-top cop Julio Ribeiro to ruefully question his status as an Indian citizen.[27] Earlier, just after he returned home from attending India's Republic Day celebrations in 2015, US President Barack Obama had said: 'Michelle and I returned from India—an incredible, beautiful country, full of magnificent diversity—but a place where, in past years, religious faiths of all types have, on occasion, been targeted by other peoples of faith, simply due to their heritage and their beliefs—acts of intolerance that would have shocked Gandhiji, the person who helped to liberate that nation.'[28] It probably assuaged his conscience about the courting of Modi on behalf of US transnationals looking at India's fast-growing consumer market.[29]

Meanwhile, the BJP–RSS jodi conjured up some interesting imagery: cabinet ministers making PPT presentations to RSS pracharaks.[30] Like a holding company, the RSS, an unelected organisation that believes in Hindu Rashtra, was calling the shots in India's parliamentary democracy.[31] Interestingly, this is what BJP MP M.J. Akbar wrote in his book *Riot after Riot*: 'RSS represents Hindu revivalism of the worst sort; the most dangerous, clandestine force, determined to provoke violence.' Today, the RSS runs the world's most exciting emerging market. The result is inherent fragilities of the sort that drove global hedge-fund manager Jim Rogers to quit investing in India lock, stock and barrel in 2015.[32]

The RSS is registered as a charitable, social and cultural organisation, but it had a translucent political agenda through Modi's first term—using the five-year window to 2019 to drive social transformation, the 'Indianisation', as it sees it, of India. The prime minister had to earn his saffron stripes if he wanted to control the RSS foot soldiers (rumoured to be 600,000 strong) as he prepared for the 2019 Lok Sabha elections. So, India's prime institutions were low-hanging fruits for Hindutva ideology infiltration—the Film and Television Institute of India (FTII), the National Council of Educational Research and Training (NCERT), the University Grants Commission (UGC), the Indian Council of Historical Research (ICHR), National Book Trust (NBT), Children's Film Society (CFS), Indian Institutes of Technology (IITs), Indian Institutes of Management (IIMs) and the like. The RSS was well pleased with their former pracharak.[33]

The RSS and the BJP are connected by an umbilical cord. Together, they represent a regressive majoritarian idea of India based on religious identity and Hindu supremacy. A comeback from this damage to Indian polity and society might take an exponentially longer time to undo than it did to inflict.

The RSS and the BJP have many non-State actors who buttress their cause. Take, for instance, Ramkrishna Yadav, a.k.a. Baba Ramdev, the self-styled spiritual guru who launched the brand Patanjali. Reports indicate that the company's advertising expenditure dwarfed that of multinational fast-moving consumer goods (FMCG) firms, which were once the big-ticket spenders. On 4 April 2016, #TalibaniRamdev trended at the top spot on social media, as Ramdev called for violence at a Sadbhavana rally organised by the RSS in Rohtak, Haryana. Referring unambiguously, if not explicitly, to Muslims, he said, 'A [skull] cap-wearing man stands there, insisting he will not say Bharat Mata Ki Jai even if you kill him. If there was no law in this country, I would have beheaded lakhs [like him].'

Earlier, the BJP had provided him with VIP Z-category security. Now, it characteristically refused to condemn the yoga guru's remark. I was reminded of the late BJP leader Arun Jaitley's absurd comparison of Ramdev to Mahatma Gandhi, flushed as he was with the 2014 victory. Presumably, even Ramdev flushed at that.[34]

At any rate, there was now an increasingly accepted marker to establish one's patriotic credentials: the proclaiming of '*Bharat Mata Ki Jai*' (often referred to by its abbreviation, BMKJ). RSS Chief Mohan Bhagwat's use of the slogan for exclusionary cultural nationalism was already gaining traction.[35] Nationalism suits the Sangh tremendously; it is an emotive subject that breaks barriers like caste and religion, region and language. And so, Hindu majoritarianism was re-jacketed as passionate patriotism. Bhagwat then performed a surprising U-turn, stating that '*Bharat Mata Ki Jai*' could not be compulsorily enforced.

This deliberate confusion keeps the debate simmering and the headlines rolling. Besides, it provides the RSS with a veneer of saintliness. Arun Jaitley was less discreet; he declared that the 'BJP had won the first round of the nationalism debate'.[36] For the BJP, nationalism is a competitive tournament where the opponent is a traitor to be quashed.

The Congress appeared confounded by the goings on. The rules of the game had changed, and India's grand old party was stunned. The BJP had a free run. India was adrift.

In the merchant banking universe, the term 'creeping acquisition' refers to a gradual takeover of corporate equity without attracting public attention or regulatory mechanisms. The RSS has followed just this tactic to assimilate its fledgling offspring into the national mainstream. (The BJP was formed in 1980. The earlier political arm of the RSS was called the Bharatiya Jana Sangh, which existed from 1951 to 1977.) The RSS—once an avuncular guardian to the BJP, ostensibly its social and cultural charitable heart—has now become central to any political conversation regarding the Sangh Parivar, the family of organisations affiliated to the RSS. TV debates are brazenly lopsided these days, as both RSS and BJP spokespersons find representation and arrive as an inseparable duo. Since there is no getting away from the fact that television shapes public opinion, it is a matter of concern that the arithmetic of talking heads is skewed heavily in favour of the Sangh Parivar.

It feels like a lifetime ago, but as recently as 2014, RSS intervention in BJP politics was considered an infringing move. Overtly political comments from the Sangh would raise questions about its stealthy influence, and observers would point to the violation of the RSS commitment to Sardar Patel that it would stay aloof from active politics. Sure, the RSS always had a considerable influence on the BJP, but since May 2014, it has dropped all pretensions of being a socio-spiritual organisation to assume operational control on disseminating information, shaping political strategy, directing economic policies and foreign policy, and monitoring campus behaviour. It even chose the prime ministerial candidate of the BJP.

By the time that prime minister was closing his first term in office, Mohan Bhagwat was providing television channels with regular sound-bites on all things, including national security. He even made the outlandish statement that the RSS could prepare an army in three days, unlike the Indian Army, which would take six months. Nobody said a word. India's chaotic democracy clearly needed detoxification. But the Congress was unable to mount a serious assault, mired in its internecine political struggles. Modi was laughing all the way to the bank. And the RSS was assuming public legitmacy.

What started with the government suddenly swooping down on JNU students, declaring some of them 'anti-national', including Kanhaiya Kumar and Umar Khalid, soon snowballed. Former Maharashtra Chief Minister Devendra Fadnavis suggested that anti-nationals should migrate to foreign lands. Just like Giriraj Singh, a cabinet minister, had earlier. Usually, they want traitors to be dispatched to Pakistan. Every now and then, RSS/BJP spokespersons on TV debates brand dissenting voices as 'Pakistani agents' and 'deshdrohis' (traitors). A complacent Opposition thought the audience would dismiss such codswallop out of hand. Sadly, they were mistaken; lies repeated often enough and loudly enough begin to pass off as the truth.

Propaganda, subtle and overt, was the BJP's principal weapon. Modi, with his flair for spectacle and style, was its best proponent. At the high tea at Hyderabad House for Barack Obama, India's humble chaiwallah transitioned to wearing flashy designer suits, rumoured to be priced at a whopping Rs 10 lakh. The monogrammed suit was eventually sold at auction for Rs 4.3 crore to a Gujarati businessman.[37] This occasion led to the birth of the '*Suit-boot Ki Sarkar*' slogan. That sarcastic sound bite from Rahul Gandhi became such a force in the farcical theatre of Indian politics that it compelled Modi to dump his free-market fetish and embrace welfare economics. Simply put, Modi began following the Congress model. Naturally, he didn't call it that.

As I observed earlier, Obama was aware of both Modi's views on minority communities and that he had been denied a travel visa to the US on account of the Gujarat pogrom of 2002. On the evidence of his speech, Obama was uncomfortable with these aspects of his counterpart too. Yet, both Obama and Modi performed a bromance. This ability to function under acute discomfiture with a straight-face is what makes political leaders unique. Earlier, on Modi's visit to the US, the non-resident Indian (NRI) community had organised an event at

Madison Square Garden, a paid-for lollapalooza with showbiz trappings. One half-expected Jennifer Lopez to drop down in a gas balloon. Indians with American passports, unlikely to ever return to India, appeared ecstatic. The extravaganza did its job: the manufactured creation of a cult status for one man. The frenzy was such that senior India Today TV journalist Rajdeep Sardesai was physically manhandled as he asked tough questions that irked the Modi toadies. But more than the NRI audience, Modi was wooing his domestic vote bank. That was always his prime obsession.

In the midst of all this celebration, Modi gave no thought to the middle name of the man he met at the White House. Obama's middle name is Hussein, a Muslim name from his Kenyan father. The American president had been elected by the world's oldest and arguably most transparent democracy. In the US, white Americans constitute an overwhelming 76.3 per cent of the population, while African Americans number only 13.4 per cent.[38] The blacks are a minority subject to discrimination even today. There is a reason why Black Lives Matter exists. During the run-up to his election, the reality TV star and real-estate tycoon Donald Trump, who would go on to succeed Obama in a shock victory in 2016, had questioned the birth credentials of the US president. Obama won in spite of the sustained vitriol of right-wing loonies, and the country's spirit of unencumbered assimilation shone bright—even if only briefly.

Interestingly, the proportion of India's Muslim minority is approximately the same as the black community in the US: 13.4 per cent.[39] They have been relegated to the status of second-class citizens post 2014, even as the RSS rages for its Hindu Rashtra.[40] Obama's sardonic parting shot about religious tolerance was a not-so-subtle message from a minority-community president to a majority-community prime minister. It was not a misplaced warning; later that same year, 2015, the lynching of Mohammad Akhlaq in Dadri, Uttar Pradesh, carried echoes of the carnage the Ku Klux Klan (KKK) had once wrought in the US.

As expected, BJP spokespersons only said, 'It is a law-and-order problem.' But they knew, as did everyone who watched in horror or in approval, that this was an ideological killing born out of morbid hate. Forensic investigations would establish that Akhlaq had lamb meat, not beef, in his refrigerator—not that possession of beef would have changed the heinous nature of the crime.

The BJP was careful not to explicitly condemn this lynching, or indeed any of the ones to follow. In fact, one leader callously declared that it was on account of 'crowd excitement', while another said it was a 'misunderstanding'.

The Samajwadi Party (SP) government in the state at the time had plenty to answer for, just as it did for the Muzaffarnagar riots in 2013. It is a travesty that the Muslims of Uttar Pradesh should have such prodigious faith in the SP's secular credentials. It usually leaves communal tensions to simmer, reaping dividends at the ballot box, much like the BJP. Hindu chauvinism and Islamic fundamentalism suit parties for whom religious polarisation is political oxygen. The Yadav family that heads up the SP thrives on the BJP's inveterate bigotry.

In his fact-finding report on the 2013 riots, Justice Vishnu Sahai indicted BJP leaders for creating a communal conflagration, but he also blamed the SP for allowing it to happen. Sixty people died, and among the 50,000 rendered homeless, many still live in miserable conditions, rooted out from their ancestral habitation. Of the two Muzaffarnagar riots accused, Sanjeev Baliyan was celebrated with a cabinet berth in the NDA government and Sanjeev Som was given the status symbol of Z+ security. Both are BJP's vote-catchers in UP.

In 2015 too, when one of the accused in Akhlaq's murder died, BJP leaders anointed him in the national tricolour, hailing him as a patriot for killing a fellow Indian.[41] India's moral fibre now hung by a thread.

Around this time, television studios underwent a palpable change—the visible face of which was that RSS spokespersons had begun regularly accompanying their BJP counterparts. A tectonic shift to saffron voices was encouraged through subterfuge, which is how the mainstream media helps manufacture a political narrative. To his credit, Modi has never tried to hide his RSS lineage. The divisive 'Ghar Wapsi' rhetoric has its origins in Modi's famous '*hum paanch, hamare pacchis*'[42] (we five, our twenty-five) speech in Gujarat about 'child-producing factories'. The beef ban got a second wind courtesy Modi's calculated mention of the 'pink revolution' during the 2014 Lok Sabha campaign. He had mastered dog-whistle politics; the foot soldiers of the RSS, Vishwa Hindu Parishad (VHP), Bajrang Dal, Akhil Bharatiya Vidyarthi Parishad (ABVP) would then create local mayhem.[43]

The late U.R. Ananthamurthy had sounded early warning bells about what was to come. He said, 'He [Modi] will create fear, and if a fearsome man is sitting there, people will just bow down to him because a bully creates cowards.' In the aftermath of Modi's win, URA was mostly ignored, his apprehensions treated as paranoid overreaction.

The prime minister quickly fell short of the dizzying expectations of Goldman Sachs, Merrill Lynch and Moody's, but he was delighting his RSS commanders and right-wing propagandists. In Silicon Valley, Modi talked of broadband penetration; in India, he courted sectarian bigots. It was breathtaking doublespeak. For all his headline management, though, the news turned away from Modi's meeting with

Facebook's Mark Zuckerberg to a nondescript Muslim man called Mohammad Akhlaq.

There would be others after Akhlaq. Soon, independent media in India began putting together lynching maps.[44] A man and a teenager transporting their cattle for a regular market auction were brutally lynched in broad daylight in BJP-ruled Jharkhand.[45] Later, they were suspended from a tree, eerily reminiscent of the lynchings of black people[46] in the US from the late 1800s to the mid-1950s. As in the US, this specific form of murder was meant to terrorise and subjugate the 'other', chiefly Muslims and, in smaller numbers, Dalits.

In step with terror on the streets was the blatant formalisation of anti-minorityism. Educational institutions, particularly schools, became prime targets because they were susceptible to indoctrination. The teaching of a twisted version of history and campus visits by proponents of the RSS/BJP ideology can easily overwhelm an impressionable soul. Schools and universities, which ought to be encouraging free thinking, were imprisoned instead in a binary contest: Left vs Right, national vs anti-national, Hindu vs Muslim, Congress vs BJP. Universities are the laboratories of a modern democracy, where ideas from the boisterously bizarre to the audaciously imaginative are explored. Some work, others don't, but it is an environment that must not be shoehorned. At JNU, the BJP government sought to flagrantly suppress independent thinking, labelling as 'anti-national' students who dared criticise the government. By giving it a hue of cultural nationalism and patriotic sentimentalism, the right-wing brigade exacted political leverage from its attack on JNU. Nobody was surprised when RSS Chief Mohan Bhagwat issued his advisory: students must be taught to say '*Bharat Mata Ki Jai*'.[47]

Narendra Modi's government had appropriated nationalism and patriotism; everyone else was a traitor to the country's agenda, whether they were opposition parties, Muslim citizens, liberals, JNU, Aligarh Muslim University (AMU), Jamia Milia Islamia, NGOs or social activists. This provided the pretext for ABVP goons and Bajrang Dal goondas to run amuck.

This appropriation also meant that criticising certain governmental actions (particularly of military assertiveness in Kashmir) was deemed apostasy. With its hyper-nationalism gambit, the BJP destroyed all possibility of civilised debate, discussion and deliberation. Censorship, clampdowns and curtailment of the natural human voice were its strategies for leveraging this muscular patriotism. At IIT, FTII, JNU, University of Hyderabad, Jadavpur University, Allahabad University, AMU, Indian Institute of Mass Communication (IIMC), there was a subterranean attempt to destabilise institutions of learning through the imposition of Sangh ideology.[48] And India had a new political calculus—NQ (Nationalism Quotient)—one the BJP had a monopoly over. As for the economy, it was not in the backseat; it was in the trunk.

If one goes to Mohammed Ali Road, Mumbai, during Ramzan, one is enveloped as much by the prodigious hospitality of the people there as the mouth-watering delicacies on offer at Sulaiman Mithaiwala. I think also of the gentle sophistication in the articulation of bearded taxi-drivers in Mumbai. They are Indians and they are Muslims. India is where they were born and India is where they will die. It is appalling that we live in times where this must be said, but here goes, all the same: Muslims are an inextricable part of India's social and cultural character, of the country's history.

Our present too is similarly enriched: three former presidents, including Dr Abdul Kalam, top-notch civil servants such as Wajahat Habibullah, lyricists and music composers such as Sahir Ludhianvi and Khayyam, musicians such as Zakir Hussain, Bismillah Khan and Vilayat Khan, the inimitable singer Mohammad Rafi, the outstanding cricketers Zaheer Khan, Mohammad Kaif and Yusuf Pathan, the cinematic charms of the three Khans, the mesmerising poetry of Javed Akhtar and Kaifi Azmi—we are not even scratching the surface of the exciting, electric, eclectic mix that Muslims have brought to contemporary cultural life. Azim Premji, who led Wipro to its position as a global software behemoth, is one of the great philanthropists of this era.

India's collective consciousness needed to embrace its resplendent multiplicity and resist the diabolical narrative of the saffron brigade. The question in 2019 was: will the vote-bank politics of the pseudo-nationalists define India's self-image? Is this to be its new tryst with destiny? The answer to that was a resounding yes.

One aspect of the project to psychologically ghettoise Indian Muslims is fear-mongering about the rising threat of the 'Muslim reproductive growth' and how it upsets the demographic balance. It is a myth that no amount of assiduous fact-checking can stem.[49]

On 13 February 2017, Union Minister Kiren Rijiju put out a mischievous tweet about the decline of the Hindu population.[50] In the BJP manifesto prepared for the UP elections that were due a few months later, BJP President Amit Shah boasted about setting up 'anti-Romeo squads' (a euphemism for 'Love Jihad' politics).[51] 'Ghar Wapsi', triple talaq, Ram Mandir, the Kairana exodus[52] were the fissiparous agendas that drove BJP's mammoth electoral factory in those elections. The

Muzaffarnagar experiment in 2013 was a political windfall for the BJP in Uttar Pradesh, and resulted in seventy-three seats in the Lok Sabha. The communal project was being assiduously executed in the plains of India's most populous state, Uttar Pradesh.

With its 200 million inhabitants, UP can qualify as the fifth most populous country in the world. It is home to about 37 million Muslims (19 per cent of its citizens)—more Muslims than reside in Saudi Arabia, Iraq or Morocco. And yet, the BJP found not one Muslim candidate to field in the 403 seats that it was contesting. The party was no longer interested in pretence. Psephologists conjecture that Muslims significantly impact results in 130 of the 403 assembly constituencies, and comprise roughly 20 per cent of the electorate in about seventy seats. In some others (thirty or so seats), that percentage rises to a significant 30–45 per cent. However, in 2014, the Modi avalanche had dismantled traditional voting projections, giving the BJP an astounding 43 per cent vote share and a lead in a whopping 328 assembly constituencies. It appeared to believe that it could abandon India's Muslims if there was sufficient consolidation of the Hindu vote. Heartbreakingly, it was proven right. Isolationism precedes persecution in societies.

The victory only led the BJP to become more obscurantist. Its trajectory was of a piece with the international trend of rising right-wing leaders playing the ultra-nationalism card cloaked in the lingo of economic autarchy. Unsurprisingly, the army's surgical strikes in 2016 inside Pakistani territory, following the Uri terror attack, became Modi's electoral calling card. Conveniently, the BJP ignored the terror attacks that happened subsequently on Indian soil, as well as the record number of Indian civil and military casualties they resulted in.[53] Cross-border terrorism cannot be obliterated overnight. Modi had introduced the dangerous game of politicising military success for the ballot box—a move that has today dismantled the Chinese Wall between military and civil leadership that has existed since Independence. Then again, the BJP has always pushed the limits of Indian democracy.

In 1992, for instance, the Babri Masjid demolition was an orchestrated act of hooliganism masterminded by the Sangh Parivar. The then UP chief minister, Kalyan Singh, had no compunctions about misleading the Supreme Court with a written affidavit assuring the court that there would be no vandalism of the fifteenth-century structure. The communal project blithely disregards constitutional propriety. 'The janata wants it' is the excuse. Twenty-five years later, by 2017, the BJP had dropped that sort of tokenism.

The taint of the 2002 Gujarat pogrom, which happened on his watch, had left Modi untroubled. The BJP rejected outright the Rajendra Sachar Committee (2006) and Ranganath Mishra Commission (2007) reports that suggested increased investment in social and economic capital to ameliorate the huge inequalities that persist among Muslims and other minorities. Economic backwardness exacerbates identity politics. And it suited the BJP to perpetuate it.[54]

Across the world, minorities and the marginalised sections have won for themselves state intervention to redress the inequalities of their condition. When a political party views welfare expenditure on Muslims as 'pseudo-secular' minority appeasement, it can only be the result of an ideological animus. This stance, unsurprisingly, is consistent with the instruction manual of the RSS. Mohan Bhagwat called for all Hindus to be united, and then took it up a notch by saying that all Indians should join the RSS.[55] The RSS has hit upon a winning formula: push the Hindu Rashtra agenda through its elected puppet, while taking the moral high ground of being a nationalistic entity promoting majoritarian interests and cultural hegemony. Thus, despite the scandals, criminal charges and allegations that occasionally mar the credentials of BJP's members and leaders, the RSS remains unblemished. From its highly protected bastion, it can do no wrong. Meanwhile, India's self-styled Pradhan Sevak carries its divisive Hindutva project forward at full tilt. Even constitutional positions have been saffronised now. In the state of Tripura, for instance, Tathagata Roy has redefined what a governor—a constitutional post deemed impartial and overtly apolitical—might do.[56] He functions, essentially, as an agent provocateur of the RSS family. In October 2020, Maharashtra Governor Bhagat Singh Koshyari would do this too when he asked the state's Shiv Sena government to open temples, asking, 'Have you suddenly turned secular?'[57]

Indian democracy is being turned upside down. The BJP, frequent winner of state elections, behaves like a graceless conqueror, contemptuous of political opponents. Elections are certainly a brutal winner-takes-all contest, but the BJP under Modi has created an environment of intense political hostility, where opponents are seen not as ideological and governance alternatives for the people, but as dangerous enemies that must be comprehensively destroyed. Ergo, Modi's call for Congress-mukt Bharat;[58] don't just defeat the enemy, exterminate them. Coexistence with differing ideologies is seen as a sign of weakness.

Earlier, Mohan Bhagwat had said that all Muslims living in India (approximately 170 million) were also Hindus. It was meant to infuriate hardliners among the Muslim leadership and elicit an equally trenchant rebuttal. That suits the Sangh Parivar, because minority hate speeches receive very wide amplification through the country's servile print and electronic media. Then the troll army stirs up a WhatsApp tornado.

In the age of social media, its actions could (and did) have destructive repercussions. As noted author Mukul Kesavan says, 'Hindutva is a bid to take over the State in the name of the Hindu majority. It is a coup in slow motion.' India's democracy is vulnerable today as its youth fall prey to maleficent propaganda. And the BJP has a ready tool to hook them: technology.

The Modi government focused single-mindedly on cashless and mobile-driven delivery, digital footprints and the internet. While India did need a digital push, the BJP's policies were, in fact, about developing for Modi and the BJP an image of technological savvy among the young and the middle class. This image is a buffer against blowback from the party's practices of archaic thinking and ethnic chauvinism that are dragging India back into the dark ages. The two-tongued messaging keeps citizens bewildered, which suits the BJP just fine.

Former president of India and senior Congress leader Pranab Mukherjee caused quite a flutter when he decided to visit the RSS headquarters. Mukherjee uttered platitudes to a poker-faced audience—the fleeting presence of this staunch secularist made not even a dent on decades of ingrained communal calcification. BJP minister M.J. Akbar has written in his well-researched book, *Riot after Riot*, 'After all, if the Hindus and Muslims live in peace, how will the RSS find another convert?' It is an astute assessment: communal harmony would cause an existential crisis for the RSS.

The author of the term 'Hindutva' is Vinayak Damodar Savarkar of the Hindu Mahasabha, the members of which were convicted for the assassination of Mahatma Gandhi. Savarkar himself barely escaped being charged, with the Jeevan Lal Kapur Commission (1969) noting: 'All these facts taken together were destructive of any theory other than the conspiracy to murder by Savarkar and his group.' Interestingly, Modi has called Savarkar a true patriot. So, was the killing of Gandhi an act of love for the motherland? Neither the RSS nor the Hindu Mahasabha took part in the Civil Disobedience movement or the Quit India movement, both of which must indisputably classify as patriotic. Savarkar, the ideological fount of the Sangh Parivar, wrote five mercy petitions to the British while in the Andaman jail—at a time when Congress leaders and workers were protesting on the streets and languishing in prisons, including the Cellular Jail in the Andaman Islands, in the thousands. Several Indian freedom fighters were thrashed and killed.

Although it poses as the torchbearer of nationalism today, the Sangh was not part of the nation-building project, nor indeed historically nationalistic. Today, its toadies beat up people who don't stand up for the national anthem, but for several decades after Independence, the RSS had opposed India's tricolour flag. Similarly, RSS leader M.S. Golwalkar rejected the syncretic nationalism that the Congress and Mahatma Gandhi espoused. Instead, the RSS lionised Adolf Hitler and Benito Mussolini,[59] who were engaged in ghastly ethnic cleansing projects.

Golwalkar had assured Gandhi that the RSS had no role whatsoever in exacerbating tensions during the Partition, which had led to the horrific killings that followed. A trusting Gandhi agreed to attend an RSS rally in Delhi soon after. Barely three months later, Golwalkar made his infamous U-turn, declaring at an RSS camp that the organisation would not let a single Muslim live in India.[60] Many decades before Amit Shah, Giriraj Singh and co. came up with the go-to-Pakistan solution;[61] Savarkar had called the Congress 'traitors and enemies' because of its secular ideology. Gandhi characterised the RSS perfectly: 'a communal body with a totalitarian outlook',[62] intrinsically intolerant and exclusivist.

The Sangh Parivar, comprising pseudo-nationalist organisations with zero contribution to our freedom movement, today uses nationalism to package religious bigotry. Dr Shashi Tharoor has painstakingly deconstructed the RSS/BJP attempt to hijack Hinduism in his exquisitely essayed book, *Why I Am a Hindu*. Hinduism is eclectic, it has universal osmosis at its nucleus; Hindutva is a regulated political mobilisation programme, says Tharoor. Segregation and ghettoisation of minorities are the markers of Hindutva.

The question then is, why doesn't the RSS just drop the elaborate charade and replace the BJP as the official political representative of the Sangh Parivar? Why should India have a political substitute in New Delhi when Nagpur is its effective capital? Why should not the RSS drop the smokescreen of a socio-cultural organisation and pass a formal electoral test? These are questions the media should have been raising, but have not.

This background in history and institutional relationships within the Sangh Parivar is essential to understanding the culture of impunity that protects gau rakshaks and lynchers in post-2014 India. While there is no denying that communalism is a deeply rooted malaise in which every political party is complicit, there is now institutional collaboration in these acts.

Will the killers of Pehlu Khan,[63] who was lynched in Alwar, Rajasthan, by 'cow vigilantes', be punished? When the fringe mob, considered a distant cousin to the principal party, becomes its patriarch, all existing logic is overturned. It is no surprise that lynching has become the new trial court of social justice. It is hardly surprising that BJP-ruled states like Gujarat, Rajasthan, Uttar Pradesh, Haryana and Jharkhand experienced gruesome escalations of mob fury.[64] An innocent man was savagely killed for telling someone to not publicly urinate in Delhi.[65] A PhD scholar in IIT Madras was thrashed for participating in a beef festival to protest against laws introduced by the Central government to effectively change India's food paradigm.[66] These violent manifestations have become the new normal—someone is always watching and can be easily offended. Hindutva politics has converted the serene Indian cow into a core ingredient of its insatiable bloodlust—a politics that killed Mohammed Akhlaq and ravaged his family.

The only way to understand human suffering is to practise empathy, to walk in someone else's shoes. The videographing of lynching crimes—a gruesome and depressingly common phenomenon—forces the participation of viewers, whether they are quailing at what they see or celebrating it. I watched the folded hands of a blood-soaked Mohammed Naeem in Jharkhand. A chill ran down my spine—Naeem was staring into the faces of his killers, a feral public court that suspected him of child-napping. I wondered what he thought of in those last moments. Did he think of the family he might never see again, did he fear that they too might be tortured to death, or did he hope that, somehow, the world's fastest-growing economy would have the resources to save him? Naeem died as the result of a fabricated WhatsApp rumour. His lynching was a throwback to the Muzaffarnagar riots of 2013, which were also triggered by fake videos.[67]

It didn't take a fake video to provoke the lynching of Junaid Khan, still a boy at fifteen years of age. Junaid had gone to Delhi for Eid shopping with his brothers. On his way home to Ballabhgarh, a hate-fuelled group of men pounced on him. He was stabbed during the attack and bled to death.[68] His brothers were assaulted too, but escaped with their lives. Beef eaters, the attackers yelled. No one in the train compartment helped them. This too is India's new social reality—the lumpen gangs are on the warpath as lynching, a primitive, spine-chilling form of public guillotining, is increasingly becoming the new norm. Between 1 January 2017 and 5 July 2018, as many as thirty-three persons had been killed and at least ninety-nine injured in sixty-nine reported cases of lynching.[69]

For the RSS–BJP combine, religious fundamentalism and bigotry are not just political tactics but an intrinsic foundational philosophy. The lynchings had a distinctive pattern. They took place sporadically to keep the communal temperature blistering, as state governments dilly-dallied and looked the other way. Social divisions worsened as inflammatory statements were liberally made by official motormouths. The PM barely spoke.

Television anchors use the misleading term 'cow vigilantes' for what are, in fact, gangs of organised murderers—the cow is just a convenient pretext. They are India's new non-State actors, and they need no provocation whatsoever. The wearing of a skullcap or the sporting of a beard is enough. And anyone transporting cattle with these newly damning signifiers is courting death. What started with Akhlaq in September 2015 soon metastasised into the killing fields of Rajasthan, Haryana, Jharkhand, J&K, Madhya Pradesh and Assam. By a not-so-strange coincidence, these were all BJP-ruled states at the time. (The party's leaders in the Northeastern states, Kerala, West Bengal and Goa, of course, sing a different tune on cow slaughter or beef consumption on account of electoral compulsions, as there are large pockets of Christian population there.)

The surest sign that the new jungle justice system of lynchings has political sanction is the blatant police inaction.

Whether it was Akhkaq, Pehlu Khan or the 'strange fruit'[70] in Jharkhand's Latehar district, there was one common factor: institutional apathy. And the perpetrators seemed confident of political patronage in the BJP-ruled states where they mostly originated.[71]

Urban India seemed barely outraged, and mainstream media seemed to not care. The #NotInMyName protest[72] across India against mob lynchings was a good start, but at best was just a hashtag. There were no candlelight marches for Akhlaq and his fellow departed. In fact, several TV channels actively propagated hate by encouraging asymmetrical panel discussions with no pretensions to either neutrality or rationality. Arun Shourie famously compared some of these suited-booted noise-makers to the anchors on North Korean State-owned TV.[73] Every night, these anchors provoked the communal mercury, adding both to their Television Rating Points (TRPs) and to mayhem in the country. India Inc. was predictably silent, its frangible moral backbone suffering from a slipped disc. Gradually, the front-page news of death by lynching slipped into a page-eleven item. At some point, the fatigue factor set in and lynching is now so routine, it is almost non-news. That was always the goal.

With rising unemployment, particularly in small towns and the rural interiors, cow vigilantism could well become the fallback option for India's struggling demographic dividend. As these young men seek social relevance under wily political chieftains, they are easy prey to the world of crime. With no occupational mobility, they become goons-for-hire and drifters, merely consuming TikTok videos and WhatsApp forwards.

To be fair, the culture of impunity comes from the very top. Politicians display aggressive and contemptuous behaviour—whether beating up airline officers or threatening police officials—which rapidly percolates down the ranks. If public figures can behave so irresponsibly and get away with it, then why not me, asks the unemployed young man twiddling his thumb.

Under Modi's NDA, one is seeing the emergence of a dark, toxic society, where lumpen elements have become the new landlords of terror. Since state elections take place twenty-nine times between two general elections, it suits right-wing political strategists to keep communal tensions high. The data compiled by data-analysis website IndiaSpend is distressing:[74] 86 per cent dead in cow-related violence since 2010 are Muslim, and 97 per cent attacks have happened since 2014. As an Ivy school research revealed, the BJP is the constant beneficiary in times of social strife.[75]

Since becoming prime minister, Modi has consistently skipped the iftar party hosted by the president of India at the Rashtrapati Bhavan, breaking a time-honoured tradition with insouciant ease. The official boycott of a religious occasion is a political dispatch; his core vote bank absorbs the message with glee. In 2017, Modi's entire cabinet avoided the Ramzan invitation from the outgoing president Pranab Mukherjee. To their credit, they were no longer pretending respect for secular conventions. India can no longer petend either.

In September 2017, two incidents captured starkly the dystopia that India has become. In one incident, Gurmeet Ram Rahim Singh, masquerading as a modern-day spiritual guru, was convicted for rape,[76] and all hell broke loose. The BJP's Haryana state apparatus, which had ignored a potentially dangerous crowd build-up of fanatical followers, totally collapsed. Thirty-eight people died in the ensuing mayhem.[77] Unbelievably, the government applauded itself for minimising casualty numbers. Meanwhile, in Bangalore, Gauri Lankesh—fiery editor of

Lankesh Patrike, a historic Kannada daily, and a scathing critic of right-wing fundamentalist ideology—was killed.

I did not know Lankesh, but had heard of her relentless battle against Hindutva ideology, obscurantist beliefs and establishment indiscretions in her state of Karnataka. It is the zealousness of social activists like Lankesh that keeps a democracy effervescent. They challenge corrupt administrative systems, keep the vitriolic venom of communal warlords under relative scrutiny, expose the insidious mafia–business nexus and fearlessly challenge political bullies. They give hope to those who live close to borderline ghettos, whether on account of material inadequacy or psychological devastation. Lankesh could have remained in her cocoon of privilege, but she chose to battle. And her resoluteness and refusal to back down threatened many in power. While investigations are still underway, there is no doubt that she was a victim of intolerance. The glee of the right-wing brigade following her death certainly points to this.[78]

Nathuram Godse may have pulled the trigger, but individual actions are often triggered by the prevailing sentiment. At that time, it was one of venomous anger. Undeniably, the perverse power of divisive politics makes people like Lankesh vulnerable. It leads to killings like those of rationalist thinkers Narendra Dabholkar, Govind Pansare and M.M. Kalburgi.[79] That India's prime minister follows many of the poisonous handles that spewed venom on Twitter after Lankesh's murder certainly makes matters worse;[80] it is tantamount to silent endorsement.

The gradual dismemberment of historical facts to suit the Hindu Rashtra narrative will mean that India's young will grow up with a foggy understanding of their social origins and cultural roots. The communal agenda is being stealthily but diligently imposed in schools, particularly government-aided institutions. Religion is centre stage in this ambitious project. RSS leaders issue intermittent diktats on the appropriate Hindu life: wear saris, eat vegetarian, and don't discuss politics or cricket during meals. Absurd as they sound, there are takers for this sage advice—believers who don't crack up with laughter when the RSS extols the virtues of making 'fair and tall Aryan babies' via some Ayurvedic formulations.[81]

Similarly, the very idea of what is 'Indian' is sought to be rewritten. Uttar Pradesh Chief Minister Yogi Adityanath stated that the Taj Mahal (the wondrous monument that drives India's tourism screenplay) at Agra is not representative of 'Indian culture'.[82] One of the seven wonders of the world is conspicuously absent from the cultural heritage plan outlined in the state budget because of its Mughal history. Bigotry is now part of the official manual too.

In reshaping the country into a monochromatic, homogenous whole, India is being shorn of its fundamental strength—plurality. These policies will, needless to say, also hurt economic growth, the reason why Modi won the 2014 elections in the first place. For example, the strictures on cow slaughter (since immobilised by the Supreme Court), caused severe losses to the beef export and leather industry.

Economic inequality is deleterious, but social discord can be fatal. 'One Nation, One Tax' (GST) may be a good thing, but 'One Nation, One Society' is what India needs more. It is what India's first prime minister was sworn to. Nehru would have been stunned to see his country today; the shrill, hyper-nationalist call that has become the dominating impulse of daily life would have crushed him. For him, nationalism manifested in a commitment to our religious plurality, our social and cultural diversity. Secular nationalism was the Gandhi–Nehru promise made in 1947 to the Muslims of India, a promise that they need not leave their homes during Partition.

It was no easy task to shepherd a country from the oppressive darkness of a post-colonial state and a savage post-Partition bloodbath in a world gripped by post-war reconstruction and political realignments. But in his seventeen years at the helm, Nehru handled this complex journey with extraordinary finesse. He had his fair share of critics, from towering personalities like C.R. Rajagopalachari, Sheikh Abdullah, Netaji Subhas Chandra Bose, down to the perennially thin-skinned RSS and Hindu Mahasabha leaders who considered him a traitor. But Nehru's vision was resolute; India's ethos, values and character as enshrined in the Constitution were to him the non-negotiable foundations for its future.

While it is not my objective to argue that Nehru was a flawless leader, I must decry the systematic and insidious campaign to vilify his remarkable political career. He is a perennial reminder to the RSS–BJP of what India truly represents: a melange, multiple and catholic. Nehru's differences with his colleagues Sardar Patel and Netaji Bose on sensitive issues have been mischievously twisted to denigrate him as a selfish man motivated by political ambition. Thankfully, these ham-handed efforts have not worked. While government fiats can force changes in school textbooks and even dictate prime-time TV hashtags, in the age of big data and limitless internet archives, the true facts are easily available to anyone who looks, and verifiable too.

One may not agree with all of his decisions, and Nehru made many mistakes (trusting China blindly being one of them), but Nehruvian ideology is what shaped the Idea of India. And that idea is not dead yet. Or is it? The rapes at Kathua and Unnao asked whether it existed anymore.

A young girl of eight was repeatedly raped in a temple in Kathua, Jammu and Kashmir.[83] Eight adult men plotted to gang-rape a child to induce her nomadic community to clear out. A Hindu religious body protested against the formal lodging of a chargesheet against the perpetrators of the rape. Several lawyers joined in to hinder due process in the case.[84] Two BJP ministers in the J&K cabinet 'allegedly attended an event organised by the Hindu Ekta Manch in support of the Kathua rape case accused'.[85]

In Unnao, Uttar Pradesh, a sixteen-year-old girl was savagely raped by Kuldeep Singh Sengar, then sitting BJP MLA. He was not brought to book. She begged for help, but the UP government refused to budge. Her father was severely thrashed by goons and relatives of the accused. He died. A car she was travelling in was hit by a truck, injuring her and killing her two aunts. Law-enforcement officers sniggered with sadistic delight. After desperate pleas, the terrified victim was given protection, but the rapist sauntered around, unaffected, unconcerned, until he was finally convicted by a Delhi court in December 2019.[86]

Violence against women has become quotidian under Prime Minister Narendra Modi, whose '*Beti Bachao, Beti Padhao*' slogan has begun to seem like a sleight of hand meant to mislead unsuspecting people into believing that the government cares. He waxes eloquent on GST, FDI and Make In India, but is mysteriously mealy-mouthed when it comes to India's falling performance in the gender disparity index.[87] He has remained mute on the rising incidence of crimes against women, especially in BJP-ruled states.[88]

Apart from this regression on gender issues, the BJP had also been ambivalent on the reading down of Section 377 (thus decriminalising homosexuality), and its ideological parent, the RSS, has often articulated that women must play a servile, secondary role to men. It was astonishing then to see the BJP position itself as a gender-justice warrior on the issue of triple talaq (instant divorce). The Supreme Court of India had already declared the practice unconstitutional in 2017. (Several Islamic countries, including Pakistan and Bangladesh, have banned this antediluvian custom.) But by making the triple talaq criminally prosecutable, the BJP provided an institutional apparatus for the harassment of Muslim men in a purely civil, marital dispute.[89] It was all of a piece: while lynching attacks against Muslim men were seeing runaway growth, the government self-righteously pretended it was a protector of Muslim women.

However, politically, the move potently contrasted with the Congress's compromised stance on the Shah Bano case (1985), where it had bent over backwards to please conservative, regressive Islamic clerics seeking a status quo on alimony and maintenance expenditure for divorced Muslim women. The Rajiv Gandhi government reversed a progressive Supreme Court judgement by bringing about a constitutional amendment, and never quite recovered from the taint of that decision. The banning of author Salman Rushdie's book *The Satanic Verses* further cemented the Congress's reputation as Muslim sympathisers. This factor had, in fact, helped galvanise support for L.K. Advani's infamous rath yatra and the Ram Janmabhoomi movement. Thirty-three years later, the BJP positioned itself as the liberal face of minority representation, even if it was an unbelievably hypocritical move.

By 2019, India was experiencing a disturbing turn towards a religious, cultural centricity that was diametrically opposed to its constitutional ethos. The fringe had been effortlessly mainstreamed, lynching murders were normalised, institutions of governance stood emasculated, media channels, by and large, kowtowed to the BJP's publicity pitch, and the RSS had no pretensions about its stranglehold on policymaking. In its citizens' silence, Gandhi's India stood vaporised. Who is surprised then that there were clarion calls for a temple to Nathuram Godse? India looked different. India felt different. Towering above all during this period of India's remarkable metabolism was one man: Narendra Modi.

2

NARENDRA MODI

A One-Horse Race

I first saw Narendra Modi on NDTV in 1996. It was the first time that the BJP had become the single-largest party in Parliament, with 182 seats. Much younger then, the future prime minister had a striking media presence, in spite of his surly expression. He listened intently to every word, and spoke with conviction in impeccable Hindi. I have always maintained that a national leader needs a certain extemporaneous brilliance in Hindi. (I can see non-Hindi-belt friends cringe at this, but it is just a practical necessity, not one I endorse.) Modi was already an ideological commander within the BJP. It was obvious that this was someone to watch. But I could not have foreseen the massive public mandate he would win for the BJP in 2014—the first time in three decades that a political party had an absolute majority. Modi had officially moved from the RSS to the BJP in 1987. Now he was the Sangh's national saviour.

His humble beginnings became political folklore. When Congressman Mani Shankar Aiyar, former diplomat and intellectual motormouth, contemptuously dismissed him as a 'chaiwala' at an AICC session, Modi promptly capitalised on the political opening. The fable of '*Chai Pe Charcha*' was born. A young RSS boy from Vadnagar, Gujarat, whose father sold tea at the local railway station, was now the prime minister. It was a heroic story, scripted for this age. In a country that had become competitive and aspirational, entitlements of birth and privilege and the elitist establishment had come to be abhorred. Modi was the iconoclast who had broken the glass ceiling set by the Lutyens durbari class. Unwittingly, Aiyar had added to the growing cult of Narendra Modi.

I have long admired Modi's inexhaustible energy, ruthless ambition and insatiable appetite for power. Under him, the BJP transformed from a modest threat to the Congress to an unassailable, monstrous machine. The Congress and Rahul Gandhi made the fatal mistake of underestimating his impact on the national stage. Modi's political destiny was linked to a horrific episode: kar sevaks returning from Ayodhya in the Sabarmati Express coach S-6 were locked in the train compartment and gasoline was used to torch it, charring fifty-six people to death. 27 February 2002 horrified the nation. It was allegedly an orchestrated attack, although there are theories that it was the result of a nasty scuffle between the travelling kar sevaks and some Muslim vendors on the railway platform. A planned anti-Muslim pogrom followed. The Gujarat communal riots lasted for weeks, the spasmodic violence uncontrollable, spreading across the state. Many called it India's first State-sponsored genocide. (Although the 1984 anti-Sikh pogrom, when around 3,000 Sikhs were massacred in Delhi following Indira Gandhi's assassination by her two Sikh bodyguards, Beant Singh and Satwant Singh, could also lay claim to that dubious distinction.)[90] The legend of Modi was born; a remorseless Hindutva proponent, RSS ideologue, a rare incorruptible politician and a brilliant administrator with a reputation for getting things done.

Modi is a smart politician and an ace communicator, with an uncannily sharp political sense. The proof of this is his reluctance to allow free-wheeling interviews with television anchors. The few that he has consented to appear too choreographed to be taken seriously. In the run-up to the 2019 elections, for instance, actor Akshay Kumar, an outspoken devotee of Modi, interviewed him on his personal life, and India made the enlightening discovery that its prime minister loves to suck on mangoes.

Although the liberal commentariat castigates him for being frightened of real interrogation—Modi has not held a single press conference in six years—he wisely plays to his strengths. What the prime minister relishes are long monologues in which he can indulge in fantastical bombasts, sardonic wisecracks and storytelling, all of which people seem to want. Unlike the Congress leadership, which spoke selectively, Modi speaks at length, cleverly repeating his main line: the Congress is corrupt, dynastic, minority-appeasing, and destroying India's economic potential with substandard governance. He travels the length and breadth of the country with unflagging energy. Modi knows he has no reason to impress a suave city journalist who touts this abstract bunkum called the Idea of India. He knows his limitations, and makes no attempt to win over what he calls the 'Khan Market gang', liberal urban elites who read the *New York Times* on their smartphones.

Modi has a fetish for razzmatazz, for extravagant spectacles that dazzle the mind, numb the senses and create a sense of euphoria. He is a risk-taker, and is keenly aware that most Indian politicians, particularly in the current Congress, are averse to big gambles. Thus, assiduously, he contrasts himself with the Congress by doing the diametric opposite of what they would do; it is a clever ploy. Seen in this context, Modi's grandiloquent announcements (Rs 15 lakh in black-money refunds in a hundred days) and tectonic policy disruptors (demonetisation, the midnight announcement of GST, national lockdowns with a four-hour notice, surgical strikes) are integral to his electoral playbook.

Since Dr Manmohan Singh had essentially withdrawn from the public gaze during UPA-2, Modi offered India a garrulous alternative. People found in this leader, accessible and animated, a refreshing change. The perception of the Congress as aloof and arrogant was cemented, and Modi's long-winded oratory, pregnant with falsehoods and melodrama, worked magic. It would go on to win him two national elections.

1991 and 1992 were watershed years that defined India's destiny. 1991 marked an unprecedented economic breakthrough that propelled India into the global economic power league. To understand how remarkable that turnaround truly was, one must remember that, in 1991, India had to airlift sixty-seven tonnes of gold to London to seek an IMF bail-out package; today, it has foreign exchange reserves of US$ 500 billion. Then came 1992, the year of the Babri Masjid demolition, which marked an ominous return to the communal tensions of the Partition era that to this day threaten our fragile secular foundations. The year 2014 has now been added to the list of memorable milestones that have changed India irrevocably.

The big buzz during the general elections of 2014 was the 'demographic dividend' factor: the 140 million first-time young voters who would exercise their adult franchise for the first time. Social media users had by then grown to jumbo-sized numbers: Facebook (112 million), Twitter (22 million), YouTube (60 million) and WhatsApp (70 million). Many of the first-time voters were not just Gen Y, but those who were 'post-1991 children'. In a sense, there is a pre-1991 India and a new order after it. With the licence raj dismantled, curbs and quotas being abolished and a market-oriented economy in place, India found the entrepreneurial adrenaline that it was looking for. In 2014, that young generation was pumping hoarsely for a man called Narendra Modi. The former RSS pracharak, who had never lost an election in his life, saw Gen Y long before they saw him.

This Young India, as it was branded, challenged the old order. It had higher personal ambition, and was a product of the economic free-spiritedness unleashed in 1991. The global technological revolution too fundamentally altered the world. Where India once had only landline connections rationed by government departments (telephone penetration was 1 per cent in the mid-1990s), it now has 1,000 million mobile connections and over 170 million television households. India is one of the world's most hyper-connected countries.[91] It is one big mass of incessant chatter. Young urban India lives in a 3M world—mall, multiplex, mobile, the new paradigms of middle-class mobility. Modi sniffed a political opportunity for the BJP. Among local politicians, he was the first to jump on to social media. He saw 2014 in his mind's eye before the others did.

All political parties are grappling with the middle-class millennial, but Modi saw this Gen Y as a trump card. When he ridiculed MNREGA (Mahatma Gandhi National Rural Employment Guarantee Act) allocations on live TV in Parliament, or the RSS mocked job reservations for the backward classes for being anti-meritocracy, they were talking to this neo middle-class India. Modi wanted the middle class to believe that budgetary allocations for the poor, contemptuously dismissed as doles, were a classic case of robbing Peter to pay Paul. On the other hand, to the poor, he sold the intoxicating Hindutva-and-nationalism cocktail, garnished with subsidies like free gas cylinders, health insurance and low-cost housing. Modi has the extraordinary ability to please conflicting constituencies, and the political panache to appeal to diverse peoples. Ironically, it was the Congress that used to do this at one time.

For the UPA, however, the growth of millennials posed an intriguing challenge. Like middle-class populations all over the world, they have a me-first attitude. They resent subsidies that provide cheap food grains to about 800 million people as a fundamental right. Yet, in a peculiar social dichotomy, it is the middle-class (estimated at 350 million to be equal to the US population) that is, in fact, the biggest beneficiary of government subsidies on LPG, diesel, electricity and the like.[92] Modi, nearing his seventies, has charmed this Yo Bro generation with his strongman braggadocio. Even his worst critics will have to admit that the man has an uncanny knack for reading his audience's mind. The absence of an alternative leader with a pan-Indian appeal makes his stranglehold on the youth a significant barometer of electoral outcomes. The sixteenth Lok Sabha in 2014 was only the beginning.

The BJP won those general elections on the promise of 'development and governance'. It was good packaging. The last few years of UPA-2 were calamitous; the Congress looked bushed, and India was ready for higher public accountability and transparent structures. The Congress fought a lacklustre campaign on the backfoot. The initial honeymoon period also ensured wins in states like Maharashtra, Haryana and Jharkhand. But the 'Achhe Din' hype was punctured early.

By the end of 2014, Modi had come a cropper on several assurances that had mesmerised the electorate. His 'governance model' had gaping holes. It was a long time before a chief information commissioner or central vigilance commissioner was appointed, judicial encroachment and Central Bureau of Investigation (CBI) interference had already commenced, and ordinances were casually promulgated. His foreign policy, particularly with India's neighbours, and especially arch-foe

Pakistan, was an unmitigated disaster.[93] Despite a sharp dip in crude oil prices, the Indian economy struggled. Crony capitalism was warmly embraced. The human resource development (HRD) ministry was rewriting history to align with the RSS fantasy.[94] Manufacturing decelerated, agriculture stress increased, social-welfare allocations diminished and job creation saw a new slump.

The sheen was wearing off. But the Modi government's fightback to the public relations (PR) damage had begun in earnest. Huge public advertisements were mounted across the country, on schemes such as the Swachh Bharat Abhiyan (which rebranded the UPA's Nirmal Abhiyan on eradicating open defecation) and Make in India, and spectacles such as the Madison Square Garden event were held. Modi was everywhere you looked. He was omnipresent. He was freely spending taxpayers' money to tell the taxpayer that he cared.[95]

Meanwhile, a phlegmatic Opposition was still licking its wounds, unable to galvanise the public against any kind of governmental bungling. For the Congress, 2014 was the year of devastation. To what degree did public disillusionment with the grand old party play a role; how much of it was Modi's unstoppable momentum? Either way, the Congress needed to rebuild, recharge and reinvigorate for the long fight ahead. Yet, such was the hubris of laidback Congress veterans that they were betting on anti-incumbency going against the NDA, a fairly predictable pattern in Indian elections.

But Modi needed no pushback from the Opposition to stir him up to damage control. He has fire in his belly, never ever letting up on his campaign mode, and he knows the art of reaping a political windfall. Like he did with the Jan Lok Pal agitation of 2011.

Anna Hazare and Arvind Kejriwal launched the Jan Lokpal Bill anti-corruption agitation. At that time, UPA-2 appeared strong, if not sturdy, and the Indian economy had remained largely insulated from the debilitating aftershocks of the great global recession on account of the mortgage crisis in the US. India had registered more than 8.5 per cent GDP growth rate the year before, remarkable given the times. Manmohan Singh's reputation was sky-high after the civil nuclear liability law was passed. China and India were considered 'emerging market darlings'. The BJP looked emaciated and enervated and almost resigned to political irrelevance. But the protests at Jantar Mantar and Ramlila Maidan upended the political equilibrium. The Congress was unprepared for the sheer scale of the movement.

Anna Hazare, a social crusader, was relatively unknown outside Maharashtra. In his own state, he had attempted novel experimentations to create a 'model village', which included bizarre practices such as tying people to a lamppost and whipping them for consuming alcohol. What started as a typical Delhi civil society agitation at Jantar Mantar turned into a tornado at Ramlila Maidan. The people of Delhi, who had voted Congress in all seven parliamentary seats exactly twenty-four moons ago, were now vociferously demanding the government's resignation. Hazare announced his fast unto death, or until the Jan Lokpal Bill was passed, and the electronic media set up 24/7 outside-broadcasting (OB) vans at the venue. The UPA made a clumsy attempt to arrest him on 16 August 2011—an outrageously ill-advised move that made him a public hero. Hazare was quickly christened the 'modern Mahatma'. Excited youngsters wore topis with 'I Am Anna' written on them. Yoga expert and spiritual guru Baba Ramdev too was arrested in an ill-handled midnight swoop at Ramlila Maidan. TRPs shot up faster than Apollo 13.

The chatterati found similarities with the Arab Spring. The anti-corruption agitation itself was mostly Delhi-centric, not collecting big crowds elsewhere in the country. But the sustained media onslaught amplified it immensely. Kejriwal saw a political window he could pounce on. An enervated BJP sniffed a chance too. And in Gandhinagar, a certain Mr Modi knew his time had come.

In short, the UPA had already lost the elections in 2011–12. The Comptroller and Auditor General of India (CAG) Vinod Rai had proposed that there were astronomical 'notional losses' from the coal and telecom-spectrum allocations scams, leading to a furious vilification of the government. Not even Manmohan Singh was spared in the vicious media trials that followed. The Supreme Court cancelled several spectrum licences, sending the entire telecom industry into a tailspin. The UPA became the visible manifestation of all that the people saw as wrong with the government apparatus. The government fumbled and bumbled and inevitably tumbled.

Ironically, it was the Congress-led UPA that had introduced the path-breaking Right to Information (RTI) Act, and even finally passed the Lokpal bill, its political bête noire. When it attempted to pass the Judicial Accountability Bill, the Citizens' Right to Grievance Redress Bill and the Whistle Blowers (Protection) Bill to augment the anti-graft infrastructure, the UPA was thwarted by the BJP. In 2014, however, optics—not facts—mattered. The BJP spokespersons would shout the word 'bhrashtachar' (corruption) at least a dozen times in every TV debate, all the way to May 2014.

The Congress, stunned and on the backfoot, had no effective response or coping strategy. That it won only a dismal forty-four seats resulted in another handicap: it was disallowed, as per constitutional rules, from being officially labelled as the leader of the Opposition. Modi had ground the Congress to dust. I can only hope he sent a thank you card to Arvind Kejriwal on 16 May 2014.

On that day, India's fleeting romance with wannabe revolutionaries was over. Its new passion was Narendra Modi.

Modi had taken a categorical position on the Indian economy; he wanted to be perceived as a free-market messiah, a right-liberal fantasy. He sought a thumbs up from foreign investors, international credit rating agencies, investment bankers, hedge funds, stock-market analysts and the upper middle class and super-rich. This mattered very much to him. A distinguishing feature of his reign has been his blatant courting of India Inc. Modi was fearless in redefining the public relationship between industrial behemoths and India's prime minister. He saw the industry as crucial to creating the 20 million jobs per year that he had promised the country's youth. For example, the prime minister featured in an ad for telecom brand Jio,[96] launched by India's biggest business house, the Mukesh Ambani-led Reliance Industries.

Big business emerged as a formidable power centre in India's political and social ecosystem. Ambitious, cash-rich and often avaricious, its questionable methods were often smoothed over by PR sophistry. In the course of NDA-1, allegations abounded of quid pro quo arrangements and extra-constitutional influence in policymaking.[97] Analysts drew parallels with the robber barons of the Gilded Age in the US. To Modi's credit, he stood by the business lobby even when Rahul Gandhi pilloried him with the '*Suit-boot Ki Sarkar*' jeer.

Undeniably, the UPA was equally guilty of using discretionary decision-making to bail out big industrialists. This became clear when two tapes involving India's biggest business houses embarrassed both the Congress and the BJP.

But if the Niira Radia tapes[98] showed the UPA in poor light, the Essar tapes[99] were explosive. They were a full-blown exposé of former prime minister A.B. Vajpayee's office being remote-controlled by business interests. Thus, when Modi featured prominently in an advertisement for Jio (which Reliance posited as a price-disruptive game-changer in the struggling telecom industry), it understandably raised eyebrows and loud protest on social media. #JioModi trended. Had Modi crossed a line in so publicly associating with a company that has serious business interests involving India's natural resources, including oil and gas? The subsequent demise of the Indian telecom industry, resulting in an oligopolistic industry (with just three surviving firms, of which two are struggling) would strengthen these apprehensions. But Modi's carefully built reputation of incorruptibility helped him through decisions that would have felled another leader. His image was his USP.

In early 2004, I was attending a corporate symposium. CEOs moved about freely, and everyone seemed to have an unusually sunny disposition. People joked that their shiny countenances mirrored the image of 'India Shining'—that clever phrase of unbridled optimism that finally spelt electoral doom for Vajpayee's NDA government. In several photo-ops, these industry honchos did a collective thumbs up. When I nervously protested that this utopia was grossly exaggerated—based as it was on just one year of 8 per cent GDP growth during the 2003–04 period, and a convenient tweak of poverty estimates—I was dismissed as a party pooper. The Confederation of Indian Industry (CII), Federation of Indian Chambers of Commerce & Industry (FICCI), Associated Chambers of Commerce of India (Assocham) are at their best when organising these five-star event management spectacles. These are social networking platforms for the big industry, where private lobbying by select groups really happens, and they are the heart of India's obnoxious oligopolies. The micro, small and medium enterprises (MSMEs) barely have a voice, although they form the bulk of the membership of industry associations.

Modi's Gujarat Global Investors Summit, held annually through his tenure as chief minister, was another such corporate shindig. He really knew how to lay out the red carpet. India Inc. publicly lauded the bearded, beaming Gujarat chief minister every year, looking smitten as they serenaded him.[100] Modi's human rights violations were long forgotten. One time, when still chief minister of Gujarat, he asked the CII to publicly apologise for Thermax ex-chairperson Anu Aga's condemnation of the 2002 'genocide'.[101] The CII promptly capitulated. When the UPA government tried to pass the GST bill, it was Modi and Madhya Pradesh Chief Minister Shivraj Singh Chouhan who delayed it, but no industrial chieftain mentioned it again.

Right from Ratan Tata to the Ambani brothers, they only sang paeans of Modi's flawless stewardship of corporate interests in Gujarat. The widening urban–rural chasm in Gujarat, its poor human development indices[102] and the utter marginalisation of its minorities were a parallel reality that the corporate sector, with its elastic moral fibre, could choose to ignore.

When the Manmohan Singh government took over in 2004, the stock markets suddenly collapsed. Merchant bankers and equity research analysts made doomsday predictions—what with a centrist national party in a fragile coalition supported by doddering Marxists. Their crystal-gazing was based on the perceived instability of a left-of-centre government. No one foresaw the huge premium that the dream combine of Dr Singh, P. Chidambaram and Montek Singh Ahluwalia could bring to India's economy and its financial markets. India grew (on the old index) at 7.75 per cent over a ten-year period, lifted 140 million people out of poverty and GDP growth peaked at 9.6 per cent. All this while the Great Recession was playing out globally in 2007. India's GDP trebled, and its stock markets peaked five times. Despite all these achievements, in 2013, the UPA story was winding up. After fifty-five years in power, the Congress party did not know how to sell itself.

The Supreme Court's Singur land verdict[103] shook up India Inc., which had long been wrangling land and subsidies from state governments through various 'arrangements'. Outrage against the takeover of land and the uprooting of poor farmers led to the ouster of West Bengal's Communist Party of India (Marxist) (CPM) government, led by then chief minister Buddhadeb Bhattacharya. The party had been undefeated for over three decades in the state. A politically astute Modi stepped in promptly and gave free land to the Tatas for the Rs 33,000 crore Nano car project. One of Modi's biggest strengths is big-ticket decision-making. He's a risk-taker, and a canny one. The Tata project was a turning point in his still developing political biography. Ratan Tata, perhaps the most revered name in Indian industry, endorsed Modi's leadership. He was now emerging as a natonal alternative.

Modi used his personal brand (I have no family, so why should I make money?) to destroy opponents. Government corruption—more than individual immorality, corporate malfeasance or institutional degradation—is an emotive issue in India. It has hampered growth, accentuated inequalities and asphyxiated efficiency. The average Indian feels short-changed by those in power. Hence, Modi's claim to incorruptibility was a potent political arsenal.

Corruption allegations are the most used strategy in Modi's playbook. He makes outrageous allegations, mustering his considerable talent for melodrama. Since television editors love him, the tirade is quickly amplified and a political narrative is created. The strategy of freely maligning opponents might seem simplistic, even tasteless, but it is effective—the dirt sticks, no matter which way the truth lies. There is no need, in the making of allegations, to submit evidence. Old issues too are given a regular airing. Robert Vadra's alleged land deals, Bofors, AgustaWestland, 2G, Commonwealth Games, all of this is close at hand when the BJP feels the urge to do some muck-raking.

The heat was finally turned on Modi with the Rafale scam. The prime minister's firm hold on big media conglomerates had spared him intense scrutiny all these years. Yet, even with a scandal as massive as Rafale, the government managed a measure of damage control.[104]

In the atmosphere of intimidation and vindictive backlash that prevails in India today, it is not easy being a whistle-blower. Strangely, the Congress, which could have mounted a massive public agitation on the non-appointment of a Lokpal, chose to let the issue drift away. It was a lost opportunity. Equally, it is appalling (and ironic) that a government that won its mandate on an anti-corruption campaign, should systematically devalue the RTI Act. Cases piled up because there were not enough personnel to handle the rising volumes. In any case, answers were routinely refused on flimsy pretexts. RTI activists were frequently threatened by political hoodlums, even murdered.[105] Decades of good work to create an important system of transparency was trashed. Paradoxically, it was the UPA that introduced both the RTI and Lokpal bills, but it was Modi—that big champion of the anti-corruption cause—who undermined these mechanisms.[106] Incredibly, people still trusted him more than they trusted the Congress.

Under Modi, India's Transparency International ranking has worsened; retail corruption is on the rise. India stumbled ten places in the Global Democracy Index, an alarming development that reflected the rising curbs on freedom of speech.[107] NDTV's

Prannoy Roy wrote an open letter to the prime minister, warning that the patently false charges against the channel, involving reputable foreign media houses, would have a deleterious impact on press freedom and the country's image.[108] Well-known editors, such as Bobby Ghosh (*Hindustan Times*) and Krishna Prasad (*Outlook*), allegedly lost their jobs. What was the occasional and subtle nudge to the management to keep journalists in check during the UPA days had been replaced by fairly direct instructions.[109]

What truly topped the corruption charts, though, was the electoral bonds scheme that the government floated—an instrument that legitimised black money and quid pro quo campaign finance from large corporations. Indian politics was no longer in a quagmire; it was in a quicksand. Transparency International listed India as the most corrupt country in Asia in 2017.[110] Yet, Modi continued to be seen as 'incorruptible': a perception that would help him paper over the Rafale allegations as well as the antics of the other Modi, Nirav (no relation to Narendra Modi).

Nirav Modi, diamond czar and glitterati fixture, stormed Indian television after it was revealed that he had duped Punjab National Bank (PNB) of Rs 11,400 crores.[111] He was soon a household name. More illustrious conmen joined the rogues gallery—Mehul Choksi of Gitanjali Gems and Vikram Kothari of Rotomac pens.[112] As skeletons tumbled out of creaky cupboards, the scope of their larceny ballooned to over Rs 30,000 crore. This was the Great Indian Bank Robbery. Prime Minister Modi chose the meditative option of pindrop silence. A jubilant Opposition dubbed Nirav Modi 'Chhota Modi'. As is the wont in such cases, junior officers at PNB were interrogated, while the big fish got away scot-free. Modi's cheerleaders used nebulous terms like 'systemic failure' and 'procedural flaws' to airbrush the proximity of Nirav Modi and Mehul Choksi with the prime minister.

India's banking universe has robust processes and a sound operating system; 'human error' is possible, of course—if the palms are well greased. The PNB scam was the result of deliberate regulatory oversight. In a departure strongly reminiscent of liquor baron Vijay Mallya's[113] red-carpet send-off from Indian shores, Modi, Choksi and their families trooped off with insouciant ease through India's immigration counters in early January 2018. Nirav Modi even made a casual reappearance in the august company of India's other billionaires during a photoshoot with Prime Minister Modi himself at Davos, only a few weeks after absconding.[114] Interestingly, the prime minister's office (PMO) had been intimated about Nirav Modi's maternal uncle Mehul Choksi's shady deals in both 2015 and 2016.[115] No action was taken. But Narendra Modi's image remained unscathed. No one is more skilled in post-truth manoeuvres.

Come to think of it, 2016 was the post-truth year. It was when Donald Trump made his hard-to-believe way to the White House. Trump's faux pas, egregious lies, profane outbursts and unambiguous bigotry found a rapt audience and, finally, a charmed voter. America and Americans became objects of global ridicule. But the post-truth age had, in fact, been ushered in three years earlier—in the general elections of the world's largest democracy. Narendra Modi had emerged victorious, despite carrying humongous baggage, including complicity in an alleged genocide. Modi and Trump displayed remarkable similarities.

Modi was a powerful regional satrap since 2002 in Gujarat, a prosperous state, even if its depressing social and economic indicators belied the trickle-down growth model of professors Jagdish Bhagwati and Arvind Panagariya.[116] As chief minister, Modi often claimed that he was being unfairly vilified by a pseudo-secular mainstream media. The media was not alone, though; the Supreme Court referred to 'modern day "Neros" who were looking elsewhere when Best Bakery and innocent children and helpless women were burning, and were probably deliberating how the perpetrators of the crime can be saved or protected'.[117] Ehsan Jafri, a former Congress MP, was killed at Gulberg Society even as his calls for help to Modi's residence went unanswered. The death toll, at a conservative estimate, was 1,200 (the NGO Human Rights Watch puts it at over 2,000[118]). India had several communal riots before, but under Modi it saw a dangerous manifestation—the State-sponsorship of organised attacks against clearly outnumbered minorities.[119] Police forces did not just abdicate responsibility, they were hand-in-glove with the murderous perpetrators of the planned pogrom.[120] Modi had calculated an electoral windfall from the human tragedy; he whipped up anti-minority hysteria (Muslims are just 6 per cent of Gujarat's population) and won three assembly elections in a row. His policy of protecting his own electoral contingent became the famous 'Gujarat model'.

Gujarat became a laboratory for testing a democratically elected police state. Fake encounter killings were carried out against suspected terrorists who were apparently on a mission to assassinate the Hindu Hriday Samrat. Police officers who valiantly protested these excesses were promptly transferred, while others faced criminal charges. Maya Kodnani,[121] convicted for the death of ninety-seven people in the Naroda Patiya massacre, was appointed a minister. The messaging was unequivocal.

If Trump wanted to 'Make America Great Again', Modi had sold #AchheDin (good days again). They were similar promises. The American economy's macro-fundamentals were actually good in 2016; Obama had rescued the US from the collapse of Wall Street and the economic meltdown following the mortgage defaults. Similarly, India, despite creeping sluggishness, had survived the Great Recession, and clocked an average of 7.8 per cent GDP over ten long years. It remained the second fastest-growing economy after China.

Modi, of course, rubbished all of this as statistical gobbledygook. He mocked the 'chicken biryani' diplomacy[122] of Dr Manmohan Singh as sweet surrender to Pakistan. He spoke disparagingly about women ('50 crore ki girlfriend' is how he referred to Congress leader Shashi Tharoor's fiancée),[123] even as he kept his own marital status a secret. To this day, there remain serious question marks over his declared educational qualifications.[124] As an aside, he even got Mahatma Gandhi's name wrong once.[125] At any rate, none of this affected Modi's popularity or dented his image. In 2014, people were far too frustrated with the Congress to notice such things.

Six months before the 2014 elections, two activist websites produced audio tapes that indicated a massive abuse of state machinery to track the movements of a woman in an alleged relationship with the Gujarat chief minister.[126] The story mysteriously disappeared from the headlines. Modi whipped out the victim card regularly and, in Parliament, the BJP was on full-throttle filibustering every time their hero appeared to be in the dock.

Like Trump, Modi offered instantaneous back-of-the-envelope solutions to longstanding problems that had no easy solutions. He even intimidated the BJP leadership through an aggressive Twitter troll strategy; L.K. Advani and Sushma Swaraj, who were seen as prime ministerial alternatives in 2014, meekly caved. In a striking parallel, some years later, Trump ran his campaign on trash-talk, with nasty nicknames like Crooked Hillary. Both Trump and Modi are reality TV superstars. Their charisma is based on being brusque and bombastic. In this strategy, clashes work better than collaboration, and cantankerousness is more effective than content. They also shared a political strategy: Islamophobia.[127] For years, the US had denied Modi a visa for human rights violations; now, he had an alter ego living in the White House.

But Modi himself lives under the shadow of India's first prime minister. He has a pathological detestation of Nehru.[128] After May 2014, Nehru became the target of an orchestrated character assassination campaign by the BJP. Over a period of several months preceding the West Bengal Assembly elections in 2016, the party unleashed a media campaign to malign him. It was insinuated that there was an attempt to cover up the untimely death of freedom-fighter and former Congress president Netaji Subhas Chandra Bose in a plane crash in Taipei, Taiwan. The BJP used right-wing stooges with literary pretensions, dubious historians, indulgent media editors and disgruntled family members of Netaji to launch a vicious assault on Nehru.[129] Modi hosted a generous reception for the BJP-supporting members of Netaji's family in his home. Soon, a member of the Bose family joined the saffron brigade, contested elections and lost. Television debates were centred on Nehru's fear of Netaji's popularity. The Sangh Parivar even created a fabricated letter wherein Nehru called Bose a 'war criminal'. Soon after the elections, the story was shelved.

Life moved on, but for all the attempts to counter these lies, citizens would still be wondering: what was the truth about Nehru anyway? That lingering residual doubt is exactly what fake news aims to accomplish. It is impossible to counter with facts. Facts such as this one: Netaji named one of his infantry brigades in the Indian National Army (INA) after Nehru.[130] Or this one: Nehru wore his barrister robes for the first time to defend INA army soldiers charged with treason by the British.[131] These stories have today been edged out of mainstream consciousness.

The Statue of Unity—apparently the tallest in the world, in keeping with Modi's penchant for the epic—has effected another masterly deception. Common sense suggests that commissioning a statue of Sardar Vallabhbhai Patel would greatly upset Modi's ideological mentor, the RSS. As India's first home minister, Patel had, after all, banned the RSS.[132] Nehru and Patel were brothers-in-arms, each other's conscience-keepers. But Modi and the BJP have told the country otherwise, and in a post-truth world, India believed them.

This unmooring of the public discourse from a shared reality has had serious consequences for the nation. The character assassination of political adversaries became the norm in the BJP's politics. Party leader Ram Madhav raised the bar of political indecency; he said the proposed coalition of the People's Democratic Party, the National Conference and the Congress in Jammu and Kashmir (which did not fructify, after the BJP-PDP coalition government collapsed in 2018) was engineered by Pakistan. The objective was to tarnish opposition parties as anti-national terror-sympathisers. Modi gave the term 'Urban Naxals', a right-wing social media invention,[133] an official imprimatur during the election campaign, because of which left-leaning intellectual liberals became targets of hate. These moves were crucial to the 2019 Lok Sabha election strategy. As was the RSS.

In 1925, K.B. Hedgewar founded the RSS. Through rigorous and long-term outreach, the organisation has gradually spread its dragnet of influence across the country. Apart from running an estimated 30,000 primary and secondary schools, the RSS has been equally active in trade unions, farmers' organisations and cultural bodies. Even Modi's appointment as prime ministerial candidate had their sign off. The RSS strategy is simultaneously subtle and blatant. Take, for instance, the name-changing spree, which signals to its constituency a power move. Thus,

Mughalsarai station became Deen Dayal Upadhyaya station, and the city of Allahabad was rechristened Prayagraj. There was even a threat to rename Meerut as Nathuram Godse Nagar[134]—although this one time, the BJP's morbid obsession with Gandhi's assassin was thwarted.

Modi's confrontationist, jaw-for-a-tooth policy stood in stark contrast to the Congress-led UPA's strategic restraint where Pakistan was concerned. In television debates, Modi's '56-inch chest'[135] became a popular reference point. India now had a biceps-triceps foreign policy model.

This muscular nationalism would only escalate as India headed into the 2019 elections. Modi pounced upon the Pulwama terror attack only months before the polls. JeM, Maulana Masood Azhar's terrorist organisation, which has the blessings of Pakistan's deep state, claimed responsibility for it. India was caught napping. How had a massive haul of 600 pounds of RDX passed undetected? Modi, however, castigated the Opposition, branding them 'anti-national' and 'the enemies of the state' for raising such questions.[136] From high-rise podiums, the prime minister spoke against giant backdrops of the slain martyrs' photos. This crude politicking around a terror attack was unprecedented in Indian history.

Modi responded to the cold-blooded massacre at Pulwama with the Balakot air strikes, which led to the capture of Wing Commander Abhinandan Varthaman in Pakistan and his subsequent release. The armed forces became a tool in the upcoming elections. In fact, even as Varthaman was being held captive, BJP's chief minister in Karnataka, B.S. Yeddyurappa, announced that the air strikes would get the party twenty-two out of the twenty-eight seats in Karnataka.[137] After Pulwama, there were twenty security personnel deaths, and a bomb was thrown in a bus in Jammu, killing a teenager and injuring thirty people—incidents that received practically no coverage. What did get plenty of play was Modi's bizarre claim that the whole Opposition, particularly the Congress, was hand-in-glove with cross-border terrorists.[138] But he was supported by vociferous retired army veterans. And this surgical strike on the Indian voter cemented a hot-headed vote bank.

Home Minister Amit Shah announced that 250 terrorists had been killed in the JeM camp at Balakot. Anyone who asked for evidence was cursorily bracketed as unpatriotic. Elsewhere, Yogi Adityanath, clearly dissatisfied with Shah's calculations, enhanced the terrorist head count to 400. Himanta Biswa Sarma, BJP's hatchet man in the Northeast, came up with the theory that, if people did not vote for the BJP, Pakistan would attack India. Joblessness, rural distress, the Rafale controversy, institutional decadence, attacks on Dalits and minorities, a failed economy, all of this faded away. A shell-shocked nation was seeking revenge against Pakistan, motivated by a virulent social media, battleground TV and a BJP on full nationalistic throttle.

The Congress, led by Rahul Gandhi, stuck to the core fundamentals of the social and economic turkey that Modi had delivered. But the ground had shifted under them.

Lt Gen. D.S. Hooda, who masterminded the 2016 surgical strikes post Uri, expressed dismay at the manner in which military endeavours were being used for political mileage. Even the families of soldiers martyred in the Pulwama terror attack demanded tangible proof of what the Balakot air strike had achieved.[139] The BJP's alliance partner in Maharashtra, Shiv Sena, questioned the veracity of the casualty numbers.[140]

This was about the time that the paramilitary forces were protesting in Delhi, demanding one-rank, one-pension (OROP)—a demand that was not met by a government under whose watch India's defence expenditure, at 1.58 per cent of the GDP, had reached a historic low after the India–China war. Several defence experts were vocal about the fact that India's military equipment qualified as 'vintage'. The government had no comment on any of these issues. It was enough that Modi should thunder, '*Ghar me ghus ke maroonga*' (I will enter your house and thrash you).

'Maha-milavat' (grand adulteration), that's how Modi dismissed his political opponents as they worked towards putting together a last-ditch effort to stop the BJP. Modi's own NDA, where the BJP was the dominant majority partner, was made up of over forty alliance partners.

Unlike business entities that tend to see mega-consolidation over a period of time, in Indian politics, breakaways and fragmentation are the norm. Yet, when one compares UPA-1 and UPA-2 with the NDA's first five years (2014–19), it smashes the myth that majority governments are good for growth and democracy.[141] UPA coalitions gave higher GDP growth rates, lower income inequalities, better social harmony, a liberal environment, enhanced national security, an independent media and democratic institutions.

India waited with bated breath to see which way 2019 would go. Would the Congress have some surprise tricks up its sleeve to upstage the front-runner?

General elections for the seventeenth Lok Sabha finally got underway on 11 April 2019, to be completed in seven phases. It was one of the most acrimonious elections India had seen, bereft of all civility. The BJP had cautioned its vote bank about a dangerous enemy that lurked in every shadow. Be afraid, very afraid, was the 9 p.m. television advisory.[142] And this one was not just about the AK-47-carrying Pakistani terrorist, but the sinister traitors within, the ones who were frequently told to migrate to the neighbouring nation. The BJP's IT cell and its WhatsApp fake news factory did the rest. Society had been weaponised to demonise Muslims as doubtful Indians.[143] For a while, Modi had tried (if not successfully) to camouflage his hard-line Hindutva constitution behind a technocratic, business-friendly image.[144] The mask had come off.

During the Uttar Pradesh elections of 2017, he talked of how electricity supply was deliberately abundant during Ramzan and deficient during Diwali, repeating his charge of 'minority appeasement' by the Congress. It was a flagrant breach of his constitutional oath as prime minister. Helpfully, the Congress responded with sheepishness. For the BJP, minority appeasement has been a stable electoral plank. (Unsurprisingly, neither the Rajendra Sachar Committee[145] nor the Ranganath Mishra Commission[146] reports, set up to examine minority economic and social status, confirm such investment in Muslim welfare.)

During the Gujarat state assembly elections of December 2017—fearing a surprise defeat in the face of a robust comeback campaign by the Congress in his home bastion—Modi gave up all pretence. This was when he charged Dr Manmohan Singh and others of conspiring with Pakistan. Few winced at this cheap jibe, certainly not the mainstream media.

The BJP's expenditure on election campaigns in 2019 was an obscene Rs 27,000 crore—among the world's most expensive, in a country that is still poor.[147] The Congress, short on both funds and imaginative marketing, was largely invisible. It also remained ill-equipped to counter the BJP's low shots, such as the one aimed at Rahul Gandhi in 2019.

Gandhi had chosen to contest (in addition to his traditional constituency of Amethi in Uttar Pradesh) from the Wayanad parliamentary seat in Kerala—a constituency and a state that has remained firmly anti-BJP. Modi quickly seized on the fact that Gandhi had chosen a 'Hindu minority seat'. The political messaging was that the Congress is a pro-Muslim party that does not respect Hindu sensibilities. Kerala, with its hard-to-crack communal harmony, has been the BJP's bugbear. Its political business model has not reaped hoped-for dividends in the state. BJP President Amit Shah wondered aloud if the Wayanad election campaign procession was happening in India or Pakistan, because of the green-coloured flags carried by the Indian Union Muslim League, the Congress's alliance partner. The Election Commission cleared both Modi and Shah of charges of using communal politics during their campaigning. Glaring evidence of another institutional takeover was out in the public.[148]

The choice of Pragya Singh Thakur as a BJP candidate was another naked and official endorsement of violence and hate by Narendra Modi, Amit Shah and the BJP. The idea of India as a secular, liberal, inclusive democracy, as enshrined in the Indian Constitution, seemed brittle just then. In 2014, there was the chimera of a 'Gujarat model' and capitalist growth—perhaps that was what voters were signing up for. In 2019, there would be no excuses.

Six years earlier, on 9 June 2013, the BJP had formally announced that Modi would be chairman of the party's campaign committee for the 2014 Lok Sabha elections, a decision that left the octogenarian Lal Krishna Advani disgruntled and Sushma Swaraj piqued. Modi had been unofficially anointed as the potential prime ministerial candidate. In the Congress camp, there was surprising exhilaration. They were positive that the Sangh Parivar had made a grave error. 'Modi is divisive; a polarising figure who is distrusted both by the Muslims and the secular Hindus. India will never forgive him for the Gujarat riots, a blot on our history. India is not Gujarat. Get ready for UPA-3,' said a seasoned veteran with a broad grin. The mood among the Congress members I knew was one of genuine hope that this was a chance for the party after years of bad publicity and electoral wipe-outs in state elections.

On 30 May 2019, Narendra Damodardas Modi was sworn in for the second time as the prime minister of India.

It was time to take stock of the last five years. Even as most of our neighbours (Sri Lanka, Maldives, Bangladesh and Pakistan, in particular) struggled to salvage their democracies, despite an occasional hiccup (the Emergency of 1975–77), India had remained a stable polity that was a South Asian outlier. Daron Acemoglu and James A. Robinson, in their epic work, *Why Nations Fail: The Origins of Power, Prosperity and Poverty*, have rightly pointed out the impact of damaged institutions, which become so enfeebled that countries transmute into banana republics, kangaroo courts take over, chaos reigns and societies become irretrievably dysfunctional. As an imperious government took heavy-handed control, India's institutions began buckling one by one.

3

INSTITUTIONS

Gasping for Breath

I think it was a Saturday evening, and I was in the drawing room watching a sports show when my otherwise unflappable younger daughter barged into the room. 'He says the BJP is absolutely right. What an insufferable bigot! I am angry.' I tried to calm her with my standard bromide that, in a democracy, one must learn to tolerate dissent, no matter how obtuse. But my robustly liberal, well-travelled, well-read girl was having none of it. Then, uncharacteristically, I cautioned her: 'Please don't say anything overly offensive or rude. The last thing I want is a right-wing mole in your group filing a case against you.' She looked stunned at my advice that she practise self-censorship—not something she had seen me do. But, like most Indians, I was worried, even fearful.

The official Emergency had lasted for twenty-one months; the 'undeclared Emergency', which began in May 2014, still continues. There has been a complete takeover of India's democratic institutions, and civil liberties have been eviscerated. An environment of fear pervades the country. Our self-censorship has been the government's true triumph. Several people I know, as well as complete strangers, have confirmed that they are afraid to speak in India today. Like a taxi driver in Mumbai.

To understand the pulse of India, you must travel by a 'kaali-peeli' (the black-and-yellow Premier Padmini taxis that are now fading out of the cityscape) in Mumbai and make conversation with the driver. On a warm October evening in 2018, I was restless and stepped into a taxi, only to be caught in a jam, even at that late hour. The city is an insomniac's dream, if that is possible. Some months earlier, making my way from the airport, I had encountered a traffic jam at an unearthly 1.45 a.m. on Peddar Road, just past Haji Ali mosque. As we gingerly crawled ahead, I discovered a nakabandi (police check-post) that forced vehicles to make a circuitous bend, even as the traffic cops stood a good distance away, blathering among themselves. Who knew what it was for, but Mumbai endured it without complaint. No one pulled down a windowpane to shout, '*Tu jaanta nahi ki mera baap kaun hai?*' (You don't know who my father is!) Mumbai is not Delhi. And its taxi drivers are treasure chests of stories.

My taxi driver that day was probably still in his early sixties, but he looked older. He wore a crumpled white kurta-pyjama, his beard was grey, his loose-fitting slippers contrasted with a snug skull cap. He appeared unfazed by the bumper-to-bumper traffic we were caught in.

'How long have you been driving in Mumbai?' I asked him.

'Around thirty years,' he said.

Suddenly, a motorcycle zipped ahead from the left. The pillion rider wore a helmet, while the young rider showed off his Mohawk cut, hair streaked golden—a ridiculousness that was hard to ignore.

'Today's youth,' he said, shaking his head in amusement. 'They are directionless.'

It was a profound observation. I looked at him. To the Shiv Sainiks, he was definitely an 'outsider'. Or would three decades mean that he was domiciled in their eyes? I asked him about his ancestral roots.

'I come from Faizabad in Uttar Pradesh.'

'Ah,' I interjected, 'the place that has captured India's imagination for so long—Ram Janmabhoomi and the now-desecrated Babri Masjid.'

He said nothing, perhaps not sure where I was leading the conversation. But I was keen to talk, especially as the Supreme Court was expected to start hearing the Babri Masjid–Ram Janmabhoomi case a few days later, on 29 October 2018.

He responded, 'There is peace over there, even if there are many trying to instigate communities to fight each other.'

It was a sensitive subject, and I did not compel him to speak about it to a complete stranger. 'What do you think will happen in the 2019 elections?' I asked instead.

His face abruptly lit up, and he said enthusiastically, 'Modi will lose.'

I pretended to be unconvinced. 'You really think so?'

'Yes. He has done nothing. Nothing. He has divided us all. We fear for the safety of our families,' he said.

Although he spoke with conviction, there was in his tone genuine dismay too. Muslims in UP have been scorched by the heat of communalism perhaps more severely than in any other part of India: 'Ghar Wapsi', 'Love Jihad', lynching, anti-Romeo squads and encounter killings, all of these have specifically targeted them. Communal politics was the elephant in the car, and I could feel the tension of it even when we screeched to a halt, to avoid a jaywalking teenager with headphones on.

'What do you think of the Congress party's chances?' I asked.

'Only if they do a mahagathbandhan (grand alliance),' he said, with the flair of a seasoned psephologist. 'I have always been a Congressi. My family has always voted for the party,' he added simply. 'But I miss the old Congress. In Uttar Pradesh, the Congress will take years to make a comeback.'

Just then, my mobile phone rang. A TV channel was calling for my views on RSS Chief Mohan Bhagwat's Dussehra speech about building the Ram Mandir. I offered my two cents in English, but perhaps the driver sensed what I was talking about—the dispute was sub judice, and we should not prejudge a religious matter pending before the Supreme Court.

I paid him the fare and asked him to keep the change. He seemed astonished at the size of the bonus. But I did not think this was the time to explain my pay-it-forward principle. He soon disappeared into Mumbai's labyrinthine jungle, one solitary brick amongst the monstrous skyscrapers—unknown, unheard, unseen, and yet, a part of its larger construct, a voice of Mumbai and one of our own.

By contrast, I spent two years with a hundred batchmates at the prestigious XLRI business school in Jamshedpur, only to discover how cut-off we were from each other. It all happened on a WhatsApp group.

These days, WhatsApp group conversations can get excruciating. Hitherto concealed biases suddenly surface and chaos reigns. In my XLRI (batch of 1984–86) WhatsApp group, the average age is around fifty-five. Most of them are successful entrepreneurs, CEOs or otherwise ensconced in corner rooms, and the majority are well-heeled NRIs, many flourishing in Donald Trump's 'Make America Great Again'. The triggers for the acerbic exchange were the Kathua and Unnao rapes, which had sickened me to the core.

Despite legal reforms following the Nirbhaya tragedy of December 2013, justice was still a long way off for survivors of sexual assault. What made the Kathua and Unnao rapes stand out in even this bleak scenario was that the ruling party in both

Jammu and Kashmir and Uttar Pradesh, the BJP, appeared to initially protect the alleged perpetrators. The ruling party's own legislators were publicly supporting the rapists, though they were asked to resign soon after, after a huge public furore and outrage.[149] As is true of much in Indian politics since 2014, this was unprecedented. At the Centre, the party maintained a stoic silence.

I wrote a piece[150] condemning the two rapes and posted the link on the XLRI WhatsApp group. Since the group had witnessed several acrimonious wars between the seemingly liberal (whom creative chauvinists had branded the limousine liberal gang) and the right-wing fanatics (whom I called the loony alt-right), it was informally understood that we would maintain a façade of conviviality by keeping politics out of our conversations. Frankly, I thought it was ridiculous. I mean, how long can you keep discussing goofy stories from thirty years ago, when giving a bucket bath to your professors from the fourth floor of your hostel was considered heroic? We were now a group of adults, many of whom had deep-seated ideological positions, and expectedly, not all these opinions were in consonance. There was simmering tension behind the boisterous hugs and birthday smileys.

Many felt that the occasional (and inevitable) angry outbursts were a transgression of the group's otherwise antiseptic atmosphere. They did not want the campus buddy network (although casual acquaintances is what most of us were now) rocked by a politically charged upheaval. And so, the spoken and unspoken rules of the group prohibited us from bickering over Trump–Clinton, Narendra Modi–Rahul Gandhi, the liberal–right, secular–conservative divides. Cold peace prevailed. My Kathua and Unnao article broke that fragile truce. For several months now, I had not posted a single one of my weekly pieces. But the Hindutva sympathisers frequently trespassed that proscription, posting hate-filled WhatsApp forwards, much like a Twitter troll's phishing attack, and a lot of it fake news. No one pointed out that they were breaking the group's code.

Moments after I posted my article, one of the right-wingers protested that I was exploiting the group for political campaigning. It was ludicrous (I have bigger fish to fry, I told him). The liberals of XLRI Class of 1984 had nothing to say. These men and women of immense privilege, whose own children were probably studying in Ivy League schools, appeared to be totally unaffected by the gory murder of a child. Christine Lagarde, the president of the European Central Bank and then managing director of the International Monetary Fund, had publicly castigated Modi about the rising incidence of sexual abuse of women in India. India's top forty-nine civil servants called Kathua 'the darkest hour in post-Independence India'.[151] This was not politics; it was about our society, our community, our future. But this group appeared not to care.

Many progressive liberals had quit the group over this particular zealot's toxic posts—a microcosm of the larger national withdrawal of liberal voices from public spaces. The remaining liberals on the group turned a blind eye to him, either living in self-denial or because they were just plain scared. The term 'Urban Naxals' was coined to make all liberals (for some strange reason, it is assumed that we are all followers of Lenin and Karl Marx) appear to be violent disruptors. Journalists, activists, politicians, students, were all dubbed Urban Naxals and called seditious.

XLRI is a great institution and has shaped me in myriad ways. But clearly, they do not teach courage of conviction there, or indeed at top business schools anywhere. A few days after the conversations got insufferably unpleasant, I quit the group, never to return.

Political culture is a by-product of the leadership, mirroring the expectations of those at the top. Ironically, the world's largest democracies, the US and India, face the same predicament—hyper-nationalism, xenophobic bigotry, Islamophobia, tribalism, contempt for the free press, proliferation of fake news and, often, blood-curling revanchism (the lynchings in India are proof of that). It is hardly astonishing therefore that, in this atmospher of mutual recriminations, there is no dialogue. Dissent? Forget it.

While catching a flight from Frankfurt, Germany, I chanced upon an enlightening piece in the *New York Times*, titled 'The New Dictators Rule By Velvet Fist'. Said the authors Sergei Guriev and Daniel Treisman, 'In recent decades, a new brand of authoritarian government has evolved that is better adapted to an era of global media, economic interdependence and information technology. The "soft" dictators concentrate power, stifling opposition and eliminating checks and balances, while using hardly any violence.'[152] They referenced leaders like Vladimir Putin of Russia, Recep Erdoğan of Turkey, Hugo Chavez of Veneuela, Viktor Orban of Hungary and others. Interestingly, I had only recently visited the Dachau concentration camp near Munich, the Nazis' first formal laboratory experiment.

The 'soft' dictator is a contemporary version of Hitler; no Auschwitz for him, no mass killings that would cause an international furore in a world where human rights violations are closely monitored. Lee Kuan Yew of Singapore throttled free speech, censored newspapers and frowned on those finding fault with the governance in his sophisticated city-state. On the other hand, he provided economic incentives to foreign investors that made Singapore an attractive destination, and its citizens quietly gave up individual liberty for efficient metro networks, a spotlessly clean city, a crime-free society and the assurance that there would be no chewing gum on train handles.

Prime Minister Narendra Modi apparently modelled himself after Yew.[153] In his first term, Modi saw himself as a free-market proponent who serenades big business and foreign investment while eschewing subsidies and big government. And he seriously abhors criticism, of his government and, more importantly, of himself. These signs were visible quite early. Following the crackdown on the NGO Greenpeace, Richard Verma, then US ambassador to India, was compelled to say, 'Because a vibrant civil society is so important to both of our democratic traditions, I do worry about the potentially chilling effects of these regulatory steps focused on NGOs.' In January 2016, Greenpeace activist Priya Pillai was prohibited from travelling to London to address British parliamentarians. Apparently, the ruling regime was worried about the damage she could do to India's brand equity.[154] NGOs receiving foreign funding through FCRA (Foreign Contribution [Regulation] Act) were relentlessly pursued, as if they were receiving slush monies for nefarious purposes.

Note that Russian President Vladimir Putin has been similarly asphyxiating NGOs in Russia.[155] Considered Marxist-leaning jholawallas, NGO workers are treated with both condescension and deep suspicion by right-wing liberal economic postulators. These allegations touched preposterous heights when India's Intelligence Bureau reported that the 'negative effects of such anti-developmental activities [by foreign funded NGOs] on GDP growth is estimated to be at 2-3%'.[156] Activists were seen as the enemy of the nation. Medha Patkar, who spearheaded the Narmada Bachao Andolan to highlight the concerns of displaced populations, and has suffered immense indignities and intimidation, wrote with new pain: 'Today, Gujarat has become a garrison state, with activists regularly being detained for 24 hours, before protests take place.'[157] It was not only activists but movie makers, environmentalists, civil servants and police officers who experienced repression first-hand for refusing to stand down against an intolerant government.

Politicians were not exempt. Arvind Kejriwal[158] and Rahul Gandhi[159] faced defamation suits for making charges against political adversaries in the BJP. For the politician, such proceedings are time-consuming, distracting, and a source of negative publicity. Kejriwal went to jail for a few days, while Rahul Gandhi had to go to distant Bhiwandi in Maharashtra to make court appearances. Oppressive states intimidate political opponents through complex legal cases, police harassment, income-tax queries, defamation cases, surreptitious snooping and wilful bureaucratic apathy. The 'soft' dictator prefers wear and tear to visible political persecution. The system browbeats the citizen into meek submission until she loses the will to push back. The space for civil society is remorselessly curtailed, and dissent is criminalised, a ploy to harass the victim. It works well for the thugs who patrol the streets and for the anonymous eggheads on Twitter who work in tandem with the goons.

India Inc. has always been a vocal endorser of whichever government is in power. A vindictive political establishment usually generates a crescendo of embarrassing adulation from craven businessmen. Some curry favour by making corporate investments in media houses that hand out pro-government propaganda. For NDA-1, 'GDP growth' was a pathological obsession. Modi spoke of development as if all India did before 2014 was export bananas and import Pepsi. When he took over, India was already a US$ 2 trillion economy,[160] the world's third largest in terms of purchasing power, the fastest growing after China for over a decade. The UPA's ten-year track record

(2004–14), despite a wobbly second-term somersault, was laudable. The NDA's ruse was to make former governments look like egregiously corrupt elitists, while simultaneously dazzling the populace with promises of lower EMIs, more multiplexes, rising skyscrapers and bullet trains. The pliant mainstream media kept a defeated Opposition demoralised, while the government obfuscated data on its own underperformance.

The weaving of nationalism into this narrative provided further cover. While visiting South Korea, Modi claimed that it was once a shame to be born in India and that this has now changed.[161] There was uninterrupted applause. The RSS called for a national renewal (mostly by infiltrating educational institutions[162] and writing a fresh interpretation of past events) and denigrated Opposition stalwarts as backstabbers (even Mahatma Gandhi[163] and Jawaharlal Nehru[164] were not spared).[165]

India began witnessing a subterranean dictatorship in the guise of a democratically elected government. The murder of rationalists Dabholkar, Pansare and Kalburgi and the ongoing fruitless investigations into who killed them caused liberals to lose faith in India's criminal justice system. Hate crimes were video recorded and shared on social media to proliferate thereafter on WhatsApp groups. The social media troll army of the BJP was a monstrous force; it could destroy reputations, invoke fear and generally run amok with no fear of repercussions.

The 2014–15 stretch was the honeymoon period, when people gave the new kids on the block the benefit of the doubt. Especially since the NDA's predecessor had been mauled at both the hustings and in general public perception. But the chickens would come home to roost.

That masterpiece of electoral salesmanship during the BJP's 2014 election campaign—Rs 15 lakh black money refund in the bank account of every Indian within 100 days—hung like an albatross around the prime minister's neck. It was at best hyperbolic overdrive, at worst a despicable lie. Amit Shah casually dismissed it as a 'jumla',[166] a slogan, an idiom, which India was dorky to take seriously.

The lackadaisical manner in which the Modi sarkar responded to a massive, global money-laundering scandal further belied the claim that it would root out corruption. The Panama Papers revealed a complex labyrinth of multi-layered transactions that were meant to obfuscate both actual ownership and the source of the funds. The sheer scale of the revelations was mind-boggling—2.6 terabytes of data, 12 million documents, over a 40-year period, covering 214,000 offshore shell companies in 200 countries. Many powerful names featured in them for direct or indirect involvement, including Syrian President Bashar al-Assad, former British prime minister David Cameron, Russian President Vladimir Putin, Chinese President Xi Jinping and the former South African president Jacob Zuma. There were many celebrity names from India too.

Compared to the promptness with which international governments responded, India appeared to be near comatose. There were a few statements from Arun Jaitley, former finance minister, but little else. Interestingly, among the illustrious names figuring in this list were those who had interests in gold mines, oil contracts and natural resources.[167] In India, access to public wealth through rent-seeking and political bribery results in monopolistic control, inefficient allocations and price disadvantage to the common consumer. While the NDA chose to dismiss the Panama Papers with casual disdain, Modi's counterpart in Pakistan, then prime minister Nawaz Sharif, was forced to resign over the allegations in the leaked papers. Even in a so-called 'failed state', these revelations had created political turbulence. Few political parties, other than the Left, put any kind of pressure on the government about its tawdry investigations. The Congress seemed blissfully oblivious. The powerful anti-corruption infrastructure that was to be the Lokpal—perhaps the issue that actually toppled the UPA—was non-existent.

The poster-boy of India's most visible anti-corruption agitation, Anna Hazare, had also gone missing. By 2020, few remembered the septuagenarian anti-corruption crusader who was the cynosure of the idiot box in 2011. Hazare put his village of Ralegan Siddhi[168] on the national map as marquee TV editors queued up almost obsequiously for his words of wisdom. Soon afterwards, the emblem of those heady times, the Lokpal, would be forgotten. Even back then, the discerning analyst had known that the India Against Corruption movement was an RSS/BJP-sponsored movement.[169]

There were two principal reasons why the Jantar Mantar affair would lead to the decimation of the Congress. One, flagrant inequalities were on the rise despite a booming economy, and two, the widespread (and quite correct) perception that several Forbes-listed billionaires had increased their net worth through rent-seeking and crony capitalism. The pent-up fury was understandable. The fact that these were worldwide problems was no consolation to Dr Singh's government or to the citizens of India. Effectively, a mere 6,000 politicians, chief executives and other bigwigs run the world.[170] Of the world's hundred largest economic entities, sixty-three are corporations, not countries.[171] The world's richest 1 per cent possesses half its wealth.[172]

The UPA could take pride in the fact that it introduced powerful legislations to combat corruption in Parliament—laws that were, of course, the result of robust civil society movements. Besides the watershed RTI Act and Lokpal Bill, there were also the Whistle Blowers Bill, Citizen's Right to Grievance Redressal Bill, Public Procurement Bill and the Judicial Accountability and Standards Bill, amongst others. But the manner in which the Congress handled the corruption charges against it was amateurish and ineffectual. Its incompetence in explaining away the atrocious CAG allegations would have a shattering—and long-term—impact on the party's electoral fortunes. Corruption and Congress became synonymous. The two huge political beneficiaries of the 2011 civil society agitation were Arvind Kejriwal (chief minister of Delhi) and Narendra Modi (prime minister of India), both in their second terms in office now. Both maintain a radio silence on the Lokpal. The Panama Paers are gathering dust. Life rolls on.

Hyper-rhetorical excesses are sadly common in Indian election campaigns, and we have all learnt to write them off as such. But during the 2017 Gujarat assembly elections, a line was crossed. Prime Minister Modi alleged that former prime minister Manmohan Singh, former vice-president Hamid Ansari, former Army chief Deepak Kapoor and a variety of retired diplomatic staff, journalists and intellectuals from both Pakistan and India were huddled together in a sinister conspiracy to impact the Gujarat election outcome and install the Muslim Congress leader Ahmed Patel as chief minister.[173] It was as outlandish as it was vile.

In an unprecedented reaction, the normally placid Dr Singh lashed out, palpably indignant at being branded an anti-national by his successor: 'Sadly and regrettably, Modi is setting a dangerous precedent by his insatiable desire to tarnish every constitutional office, including that of a former prime minister and Army chief. I sincerely hope that the prime minister will show the maturity and gravitas expected of the high office he holds instead of concentrating his energy solely on erroneously conceived brownie points. I sincerely hope that he will apologise to the nation for his ill-thought transgression to restore the dignity of the office he occupies.' Modi, of course, did no such thing. Every prime minister in the future will now inherit an office that has been grievously diminished.

The Rs 59,000 crore Rafale scam dealt another severe blow to the flagging reputation of the prime minister's office. Former senior leaders of the BJP, Yashwant Sinha and Arun Shourie, having openly rebelled, called it 'the biggest defence scam in India's history'. Comparisons were made to the Bofors corruption case (which was dismissed by both the Delhi High Court and the Supreme Court, and which had irreparably damaged the Congress and former prime minister Rajiv Gandhi in 1989). The government obdurately refused to order a joint parliamentary committee inquiry into the Rafale scam.[174] In revelations made by the *Hindu* newspaper,[175] several questions were raised, but the BJP stonewalled them all. A biopsy of the deal is in the interest of the nation, said the Congress in its election manifesto.

The Rafale corruption charge against Modi was expected to be a major election issue in 2019. Then came the Balakot air strike, and the public mood changed dramatically. National security was now the prime driver—and it was Modi and the BJP who had come to be associated with muscular nationalism. They had successfully painted the opposition as Pakistan-friendly. So, the core issues of a failed economy and of the Rafale scam steadily lost momentum. In 2014, the Congress's alleged corruption had burnt the party; the BJP's legerdemain, on the other hand, led to an even bigger haul—303 seats, up from 282.

The Panama Papers and the Rafale scam were no anomaly. The NDA government had been systemically bulldozing India's most sacred institutions into timid submission.

Within the CBI—the much-maligned caged parrot of every regime at the Centre—there were symptoms of a fightback, as if the crumbling edifice of that institution was battling for a resurrection. The Alok Verma vs Rakesh Asthana ego tussle[176] was a new low in the history of the country's premier anti-corruption investigating body. The NDA may well have destroyed the caged parrot altogether.

There was also tumult in India's central bank, the Reserve Bank of India (RBI). Then deputy governor Viral Acharya, making no concessions even in this age of fear, took the government head-on. His message was clear: repeated interference in the operational autonomy of the RBI would force a severe backlash from the financial markets and create an unmanageable crisis. His analysis was based on hard data. October 2018 saw a massive outflow of foreign capital, aggregating Rs 35,000 crores. The stock markets had until then appeared to inhabit a different planet, seemingly cut off from the wobbly economy they operated in. Finally, they were on a downward trajectory. The government's response to Acharya's outspokenness was churlish, of course. Jaitley launched into a tirade against the RBI (reminding them of Section 7 of the RBI Act, which empowers the government to issue directives to the central bank).

Absurdly, Jaitley alleged that Acharya had wilfully camouflaged non-performing assets (NPAs) in 2014–15, understating their magnitude by an astronomical number. According to Jaitley, the NPAs that the NDA inherited from UPA, of Rs 2.6 lakh crores ballooned to Rs 850,000 crores after asset quality review in 2015—a mind-numbing 300 per cent rise in one year.[177] This was an unparalleled confrontation; India's finance minister was publicly accusing its central bank of deliberate fraud. The concealment of NPA data by RBI (in cahoots with banks) would be tantamount to an act of criminal culpability under both Section 406 and Section 420 of the Indian Penal Code (IPC), an open-and-shut case of cheating. The RBI, another independent institution, with an immaculate reputation, was on the verge of being decapitated.

Jaitley's political tirade could have had damning consequences. It may well have irreparably damaged the credibility of the RBI in global markets. But the RBI, which was under tremendous pressure, did not refute this outrageous allegation. If NPAs crossed 400 per cent to over Rs 10 lakh crore since Modi became prime minister, it was clearly due to the rampant evergreening of loans and the creation of new doubtful assets.[178] Nirav Modi and Mehul Choksi—two high-profile NRI absconders who allegedly duped public sector unit (PSU) banks (Punjab National Bank is jokingly referred to as Pure Nirav Bank) of over 16,000 crores—got away because they had political cover. A cornered government began scapegoating.

In his letter to Dr Murli Manohar Joshi, who heads a parliamentary committee on estimates, former RBI governor Raghuram Rajan, who was rudely jettisoned by the Modi government, stated that he had given a list of wilful defaulters—the who's who of big business—to the PMO as early as 2015. An RTI query confirmed this. The PMO did nothing about it. Why? Why were the identities and liabilities of these big kahunas not being made public if they were the biggest consumers of bad debts? The RBI staff was demoralised. The All India Reserve Bank Employees' Association protested the erosion of the institution's autonomy—an untypical reaction from a usually pliant crowd. Earlier, RBI employees had written to then governor Urjit Patel that they had been 'humiliated' by the events since demonetisation.

Patel had earlier been widely ridiculed for his utter silence on Modi's whimsical demonetisation policy. Belatedly, the RBI had understood that silence would mean acquiescence with the government's reckless programmes and lead to the further stifling of its autonomy. The fact is that the Modi government had been blithely indifferent to the looming NPA crisis. The RBI insisted on a red flag if there was even a single day's default by a corporate borrower. It was a legitimate call, given the sordid saga of conmen had left the banks haemorrhaging. On a TV show in which I occasionally appeared, one market analyst called the RBI's prompt corrective action (PCA) framework a 'bizarre overreach'. In the same breath, he lamented the defaults that left banks bleeding. You can't have the cake and eat it too, unfortunately.

On its part, the RBI seemed cognisant of the fact that the government was spinning the bank crisis as the central bank's 'due diligence failure'. That was what led to Viral Acharya's outburst. This scapegoating was necessary for the BJP and Modi in an election year when the Congress's crony capitalism charge and the '*Chowkidar Chor Hai*' slogan had gathered momentum.

Ninety-six hours before the congregation of the RBI board in November 2018, a beleaguered Patel submitted his resignation, citing 'personal reasons'. It was a fait accompli, given the acrimonious public spat, especially after the government invoked Section 7 of the RBI Act. Another issue was the RBI's sizeable reserves of Rs 9.69 lakh crore; the government wanted to appropriate a large chunk of it, almost as if that was their right. The RBI refused, insisting that it needed capital to stand as buffer for market volatilities. But the myopic, fiscally starved government was desperate. In the end, this issue of protecting the reserves was surely at the heart of Patel's resignation. Another institution had bitten the dust.

The new RBI governor, Shaktikanta Das, conceded RBI's precious reserves to a struggling government that had already crossed 103 per cent of its fiscal deficit target by October 2018. Was the NDA hoping to utilise this windfall for some generous sops in an election year to save the prime minister's fast-dissipating credibility? Was the future of the RBI to be determined by voodoo economists, RSS ideologues and government-appointed cheerleaders with no knowledge of foreign-exchange markets, interest rate risks and regulatory mechanisms? Under Modi, there has been an organised paralysis of institutional independence.

In a democracy, the government is tasked with the protection of the country's institutions of governance, policy and public service. In a dystopia, it becomes instead a predator, cannibalising the core structures of the nation's foundations, posing a challenge to its suzerainty.

The RBI, it turns out, was in august company; the institutions that had come under attack included, among others, the CBI, Election Commission, Enforcement Directorate, Chief Vigilance Commission, Income Tax Department and the NIA. To understand the gravity of the institutional meltdown under the NDA, it is worthwhile to point out that a senior officer of the CBI, Manish Kumar Sinha, wrote in a petition that the bureau faced the threat of becoming the 'Centre for Bogus Investigation'.[179]

Three esteemed members of the National Statistics Commission quit because the government tried to suppress dismal jobs data[180] (joblessness is reported to be at a staggering forty-five-year high).

The fourth estate, the pillar of modern democracy, was another institution railroaded by the Modi government. Journalists were killed in cold blood, particularly those in the vernacular media working to expose corruption and State repression of human rights.[181] Gauri Lankesh was killed on 5 September 2017. Paranjoy Thakurta, editor of *Economic and Political Weekly*, a left-leaning magazine that repeatedly took on corporate leviathans, was politely asked to step down. India's ranking in the World Press Freedom Index tanked to 142 out of 180 countries by 2020,[182] reflecting the chilling impact of intolerance.

My driver, who is from Uttar Pradesh, wishes me a Merry Christmas, as does the security guard from the rural interiors of Maharashtra. This is the spirit that has bound 16 per cent of the world's population into one multicultural, multi-religious whole. It is in grave peril today. In a strongly worded indictment, Human Rights Watch said, 'Between May 2015 and December 2018, at least 44 people—36 of them Muslims—were killed across 12 Indian states. Over that same period, around 280 people were injured in over 100 different incidents across 20 states.'[183]

The BJP, unmoved by criticism from the outside, worked to suppress dissent within the country. When the iconic actor Naseeruddin Shah spoke up in the context of the violence in Bulandshahr, Uttar Pradesh, and the killing of police officer Subodh Kumar, he touched a raw nerve among the thin-skinned right-wing brigade. It went after him with a vengeance—he was swiftly declared an anti-national. Shah was hectored, his family was humiliated, and they were promised a grand see-off to that tourist destination the BJP promotes with gusto: Pakistan.[184] Overnight, one of India's finest actors ever, one of the fiercest champions of Indian theatre, an inspiration to generations of theatre and cinema aspirants, was accused of seditious conduct. This was not without precedent. Aamir Khan and Shah Rukh Khan had both been attacked and had since retreated into their shells.

There is one actor who symbolises the 1970s for me: a Buddha-like calm on his face, the quintessential middle-class man, awkward of manner when making conversation with the object of his affection. (This is the pre-Tinder, pre-Ashley Madison era, no doubt prehistoric to the young of today.) Amol Palekar, the lead in timeless romantic classics such as *Gharonda*, *Chitchor*, *Rajnigandha* and *Gol Maal*, is now a seventy-four-year-old, and still very active in the national conversation. During a public event at the National Gallery of Modern Art (NGMA) in Mumbai on 9 February 2019, he was told to shut up.[185] Palekar replied that author Nayantara Sahgal had been similarly prevented from speaking at a literary event in Yavatmal, Maharashtra, and bemoaned the loss of freedom of speech in India. The organisers forced Palekar to halt his speech midway, even though the legendary film-maker, actor and producer was the chief guest. This happened in front of a distinguished audience of creative artists and aficionados of the arts.

Democracy may not yet be completely dead in India, but it is on life support. Palekar, Shah and the Khans were celebrity victims, but there are countless others, many of whom have self-censored and withdrawn from the public sphere.

On a WhatsApp group that I'm part of, someone posted a column critical of Modi, written by an unknown author on an unknown blog portal. Within minutes, someone advised him to delete the post, with the warning that Big Brother's mole in the group could target him for propagating slander. An FIR might be registered. I was flabbergasted at how people had begun to adapt to this unconscionable level of intimidation. Snooping by powerful government agencies[186] was being legitimised, and online patrolling had official approval under the pretext of 'national security'. Civil liberties could not be taken for granted anymore. The NDA government had argued before the Supreme Court that the right to privacy was not a fundamental right in India. In Kashmir, following the abrogation of Article 370 on 5 August 2019, an internet blackout was implemented—more than a year later, it is still in place for all practical purposes. Only dictatorial dispensations, such as Myanmar and China, have a worse track record.

Speaking of tracking records, that too has suffered a body blow. On 25 July 2019, the RTI Act was amended, radically diluting it.[187] And resolute RTI activists who still doggedly pursued the truth have been murdered. The Commonwealth Human Rights Initiative has been tracking attacks on RTI users and, as of early October 2020, reported eighty-seven deaths and 451 attacks overall.[188] Democracy truly dies in darkness.

During a chat with former JNU president Kanhaiya Kumar in Mumbai in December 2018, I asked him about the alarming toxicity in India and the deliberate fuelling of polarisation politics. Kanhaiya's stunning diagnosis of the situation is worth recalling: 'If the prime minister of India uses "*kabristan-shamshan*" in an election speech[189] to fracture society and win votes, it means that we are even being divided in the period of maximum grief: death. This is political immorality at its conceivable worst.'

It is also a very effective course of action. With every climbdown, every new evidence of a liberal voice backing off, a new normal is established. At some point, numbness begins to set in.

Thought-policing is a core strategy of fascist regimes. Once fear is injected into the body politic, it stops complaining and it stops protesting. The threat of an FIR, defamation suits, criminal charges, social-media trolling and relentless hate-mongering can frighten the bravest soul.

Sudheendra Kulkarni, author and former advisor to L.K. Advani, was attacked with black ink by right-wing activists for hosting the book launch of a former Pakistani foreign minister. Bollywood's silence was deafening when the Karni Sena threatened to behead popular actor Deepika Padukone during the release of Sanjay Leela Bhansali's *Padmaavat*. Well-known journalist Atish Taseer, who wrote the masterful but unflattering profile of Prime Minister Modi, titled 'Divider-in-Chief', in *TIME* magazine, suddenly found his Overseas Citizenship of India (OCI) status revoked. Non-State actors have been on a rampage because of a non-acting State. How else could someone murder a man, shoot a video, post it on social media and still be able to successfully raise funds to fight an election?[190]

After creating a troll army on social media, brutalising TV channels into submission and subsuming the print medium, the right-wing faction turned its attention to the next platform: 70mm cinema. It proved to be a potent weapon of political propaganda, as the films *The Accidental Prime Minister* and *Uri* (with its commercial marketing of surgical strikes as #HowsTheJosh?) show.

Media and regulatory capture were part of the government's institutional takeover during 2014–19. India's universities were brutally silenced, including several marquee centres of learning.

As the BJP became less and less interested in probity and transparency, the highly dubious electoral bonds came into play. It was a move that the RBI had opposed.[191] But the BJP rode roughshod over all objections using its absolute majority in Parliament. The result is that, even as Indians have become poorer and are worse-off than before, the BJP has become richer than ever. The party has a near monopoly on electoral bonds: 95 per cent. It is a government of the 1 per cent, by the 1 per cent, for the 1 per cent. Big business, campaign finance donors and rent-seekers (one industrialist got a sweeping mandate for several domestic airports at one shot[192]) have a field day.

The defining characteristic of this ingenious financial instrument—perhaps the most outlandish one in existence—is that the donor's details remain anonymous by law. There are other provisions, too, that ought to set the alarm bells ringing, such as the removal of the provision that the maximum a company can invest is 7.5 per cent of its net profit, and the fact that foreign contributions have been made permissible, or indeed that there is no need to declare the name of the political party in the annual reports of the company's balance sheet. The matter of the illegality of electoral bonds has been pending before the Supreme Court since 2019.

Unless campaign financing is made 100 per cent transparent, with full public disclosure, Indian politics will continue to stink. Political funding is the principal factor behind India's ugly politics of quid pro quo deals, crony capitalism and rent-seeking. Gangsters and crooked businessmen become elected representatives, and corruption and government malfeasance increase. Every now and then, the issue of electoral bonds surfaces in the public domain, and a few heated television debates follow, where everyone appears self-righteous. Soon after, it conveniently slips back into the shadows. There is an expenditure limit of Rs 70 lakh per candidate contesting a Lok Sabha seat—a limit that is brazenly flouted. That limit is considered a pittance in a world where free booze, cash distribution, monetary inducements, buying airtime, billboard promotions, posters, organising rallies and so on are considerable expense heads. The Election Commission intermittently wakes up to issue a show cause notice for a poll violation. Frankly, no one cares. At best, the official cap is a notional one.

The late BJP leader Gopinath Munde publicly declared that he had spent Rs 8 crore in his parliamentary constituency. Most political parties, therefore, choose candidates who are able to self-fund their election campaigns, which means that the quality of candidates is invariably lower than it can be. Tickets are often given to certified criminals, opportunistic carpetbaggers and other shady characters. Since most of these election-related transactions are in cash, India runs a parallel economy that does not have an audit trail. Moreover, the Election Commission does not have the wherewithal for forensic investigation of such financial impropriety. This is the reason that politicians happily defect from one party to another, the *aaya Ram gaya Ram* character of Indian politics. Ideology? What the hell is that? This is how it has been for decades, and no political party has shown a serious inclination to change it.

Unlike individuals, there is no limit on how much political parties can spend on elections. After the 2019 Lok Sabha elections, it was estimated that approximately Rs 60,000 crore was spent—an amount that exceeds what was spent in the US presidential elections of 2016. It needs hardly be said that most of it was black money. The BJP was, by far, the biggest spender.[193] For a country with 22 per cent of its citizens living below the poverty line, and one where there was such an animated debate on where funding for the NYAY (minimum income guarantee) scheme for the poor would come from, there was deathly silence on the BJP's seemingly inexhaustible source of funds.

The bonds are a way of industrialising corruption, formally institutionalising it. The equivalent of wearing a 'We Are Corrupt' T-shirt with a winking smiley. India Inc. is an accessory in this crime, its platitudes about corporate governance notwithstanding. Corporates prefer anonymity in political donations for fear of reprisals if the rival party triumphs. Some of that apprehension is justified, given the current political climate of fear and intimidation. It is tragic indeed that industry bodies succumb meekly to the powers that be. They should try to bell the cat. With all their resources, they actually have a shot at it. Perhaps the agitating JNU students can serve as inspiration. But this is a foolishly optimistic hope, of course.

Big business needs politicians for favours in order to access public assets like land, water, spectrum, coal, forests or mines. So, corporate donors fund all political parties proportionate to their winnability projections. The electoral bonds now provide protective guard.

In July 2019, *Guardian* columnist George Monbiot wrote, '[E]verywhere the killer clowns are taking over. Boris Johnson, Nigel Farage, Donald Trump, Narendra Modi, Jair Bolsonaro, Scott Morrison, Rodrigo Duterte, Matteo Salvini, Recep Tayyip Erdoğan, Viktor Orbán and a host of other ludicrous strongmen—or weakmen, as they so often turn out to be—dominate nations that would once have laughed them off stage. The question is why?'[194] He goes on to answer that question in his inimitable style, and there are many different answers out there. But this much is an irrefutable fact: there is a global rise in authoritarian leaders.

As discussed earlier, they are not quite like the tinpot dictators of yore, but in effect they are not very different either. They have created a new political-government structure—illiberal democracy, which is essentially a diluted dictatorship. Like Adolf Hitler, these leaders are democratically elected, so their acts of despotism are seen as having public backing.

In Vladimir Putin's Russia, several dissenters, such as Denis Voronenkov, have been assassinated in mysterious circumstances. Rodrigo Duterte of the Philippines indulges in macabre braggadocio, claiming that he has killed drug peddlers with his own hands.[195] Manila recoils in fear because suspected offenders may be summarily jailed and executed just like that. Turkey's Recep Tayyip Erdoğan has crafted a draconian law that sets him up almost as a ruling monarch with unbridled powers.

Authors, journalists, social activists, public intellectuals, dissidents and political rivals are being jailed as part of massive crackdowns in these countries. In Peru, Venezuela, Malaysia and Indonesia, hardliner positions are being taken. Donald Trump's witch-hunt for political adversaries borders on extreme paranoia. Under Modi, there have been so many crackdowns, it's hard to keep count. For instance, the Bhima Koregaon case, with its ever-increasing list of suspects, has seen some of India's most respected intellectuals and activists thrown behind bars during a pandemic. The government's modus operandi seems to include filing FIRs, criminal defamation suits, using the CBI/Enforcement Directorate, income-tax raids, sting operations, fake news and the plain issuing of threats. The Elgar Parishad case (relating to the violent clashes at Bhima-Koregaon on 1 January 2018) is a classic example, where despite being arrested for over two years, several left-leaning activists such as Sudha Bharadwaj, Arun Ferreira and P. Varavara Rao continue to be in jail, despite the fact that no incriminating documents have been found to establish the charge of a plot to assassinate the prime minister. These activists allege that the NIA, which reports to the home ministry, is wilfully harassing them.[196]

Television editors who fail to charm Big Brother with their dulcet tones are treated as betrayers of Mother India. As a spokesperson of the Congress, I was often asked why I wouldn't give 'full marks to Mr Modi' for this scheme and that policy? I was amused, but keeping a straight face was a prerequisite of the job. In my view, digital platforms and online portals, like the *Wire*, *Scroll*, *Quint* and the *Print*, are the new heroes of journalism, filling the gap left by the mainstream media. 'Four hostile newspapers are more to be feared than a thousand bayonets,' said Napoleon Bonaparte. He would have been shocked at the scene that the craven Indian media presents today.

The one institution that the ordinary people of India still had faith in was the Indian judiciary, despite the nearly 38 million pending cases. The Supreme Court of India appeared to be infallible, despite the occasional allegation of political compromise. That was shattered on a cold winter morning, 12 January 2018, when four of its most senior judges (J. Chelameswar, Madan Lokur, Ranjan Gogoi and Kurian Joseph) held an unprecedented press conference, questioning the brittle independence and compromised standards of the highest court of the land. They alleged that certain 'benches' could be manipulated, and that the appointment of judges itself was prone to nepotism and favouritism. It sent shockwaves down the haloed corridors of justice. After the controversial term of the then chief justice of India (CJI) Dipak Mishra, Justice Ranjan Gogoi replaced him. A sexual harassment case against the new CJI was handled in a manner that would have embarrassed even the thick-skinned Donald Trump.[197] In his thirteen-month tenure, he presided over some crucial, sensitive decisions of the highest import: the Rafale scam, the CBI fracas, the Ayodhya land title dispute, the abrogation of Article 370, NRC in Assam and electoral bonds, among them. The BJP had a huge political investment in all these decisions.

Four months after his retirement, the Modi government appointed Gogoi as a Rajya Sabha member. He happily acquiesced with the post-retirement sinecure. Even his brother was given an official position in the Assam government. The cataclysmic end of Indian institutions was finally in full public view.

This all-round institutional collapse was one of the factors behind the economic reversals of the past six years. Political parties charm voters with bombastic promises in their election manifestos. From providing farmers with remunerative prices, millions of jobs for India's educated unemployed youth, tax concessions for the middle class and a slew of benefits for start-ups and industry, the economy becomes a competitive differentiator. Modi won the 2014 elections as a 'vikas purush' (development man), but by the 2017 Gujarat assembly election campaign, the slogan '*Vikas Gando Thayo Chhe*' (development has gone crazy) had become a blockbuster hit. Because the Indian economy under Modi had flattered to deceive.

4

ECONOMY

A Season of Blunders

It was a gathering of Mumbai's finest—CEOs of large companies, niftily dressed investment bankers, social celebrities, policy wonks and economists. Dr Montek Singh Ahluwalia's book *Backstage: The Story Behind India's High Growth Years* was to be released on 24 February 2020 at the Taj hotel. Dr Ahluwalia is credited with shaping India's economic policy during the turbulent decades that reconfigured India—an esteemed member of the dream team that included former prime minister Dr Manmohan Singh, former finance minister P. Chidambaram and former RBI governor Raghuram Rajan. In the deep and lively conversation that evening, one statement of Dr Ahluwalia's stood out: 'The UPA refused to take credit for many of its achievements.' That statement told a whole story. The party's reluctance to advertise its good deeds was mysterious. Rest assured, Modi was not complaining.

The Congress has appeared to be on a suicide mission since 2011, when it appeared clueless in taking on the anti-corruption movement with its clear political agenda. At the slightest whiff of a scandal, it would express righteous indignation and ask the accused leaders to resign. This strategy boomeranged. With the CAG's allegations, the Jan Lokpal agitation and Radia tapes making negative headlines every day, the resignations of leaders like Shashi Tharoor, Pawan Bansal, Ashwani Kumar, Ashok Chavan and Jayanthi Natarajan only confirmed everyone's worst apprehensions. They saw these moves as sanctimonious window-dressing meant to hoodwink them.

'You gave the Congress sixty years, give BJP just sixty months,' Modi told people in 2014. (The Congress had, in fact, had fifty-five years, but why let facts stand in the way of a catchy line?) The crucial word was 'just'. Modi loves slogans, even shouting 'Yes, We Can', à la Obama, during his campaign. And he knows the power of formulaic clichés—'Minimum Government, Maximum Governance', for instance. After the calamitous last few years of UPA-2, the idea of minimum government had everyone hypnotised.

When India gained independence, 70 per cent of her citizens were living below the poverty line. That figure now stands at 22 per cent. India's adult literacy level was just 18 per cent back then; now it is 76 per cent. The average Indian's lifespan was just twenty-seven years; it has risen to seventy-four years. In the 1950s, agriculture contributed 50 per cent of the national output, but only 1 per cent of India's villages were electrified. Now, 100 per cent of its villages are covered. Undoubtedly, Congress, the party that governed the country for the bulk of its history, must receive a major share of the credit for this remarkable transformation.

But as Modi relentlessly targeted the Congress for under-performance and personal profiteering, the party's response was unusually defensive and ineffectual. This helped fortify his story. He promised a bouquet of high-profile goodies to Indian voters: bullet trains, 2 crore jobs per year, solar energy and power plants, manufacturing centres, roads, airports, ports and hundred 'smart cities'. '*Na khaunga na khane doonga*' (Neither will I take a bribe nor will I let others do it), Modi thundered—words that helped cement the Congress's reputation as incorrigibly corrupt. At an election rally in Jharkhand, Modi made a chimerical promise to voters that he would regret throughout his tenure: 'We will change the minimum support price. It will be the entire cost of production plus 50 per cent profit.'[198] The farmers were naturally ecstatic.

India's GDP grew at 7 per cent per annum in real terms between 1993–94 and 2011–12, and poverty declined from 37 per cent in 2004–05 to 22 per cent in 2011–12. Both were turnaround success stories that went unheralded because of the UPA's lousy communication skills. In the first seven years of UPA, often described as the 'golden period of India's economic growth', India registered a phenomenal GDP growth of 8.5 per cent. Manmohan Singh's first-generation reforms of 1991 were beginning to pay off. In 2010, India moved out of the World Bank's low-income countries classification and into the group of middle-income countries; a remarkable leap. In UPA-1, between 2004–09, the average GDP growth was 8.4 per cent, one of the reasons why the Congress returned to power with 206 seats. The rate of private corporate investment rose from 6 per cent of the GDP in 2003–04 to 14.3 per cent in 2007–08, resulting in the industry bigwigs backing Dr Singh. The GDP grew handsomely—at 8.6 per cent in 2009–10 and 8.9 per cent in 2010–11—as well before the policy slowdown paralysed the government. Then, in 2012, Pranab Mukherjee, finance minister at that time, decided to amend the Income Tax Act retroactively to force Vodafone to pay taxes in spite of a ruling by the Supreme Court in favour of the company. It was a terrible miscalculation. Both the right-liberal policy wonks and foreign investors were stunned by that one-sided, peremptory decision.

The UPA pushed for foreign direct investment (FDI) in insurance to be raised from 26 per cent to 49 per cent; the BJP opposed it with all their might. In 2015, the NDA passed that bill after a delay of ten years; a delay they were responsible for. The GST Constitutional Amendment Bill was introduced in the Lok Sabha by then finance minister Mukherjee in March 2011. It was forced to lapse. Ultimately, at the midnight hour on 1 July 2017, it would get a razzle-dazzle red-carpet welcome by the NDA. FDI in multi-brand retail, with big names such as Walmart, Carrefour, Target and Metro, would have had a multiplier effect on a slowing economy, but the BJP opposed it tooth and nail. In its time in the Opposition, the BJP effectively jeopardised every major reform proposed by the Congress.

In 2013, India became part of the infamous 'Fragile Five', as Morgan Stanley described it. The others in that dubious compendium were Indonesia, Brazil, South Africa and Turkey. A concerned Moody's (the credit-rating agency) put India on a negative outlook. The May 2013 announcement by the chairman of the US Federal Reserve Bank Ben Bernanke that quantitative easing (the Fed buying long-term securities and bonds to increase money supply) would be tapered lacerated emerging markets even as American growth rates stabilised. The rupee crashed to Rs 67 against the dollar. But by the end of March 2014, it had improved to Rs 60. The current account deficit was also under control—down from 4.8 per cent in 2012–13 to 1.7 per cent in 2013–14. The UPA failed to publicise an outstanding turnaround, one that was recognised by global economists.

There was indeed much to celebrate. The UPA's policy approach was to establish rights-based laws meant for citizen empowerment, and a true effort at the democratisation of institutions. Take, for instance, these policies: the mid-day meal scheme, National Rural Health Mission, Integrated Child Development Services, Jawaharlal Nehru National Urban Renewal Mission, Mahatma Gandhi National Rural Employment Guarantee Act, the Right of Children to Free and Compulsory Education Act or Right to Education Act, the RTI Act, Food Security Act (FSA), FDI, enactments on forest rights, among others. Or consider this: in the 2008–09 budget, then finance minister P. Chidambaram announced a loan waiver of Rs 60,000 crore for small farmers.

The FSA, passed in 2013, in particular, was a continuance of the Congress party's long history of anti-poverty schemes. The Congress had, in effect, implemented the 'Garibi Hatao' (remove poverty) slogan of former prime minister Indira Gandhi. The FSA covered two-thirds of the country's population, allotting 5 kg subsidised essential food grains per person, the total cost of such allocation being only 1 per cent of the GDP. Although they initially opposed it, the BJP quickly realised the huge political cost of opposing the FSA, and eventually supported its passage in Parliament. Similarly, when the Aadhaar Bill was introduced in 2010 to give the Unique Identification Authority of India (UIDAI) statutory status, the BJP vehemently opposed it. Aadhaar was meant to facilitate direct benefits transfer for scholarships, pensions, maternity benefits, wages, and so on. Once Modi assumed office, the NDA was quick to pass the bill.

The UPA was a victim as much of the BJP's planned filibustering as its own shoddy communication skills. A combination of sloppy governance, poor image management and substandard political articulation destroyed the UPA in 2014.

In UPA-1, agriculture grew by 3.1 per cent, and in UPA-2, by an impressive 4.3 per cent. At their core, the Congress and its allies remained focused on the social amelioration of the disadvantaged. Even though India had registered high GDP growth rates during 2004–09, almost 350 million were still below the poverty line in 2009–10. The Manmohan Singh government's economic policy was aligned towards addressing this issue. By 2011–12, UPA policies would result in the reduction of poverty by 138 million (an estimate that the World Bank has since revised to 270 million).

No wonder then that Dr Ahluwalia was puzzled about why the Congress was so reluctant to truly own the credit for this humongous accomplishment. To announce this landmark reduction[199] in poverty, on 25 July 2013, Bollywood actor and Congress leader Raj Babbar was tactlessly thrust forward to address a press conference. Babbar made an anecdotal observation that food could be had for just Rs 12 in Mumbai. The BJP promptly pounced on the Congress for mocking the poor. An extraordinary Congress accomplishment became an object of derision. It was a self-goal.

The clearest explanation that presents itself is that the Congress had lost self-confidence early in UPA-2. The Niira Radia tapes, which hit the headlines in November 2010—and made it look like the Manmohan Singh government had been taken over by slimy power brokers and sleazy lobbyists—was another mortifying moment for an already beleaguered government. When, later that month, Telecom Minister A. Raja was accused of procedural violations in the 2G scam, all hell broke loose. The BJP forced a joint parliamentary committee to be constituted, the party sniffing an unforeseen windfall. Although, in 2013, the joint parliamentary committee correctly repudiated the absurd 'presumptive loss' theory of the then CAG Vinod Rai, the damage to the Congress had been done.[200] The party had become synonymous with corruption. In fact, it was perhaps the biggest reason why the India Against Corruption movement got the Indian media—unafraid in those days to lay into the government in power—really going.

In the 2G spectrum case, perhaps in response to the uproar around the country and in the media, the Supreme Court cancelled all 122 telecom licences in February 2012, sending the ballooning sector into a tailspin. It was an act of judicial overreach. Combined with the UPA's internal skulduggery, it made a mess of a critical sector. In 2017, a special court judge acquitted all the accused in the 2G scam, citing lack of evidence, but by then the Congress's reputation was in tatters. Inexplicably, the party failed to capitalise on this judgement, to use it as an opportunity to tell people that the charges were fabricated and that there had been an orchestrated smear campaign against the Congress. This was a tactical PR blunder, one in a long history of faux pas.

Not only did the Congress not sell its accomplishments aggressively, it de-marketed itself. Infrastructure expenditure increased from 5 to 7 per cent of the GDP. Rural highways and interior roads expanded by 2 lakh km—a crucial success. India's per capita consumption of electricity went up from 559 kWh to 813 kWh, exhibiting higher commercial activity and better household connectivity, signs of economic progress. Under the UPA, in terms of purchasing power parity (PPP), India's economy became the third largest in the world. The BJP would have booked billboards in advance for such an announcement, but the Congress did not even hold its daily press conference. India successfully eradicated polio in 2014, but no one noticed because few were told. To cut a long story short, the UPA self-annihilated.

Compounding the Congress's own crisis of communication was the fact that India suffered a double whammy just as elections came around: slumping growth in the last two years of UPA-2, and an average inflation rate of 9.7 per cent. Thus, both Indian industry and households were feeling let down by the party when it came time to vote. The Congress gave up 7, Race Course Road to Narendra Modi on a platter.

It is, therefore, necessary to assess what Modi and the NDA did with that mandate—especially because the people of India had voted in big numbers for Modi's 'development' agenda. While several experts believe, in retrospect, that the one policy decision that defined the Modi government was the short-sighted voodoo experiment of demonetisation, it is important to review the NDA government's performance under several heads. A dispassionate appraisal of India's economy during the critical phase of 2014–19 will answer the question: did his government deliver on its promises?

AGRICULTURE

Gajendra Singh Rajput was just another farmer until 23 April 2015, but by late afternoon of that day, he became emblematic of Indian's worsening rural crisis. Rajput committed suicide by hanging himself from a tree during a political rally of the Aam Aadmi Party (AAP) at Jantar Mantar, New Delhi. Heartbreakingly, his suicide note ended with the slogan that defined the 1960s: '*Jai Jawan, Jai Kisan*' (hail the farmer and the soldier). He left behind a family, including three children. 'I was driven out of my home after my crops were destroyed by bad weather. Please tell me how I can go home,' his note said, laying out his anguish. Deadly unseasonal hailstorms had lashed Rajasthan in February and March that year, destroying his crops and leaving him destitute. In the two months preceding Rajput's suicide, the state had logged an alarming forty-two farmer suicides. Just as the barbarous murder of Nirbhaya made her the symbol of the violence of rape, Rajput's death, in the presence of 5,000 people, captured remorselessly by 24x7 broadcast networks, became the face of farmer suicide. The moment was eerily reminiscent of the satirical film *Peepli Live*, a slapstick take on the vulture-like Indian media and its tendency to prey on sensationalistic content.

Agriculture contributes just 15 per cent of our GDP, but it supports 55 per cent of India's population. In the already precarious lives that small farmers lead, unseasonal or unevenly distributed rain wreaks havoc. The impact on cash flow is massive, and there is no backup or contingency fund. The cost of education, weddings, spending on social customs and religious festivals must still be met. Debts mount. A severe illness in the family could worsen things rapidly. The local moneylender—usually a politically connected local don—charges exorbitant interest rates. Failure to repay loans might result in not just loss of agricultural property but also physical intimidation and public humiliation. Suicide is the culmination of the extreme despair of this situation.

The social schisms in rural India are huge, and widening further. About 80 per cent of India's farmers are marginal,[201] with small holdings that get further fragmented with every generation until the holdings become uneconomical.

In 2013, UPA passed the Land Acquisition Rehabilitation and Relief Act, which reformed an archaic British-era legislation from 1894. It was a timely intervention meant to protect vulnerable landowners. Farmers live with the fear of their land being forcibly acquired by giant corporations in cahoots with a compromised government. For projects concerning the defence sector or national security, the State has preferential rights anyway. Initially, Modi and the BJP resisted the law, and then quietly backtracked as rural protests mounted. Less than 20 per cent of India's farmers are insured,[202] but as noted earlier, 55 per cent of India's workforce is still dependent on farming, either fully or partially.

Farmers would have benefited from FDI in multi-brand retail, which the BJP vociferously opposed in order to protect its traditional vote bank of small traders. FDI would have introduced into the Indian agricultural chain the farm-to-fork model. That could have been the panacea for agricultural modernisation: cold storage, sophisticated warehouses, quality control, contract farming, scientific processing, distribution chains, direct purchasing without corrupt third-party intermediaries, among other things. It could have reduced the wasteful damage of fruits, vegetables and food grains.

Even given its history of disregard for the distress of farmers, the BJP's nonchalance at the abysmal growth rate—an abject 0.2 per cent during 2014–15[203]—in the agricultural sector was astounding. Farmer suicides in Maharashtra alone crossed 3,200 in 2015. The data miraculously disappeared from official records thereafter. As many as 302 of India's 676 districts faced droughts.[204] Rural wages, which had shown rapid growth in the preceding years, were down to a miserable 3.8 per cent growth rate in 2015.[205] Sales of tractors (20 per cent) and motorcycles (4 per cent),[206] which are markers of rural market buoyancy, were down in the first half of the fiscal year 2015–16. The NDA government appeared to not notice.

Important economic gains in the sector had been lost. The UPA's pro-farmer policies had begun paying dividends. Farmer incomes had increased 5.13 per cent per annum during the ten years between 2004–05 and 2014–15, and real wages in rural areas increased by more than 8 per cent per annum between 2007–08 and 2011–12. Four years into the Modi government's term, the annual growth rate in agriculture declined to 1.86 per cent—less than half of what was achieved during the UPA regime. Real wages of agricultural labourers declined at 0.3 per cent per annum between 2013 and 2017, whereas non-agricultural wages declined 1.1 per cent. The stagnation in farmer incomes coincided with a decline in real rural wages (which, during the UPA regime, had grown at 6 per cent). The agrarian distress had worsened because of the government's mulish approach to the UPA's game-changing legislation, MNREGA. Modi had ridiculed it thus in Parliament in February 2015: 'My political acumen tells me that MNREGA should not be shut down. I will not make such a mistake because MNREGA is a living monument of [the Congress party's] failures. Sixty years after independence, you still have to send people to dig holes in the ground ... I will tell the world that these holes you are digging are for your own sins.' The year 2015, two years into the NDA government's tenure, was the tenth anniversary of MNREGA. In a dramatic U-turn, in 2015, the government discovered salutary attributes to the UPA's landmark employment scheme, which had been internationally accepted as the world's largest social security programme. The Modi government belatedly acknowledged the significance of rural employment and capital-asset creation as farmer distress rose and the rural economy crashed. MNREGA was its new lifeline.

As private jets flew into the Swiss Alps at Davos for the annual World Economic Forum summit, in 2018, and India was doing a showstopper walk, an eighty-four-year-old farmer from Maharashtra committed suicide at Mumbai's state secretariat. His name was Dharma Patil. As India's stock markets breached 35,000, prompting pink papers to go into uncontrollable euphoria, Dharma Patil lay dead at JJ hospital. He had come to Mumbai to protest the low price offered by the state government while acquiring his land for a solar project. The government of Maharashtra had ignored his repeated entreaties for help. The Opposition accused the BJP government led by Devendra Fadnavis of culpable homicide.[207] Gajendra Singh Rajput's death was on everyone's minds again.

The late Arun Jaitley, India's finance minister at the time, who had declared that India would double farmers' income in five years, was uncharacteristically silent. Perhaps that was understandable: after four years of the Modi government, the average agricultural growth was at a low of 1.9 per cent. To achieve the government's ambitious growth projections, a minimum of 12 per cent growth was needed. But it was only hot talk.

Take, for example, the BJP's high-pitched assurance to farmers that they would increase MSPs by 50 per cent over and above the cost of production. Its very foundation for measuring MSP was flawed to begin with; instead of taking the comprehensive cost (C2), they absorbed only a part of it (FL, or family labour).[208] While FL only factored in actual paid-out costs and an imputed consideration of unpaid family labour, C2 additionally considered rentals and interest earnings foregone on land owned and fixed assets. To put it simply, the government chose a lower denominator. More simply still, it was a sleight of hand.

In most places, the market price was below the MSP because of excess produce and low procurement (which means the government may not procure the produce). The farming community was faced with a catastrophic situation, but an intoxicated, arrogant government refused to recognise it. A frustrated Maharashtra farmer sent a cheque of Rs 1,064—the price he got for 750 kg of onions—to the prime minister. There could not have been a more choleric exhibition of rural angst. Procurement levels remained extremely low. In a cruel paradox, the farmer was being guillotined for plentiful production. Many farmers dumped their vegetables, fruits and milk on highways to express their dismay and desperation. Increased farm output did not lead to higher income levels, but did add to costs substantially. That explained why farmers marched from all over the country to Delhi, demanding a special session of Parliament—they wanted to be heard by a government that appeared oblivious to their worsening problems.

By 2015, the farmer crisis was coming to a head. Even in the crop insurance scheme, private insurance firms made whopping profits (over Rs 10,000 crore), while claim settlements were very low.[209] Farmers were being short-charged, their premium payments providing little buffer in contingencies. Figures clearly show that India's gross investment in agriculture came down drastically from 17.7 per cent in 2013–14 to 15.5 per cent in 2016–17. The value or profitability of major crops had diminished by over 30 per cent in 2017–18. The gross margins on several commercial crops and agricultural commodities shrank. The terms of trade got worse for farmers; their price realisation and thus their incomes saw a downward trajectory. The National Crime Records Bureau reported an eight-fold increase in farmer protests in only the first three years of the Modi government—from 628 in 2014 to 2,683 in 2015 and 4,837 in 2016. The government mishandled trade policies, MSPs, and procurement and storage management. Thus, despite a bountiful supply after two years of drought, farmers were worse off than they were before.

The slogan '*Narendra Modi Kisan Virodhi*' (Narendra Modi is anti-farmer) rang through the farmer protests. His obstinacy in attempting to see through the anti-farmer Land Acquisition Ordinance, promulgating it three times, is an example of why this slogan was justified. Ultimately, Modi had to let the ordinance lapse, claiming he had done so in response to farmer concerns.[210]

After living in denial for five years, dismissing farmer protests as politically motivated movements, in the last days of its first term, the NDA government woke up to the agrarian crisis. What they offered, though, was a sham compensation of Rs 500 per month per household, which works out to Rs 17 per day under the PM Kisan Yojana scheme. Assuming an average size of four persons per family, the number shrinks to a laughable Rs 4 per day per person. It was adding insult to a burning injury. Life had come a full circle for the prime minister, who had run his 2014 campaign on the promise of a guaranteed minimum financial return for farmers—a commitment he had comprehensively broken with.

INDUSTRY AND NPA

On 16 May 2014, the stock markets caroused, expecting an exhilarating acceleration, as the harbingers of 'Achhe Din' overwhelmed political adversaries. By repackaging the UPA's sombre-sounding 'new manufacturing policy' with glittering branding, Modi positioned himself as the messiah of manufacturing (an industry that contributes 17 per cent to India's GDP). Ironically, under the BJP's watch, even the manufacture of the world's tallest statue, the Statue of Unity, was outsourced to a Chinese foundry. The much heralded Make in India was marketed aggressively, building further on the prime minister's rock-star image. The bespoke lion logo—inspired by a Swiss bank emblem, in a nice little piece of irony—walked majestically. How did it matter that manufacturing activity nosedived to a twenty-eight-month low,[211] exports tumbled like Jack and Jill for twelve successive months[212] and private investment remained as flat as a table in 2016–17. This in spite of the fact that global oil prices had crashed to approximately US$ 27 a barrel in January 2016, giving the government a lot of headroom.

The 'twin balance sheet problem' was the UPA's epitaph. Large corporates had borrowed extensively to invest in infrastructure projects during the boom years, and PSU banks had indiscriminately lent substantial funds. However, in the boom and bust phase of UPA-2, many of these investments soured, and banks were left holding either dud assets or toxic assets that required rescheduling to prevent the debtor's bankruptcy.

India's stressed-debts problem was concentrated in fifty large defaulters who forced banks to take huge write-offs in their already bleeding balance sheets. Stalled projects were up at a staggering fifty-two-quarter high in 2018. PSU banks made a mammoth loss of Rs 85,369 crore in 2017–18. The RBI's financial stability report, released in June 2018, warned that the gross non-performing assets (GNPAs) of scheduled commercial banks could rise from 11.6 per cent of total assets in March 2018 to 12.2 per cent in March 2019, which would be the highest level of bad debt in almost two decades. The NDA refused to reveal the large corporate wilful defaulters' list given to the PMO by former RBI governor Raghuram Rajan, even as industry debt write-offs touched Rs 3.5 lakh crore and swelled beyond. The NPAs of PSU banks crossed a staggering Rs 11 lakh crore. Meanwhile, the government struggled to extradite the flamboyant poster boy of NPAs, Vijay Mallya, who clearly had more pressing problems in London, such as rebranding his Formula One racing team.

By 2019, the banks' recapitalisation requirement was estimated at US$ 90 billion, of which the government had committed only US$ 10 billion in fiscal resources. The total market value of all the public sector banks (PSBs) put together was at one point Rs 4.83 lakh crore—less than that of just one of the private sector banks, HDFC, which was Rs 5.69 lakh crores.

In October 2015, Raghuram Rajan had completed the Asset Quality Review (AQR), meant to prevent the evergreening of loans—a trick to perpetuate bad loans, which had increased exponentially following the economic downturn. The PCA framework was also Rajan's idea. He seemed intent on bringing to book India's crony capitalists who had monopolised PSB loans. NPAs shot up from 4.62 per cent in 2014–15 to 10.41 per cent by December 2017.

Swaminathan Gurumurthy, a sixty-nine-year-old chartered accountant and an RSS ideologue, joined Rajan on the RBI board, manifesting the government's ideological shift. He had been among the principal proponents of demonetisation. Gurumurthy criticised Rajan for raising the red flag on NPAs in PSU banks; according to him, it was a clever trick to give foreign banks an entry into India. Clearly, Rajan had his hands full.

The Modi government responded to the situation by passing the Insolvency and Bankruptcy Code—a game-altering, big-bang legislation, for which the government deserves salutations. Under the new law, once the process of declared insolvency is triggered, it has to be decided within 180 days (extendable by another ninety days) whether the company will be liquidated or revived and sold to a new owner. It was a right step towards resolution of sticky loans, but was soon caught in legal and bureaucratic tangles. The Economic Survey of 2014 quantified bad loans, or NPAs, at Rs 2.05 lakh crore. Then, in October 2018, Jaitley shifted the blame to the previous government, saying that when Modi took office, NPAs stood not at Rs 2.05 lakh crore but Rs 8.5 lakh crore. Did he then lie to Parliament in 2014? If he did, a privilege motion was needed against the finance minister. In any case, it was not merely bank credit that had stifled Indian manufacturing, which needed much more help than smart packaging like Make in India.

Ultimately, Make in India was hollow hyperbole, with corporate India unable to leverage the improved ranking of India's Ease of Doing Business. Although the government blamed the RBI for not reducing the repo rates faster, the fact was that neither the banks nor the borrowers had any incentive to invest. Demonetisation and GST would erase it altogether.

By 2016–17, India's suspect, over-inflated GDP had slumped to 6.1 per cent[213] following demonetisation—the first time in five years that GDP growth had slowed. Thereafter, it has been on a downward spiral, with no sign of recovering. In the fourth quarter of the last fiscal of 2016–17, 1.5 million were rendered jobless.[214] Unemployment levels were soaring high, with virtually negative accretion—a sharp negation of the 600 lakh jobs in three years that the Modi government had promised voters. Even the IT sector was sacking young software engineers, resulting in massive stress. Rural distress had led to a pan-India revolt. The mayhem in Mandsaur, Madhya Pradesh, where several farmers were shot dead during a protest was only the tip of the iceberg. Farmer suicides had crossed 37,000 deaths since 2014.[215]

Most macroeconomic indicators told a grim story for 2018–19, the election year. Current account deficit was at 2.9 per cent of the GDP. India's exports performance was sub-par. India's investment rate (gross fixed-capital formation as a percentage of the GDP) slumped from 33.4 per cent under UPA to 29 per cent under Modi.

On large projects, India experienced a double whammy—very low new projects valued at Rs 15.8 lakh crore, while concomitantly, the value of stalled projects was up at Rs 11 lakh crore. Despite the RBI lowering repo rates over the years, overall lending growth was 10 per cent in 2018, far lower than 16 per cent in 2014. After ignoring the PSU banks' ballooning NPA problem (over Rs 11 lakh crore) for its entire term, the government finally woke up to bank recapitalisation—but it was closing the stable door after the horse had bolted. For all the hype on stock-market exuberance, corporate profits to GDP ratio was at a fifteen-year low, at 2.8 per cent. Lower inflation (mostly due to fuel and food) accompanying lower demand suggested the beginnings of a clear slowdown. Disturbingly, government debt stood at Rs 82 lakh crore in September 2018, up by 49 per cent since Modi became prime minister.

Thus, India entered 2019 with the ominous headwinds of a slowing world economy, a trade war between the US and China, Brexit uncertainty, and the threat of rising oil prices. A new government in 2019 would have to troubleshoot through a hotchpotch legacy of policy failures. It wouldn't be easy to wash away the problems as 'legacy issues'. India would need an assurance that it would never see dorky decisions like demonetisation ever again.

GROWTH MODEL AND INEQUALITY

The Modi government's rather naïve belief in the trickle-down growth theory—propounded by Columbia University professors Jagdish Bhagwati and Arvind Panagariya, who advised the government on economic policy matters—had not worked. High growth alone cannot reduce poverty levels; it needs to be accompanied by a structured strategy for income redistribution, especially in an emerging market with economic inequities. India's ranking in the Inclusive Development Index had slumped to sixty-two: an appalling commentary on the skewed policies of the NDA government that increased social disparities. Not surprisingly, the ranking seemed to synchronise with the astonishing fact that 1 per cent of Indians now owned 60 per cent of India's aggregate wealth.[216] As Nobel Prize-winning economist Joseph Stiglitz and French economist Thomas Piketty have pointed out, inequality hinders growth. About 35 per cent of urban India lives below the poverty line even as the NDA goes on about smart cities and bullet trains. As Piketty says, unfettered globalisation founded on free capital flows, fresh markets, portable technology and cost competitiveness have accentuated income inequalities. Even the World Economic Forum, that incestuous club of the super-rich at Davos, was worried about the worldwide pushback. Occupy Wall Street was a manifestation of anger against the specious belief that capitalism based on free markets is a silver bullet for all woes. Far from it. The global financial meltdown of 2008 showed how the sophistry of the super-rich had intentionally misled the common people. Far from being the universal panacea that right-wing economists touted it to be, globalisation had opened up a Pandora's box. There are obviously intrinsic advantages to greater multilateral trade, to open societies encouraging cultural pluralism, the unshackled flow of foreign funds and resource or technology transfers, but each country needs to take a considered and calibrated position on the liberalisation graph and the progressive internationalisation of its economic landscape.

Travelling in Leh, Ladakh, I saw MNREGA projects in operation across the rural interiors and under-construction roads. Modi had once jeered at UPA policies, including MNREGA, as 'povertarian economics'. Yet, when faced with elections in 2017 in Uttar Pradesh, he himself sold loan waivers[217] to farmers. The much-trashed 'UPA doles'—MNREGA, Aadhaar, Direct Benefits Transfer, GST and food security—became the NDA's lifeline when it came to combating the damage that its '*Suit-boot Ki Sarkar*' image had caused.

Yet, the Modi government is yet to accept another important fact: that economic growth and social harmony cannot be decoupled. Congress leader Shashi Tharoor famously said that cows are safer than Muslims in India. A fractured society living on the precipitous edge of communal strife cannot deliver mind-boggling growth figures. The cottage industry of bigoted fanatics saw a burgeoning growth rate during 2014–19. Declining GDP growth was the collateral damage this raging tribalism delivered. It goes without saying that the poor suffered the most as government resources dried up.

Arvind Panagariya's resignation as vice-chairman of Niti Ayog was the formal abandonment of the pure growth model that had pleased free-market analysts and liberal economists lobbying for corporate tax cuts, free trade, cutback in subsidies and lesser welfare expenditure. They had loved the 'Minimum Government, Maximum Governance' dream that Modi marketed. With Panagariya's resignation, that cookie crumbled. Panagariya returned to Columbia University, perhaps chastened by the severe limitations of a sterile capitalistic model in a country grappling with extreme poverty (22 per cent of its citizens live below the poverty line[218]) and unrestrained crony capitalism.

In India, economic growth has only led to an enhanced concentration of public resources and economic wealth in the hands of a few. Principally, the growth model has a compelling argument—booming economic activity increases national output, which concomitantly results in higher budgetary revenues on account of buoyant tax collections. The latter can then be allocated for social welfare and public expenditure, thus ameliorating living standards for those at the bottom of the pyramid. Among other things, Panagariya and Bhagwati probably underestimated the systemic corruption that is deeply embedded in India's complex political-bureaucratic-business-media nexus. The trickle-down effect does not take shape as large corporations employ their gravy trains to usurp government contracts, in effect appropriating public assets for private consumption. The bottom line is then magnanimously distributed as high-dividend payouts (the owners are the largest shareholders and thus get a double bonus). And since most big corporates are ideologically agnostic and fund political parties across the spectrum, they stealthily dictate policy prescriptions even if governments change. Political parties risk a five-yearly unceremonious purge, but big business balloons. They are the stationary bandits who rule permanently, irrespective of which party wins the elections.

JOBS

Sometimes, social media memes have an uncanny knack for reflecting the popular narrative. On the day Bollywood actor Vivek Oberoi proudly announced that he would play Prime Minister Narendra Modi in an eponymous biopic, Twitterati sardonically captioned it as 'Modi's job creation scheme for the unemployed'. Sadly, the joke was on the jobless. The alarming escalation in joblessness has obliterated the demographic dividend advantage India marketed globally some years ago. The BJP's reaction was to abruptly announce a 10 per cent job reservation for the 'general category' in early 2019—an attempt to attract upper-caste votes and also, essentially, a pre-election headline-diversion tactic. The party had belatedly recognised that India's youth were feeling betrayed.

The government then attempted to control the narrative through a suspect bit of research published by an IIM-SBI collaboration that propped up EPFO (Employees' Provident Fund Organisation) data to claim that 7 million jobs had been created. 'Job creation is not the problem. The only snag is that the government has not captured job data,' the government declared in feeble defence. In reality, the increase in that data is accounted for by the number of micro and small enterprises that had registered for GST after reaching the threshold number of twenty workers because it had now become compulsory to do so. The government treated the entire workforce of these new entities in EPFO data as 'fresh jobs' when all it showed was the formalisation of the economy.

It was an embarrassing and transparent spin. Meanwhile, well-off and formerly prosperous communities, such as the Jats (Haryana), Patidars (Gujarat), Gujjars (Rajasthan) and Marathas (Maharashtra), had been protesting on the streets for a better deal. The Centre for Monitoring Indian Economy says that 12.7 million jobs were destroyed in the month after demonetisation. As of July 2018, the number of youngsters trained under the Modi government's much-vaunted National Skill Development Mission had not even touched 2 crore, as against a target of 40 crore.

It is elementary developmental economics that, if there is GDP growth, there ought to be a reasonably proportionate job expansion too. The bulk of new job creation happens in the manufacturing sector, which saw little traction in the 2016–18 period. In fact, factory production growth in November 2018 fell to a seventeen-month low (just 0.5 per cent), with manufacturing sliding into a negative growth rate (-0.4 per cent). Even capital goods and consumer durables slumped. It was hardly surprising that, in the absence of private capital investment, job growth plateaued. The global trend has moved to boosting domestic jobs (a political hot button post the globalisation backlash). India's demographic dividend advantage has become an onerous liability: an ill-equipped workforce,[219] hampered by poor health and inadequate knowledge and skills exposure. About 1.5 million of India's young die before attaining the age of five.[220] Over 25 million, including engineers, MBAs, PhDs and postgraduates, applied for 90,000 clerical jobs in the Indian Railways. According to a survey by the All India Manufacturers' Organisation (AIMO) on local industries, 35 lakh jobs were lost post demonetisation. A slowdown in construction, a source of alternative employment, worsened the job crisis. The construction sector grew at 9.4 per cent between 1999–2000 and 2004–05; at 7.9 per cent per annum between 2004–05 and 2012–13; and 3.5 per cent between 2014–15 and 2017–18. Once again, the government argued that the real problem was inadequate data points to capture recruitment figures.

The data, however, is clear. Under Modi's NDA, India experienced seismic job-loss growth; in 2018, 11 million Indians lost their jobs.[221] It was an electric shock to the Indian economy. At a 7.4 per cent unemployment rate (the highest in four years), the demographic dividend story is no longer sustainable. The pandemic has only exacerbated the situation, with unemployment rates shooting up to 8.4 per cent in August 2020.[222]

For the record, the BJP had promised young India 100 million jobs by the end of its first term, but that project was a failure, with the government accomplishing less than 1 per cent of its target. Infuriatingly, reports suggested that there were 24 lakh government jobs that remained vacant during this period—including jobs with state governments, PSUs and the armed forces.

The Modi government had little to say about jobs. When the prime minister did talk, he suggested that frying pakodas was a job too, because there was demand for it. That remark did not go down well with a desperate populace. A report by the National Sample Survey Organisation (NSSO) stated that India faced distressing and record unemployment levels: 6.1 per cent in 2017–18, a stunning forty-five-year high. Compare this to the astonishing fact that unemployment levels were at 2.2 per cent in 2011–12, one of the toughest periods during UPA-2, when India was pulling itself together in the aftermath of the recession of 2008. A panicky NDA government tried to suppress the NSSO figure,[223] forcing the resignation of two senior members, including the chairman P.C. Mohanan, from the National Statistical Commission, which is responsible for declaring the official figures.[224]

'Where are the jobs?' A rare moment of honesty was on record—even Highways Minister Nitin Gadkari seemed worried in August 2018 while addressing the media.

OIL

As the Turkish lira did a whopping nosedive against the dollar in August 2018, the Indian rupee plummeted to a historic low, breaching the psychological hurdle of seventy. All hell broke loose. Emerging market economies, many still long on dollar-denominated foreign currency borrowings, had good reason to panic. The ghost of the Asian currency crisis of 1997 as well as the 'taper tantrum' of 2013 were haunting reminders of the ravages an external uncontrollable can do to domestic economies.

In India, expectedly, the debate turned both puerile and political. A television chat I was participating in transformed into the theatre of the absurd, with a BJP political heavyweight saying, 'The Congress party loves the American dollar. We believe in the Indian rupee. We have pride in our local rupaiyya, while the Congress has a penchant for foreign things.' He stopped just short of calling me anti-national. It reminded one of Narendra Modi's unmatched hyperbole when, as chief minister of Gujarat, he had called the depreciating rupee a national humiliation.

Convertible traded currency, of course, has little connection to this kind of chest-thumping. India's exchange rate is greatly influenced by oil prices. Prime Minister Modi's government cruised through its first tenure on the back of falling international crude oil prices. To understand the magnitude of that economic tailwind, consider this: under the UPA, the per barrel dollar price had peaked at a staggering US$ 147, while under the NDA, the price had bottomed out at US$ 28. This was not a steep discount, it was virtually a distress sale. A smart government would have done two things—one, passed on the benefit of falling prices to consumers as part of principled mark-to-market pricing (a transparent mechanism), or created a price equalisation fund as a financial buffer for the unforeseen future when global crude oil prices would surge again (India imports 80 per cent of its crude oil requirements, making it susceptible to global volatilities). They did neither.

The NDA frittered away an oil bonanza, which Modi once haughtily described as his naseeb,[225] or destiny, perhaps revealing a sliver of his megalomaniacal self in the process. As petrol and diesel prices shot up sharply after a three-year lull, BJP spokespersons made a feckless attempt to blame it on worldwide developments. No one could explain where the Rs 16 lakh crore savings from the crude oil price crash had been deployed—in capital expenditure, reducing fiscal deficit, creating an oil-shock absorber buffer or on welfare schemes. TV channels played on a loop Modi's and the BJP's absurd hypothesis that the sturdiness of the Indian rupee in the FX market was directly proportional to its nationalistic zeal and patriotic ambitions. This play of irrational economics masked missed opportunities and the massive catastrophe that was coming.

GDP

Within a year of assuming power, the NDA started manipulating data readings.[226] In January 2015, the Central Statistical Office (CSO) changed the methodology for calculating GDP. The base year for estimating national accounts aggregates, such as GDP, changed from 2004–05 to 2011–12. The CSO shifted to calculating economic output at market prices as opposed to factor costs, as was done earlier. During Modi's first year, growth picked up to above 7 per cent, fiscal deficit declined to 4.1 per cent of GDP, inflation fell sharply to below 5 per cent and the current account deficit ended up close to 1 per cent of GDP. It was a good start. While some did question the abrupt 'inflated GDP', the BJP propaganda machine was in full throttle, horn blaring and headlights on.

At the World Economic Forum in Davos in 2015–16, India became 'the world's fastest growing economy'. Modi sold himself as the miracle man, and no one at the forum asked how such a dramatic turnaround was even theoretically conceivable within a year (between 2013–14 and 2014–15). This ought to have been an especially pressing question in view of the fact that only the previous year, the BJP had trashed the UPA, claiming that 'India was on the verge of a collapse'. The proposition that a large emerging market economy could make such a dramatic turnaround within one year was patently absurd.

Facts, it appeared, no longer mattered. But, according to the Modi government's own revised figures, the NDA had inherited from the UPA a very impressive GDP of 6.9 per cent[227] (later readjusted to 6.4 per cent)—clearly, a robust economy on a strong rebound from 5.1 per cent in 2012–13. Manufacturing growth stood at 6.2 per cent and not at -0.1 per cent, as was earlier estimated. In its statistical acrobatics, the BJP had scored a self-goal. Its motivated attacks on former prime minister Manmohan Singh and the Congress had boomeranged, thanks to the BJP's own revised numbers. The fact is that the Congress/UPA had registered an average GDP growth rate of 7.6 per cent over ten years, despite a coalition government, skyrocketing oil prices, a parliamentary gridlock, wholesale inflation and a volatile world economy.

The BJP had blown up this strong inheritance from the UPA, as well as the tailwind of low global oil prices, through sheer headline-hunting and dreadful governance. All crucial economic indicators, such as job accretion, core-sector growth, merchandise exports and agricultural productivity, were languishing. Despite massive ad spends for government branding of popular schemes (all of which were erstwhile UPA launches),[228] there was little incremental momentum. Make in India, Digital India, Swachh Bharat, Jan Dhan Yojana and the like were only seductive slogans. Modi was a globetrotter who boasted of attracting higher FDI, which in all fairness, did rise appreciably.

If the NDA were to adhere to the old index of calculation, India's GDP today would be lower by at least 250 basis points. It cherry-picked data, exaggerated claims and adopted new methodologies to massage numbers.[229] Thus, India was at once the world's supposedly fastest-growing large economy, while also a country where all of this was true: children died due to negligence in government hospitals,[230] train accidents were shockingly routine,[231] child malnutrition was on the rise,[232] joblessness was forcing MBAs, PhDs and engineers to apply for jobs as peons and constables,[233] and a record number of farmers were committing suicide.[234]

The true health of a country can only be determined through a biopsy of economic and social indicators, among them, job creation, per capita income, export performance, gross fixed capital formation, reduction in poverty levels, and per capita expenditure allocations to health and education. On all these factors, the NDA had slipped. On the Human Development Index, India was at a lowly 134,[235] and on the Global Hunger Index, it ranked 100.[236] It was at 138 on the Press Freedom Index,[237] and on the Gender Disparity Index, it trailed at 108.[238] Transparency was buried deep, opaqueness got the red carpet. India's GDP had become a conundrum; everyone had their own GDP of India.

DEMONETISATION

I remember the evening of 8 November 2016 in minute detail. There were no television show commitments—a rare free evening. I was in the middle of a serene walk-cum-jog when someone from the Congress media team called. They have to continually juggle allocations of spokespersons to various shows at short notice. I thought it was just another last-minute shift because someone had pulled out of a programme at the eleventh hour. The voice on the other side had an edge of panic.

'What's the news break?' I asked.

'Mr Modi is making a big announcement on national TV across all channels at 8 p.m. We need to be prepared to respond.'

'To what?' I inquired.

'Something about black money.'

Black money? Had the prime minister fulfilled his irrational, impossible election pledge? Modi had promised that he would bring back illegal monies stashed abroad and credit every Indian's bank account with Rs 15 lakh within one hundred days of assuming office. Was it no longer, as his lieutenant Amit Shah had called it, an electoral 'jumla'?

It was not to be. Instead, Modi announced demonetisation with characteristic melodrama and theatrics. Rs 500 and Rs 1,000 notes would be deemed cancelled with effect from the midnight hour. Together, the two denominations accounted for 86 per cent of the currency in circulation. BJP spokespersons called it a 'surgical strike on the black economy'. The government expected that Rs 4–5 lakh crore would not be returned to the banking system (and thus become a monetary profit that could then be used to distribute freebies to the electorate).[239] The end goal was always political.

What followed is now well known. In the months to come, ATMs ran dry within hours every day as the government was unable to print enough new currency. The machines also had to be rejigged to handle the newly announced Rs 2,000 notes.[240] Panic ensued. But, overnight, Modi had grabbed headlines that projected him as a leader who was cleansing the system of ill-gotten wealth[241]—an image that would endure the revelation that demonetisation was an unmitigated disaster.

Modi tore into critics of demonetisation as being in bed with crooks and criminals. All opponents of the move were declared anti-nationals who deserved to be packed off to Pakistan. Hyper-nationalism is the real currency of the Modi era anyway. The prime minister was hailed as a big-thinking Superman with a risk-taking propensity that only the bravest leaders are capable of. Meanwhile, a certain wise man called Manmohan Singh warned that demonetisation was organised loot and legalised plundering,[242] but he was ignored. Singh also correctly predicted that the GDP would decline by 2 per cent during the financial year.

There was frenzied speculation that even then finance minister Arun Jaitley was unaware of the decision until the last moment. The nation was gasping, struggling to cope. Long lines formed outside petrol pumps. It is reported that wealthy housewives hit Louis Vuitton stores with Gucci suitcases carrying cash. Going by the track record of income-tax raids and sundry recoveries, it was a fair estimation that, at best, the government could hope to recover only 5 to 6 per cent of the demonetised currency as black money. Besides, black money was rarely hoarded in cash. Those involved in large-scale tax evasion usually park their money in overseas tax havens to avoid being vulnerable to tax raids.

A further question must be asked: if Modi had meant business, why did he not go the whole nine yards and attack the source of black-money generation? Financial skulduggery is most prevalent in gold and bullion trading, export–import under-and over-invoicing transactions, real estate deals, P-notes (participatory notes) in stock markets and business corruption. The last of these morphs into a monstrous force when it contributes to political funding through instruments like electoral bonds and underhand cash donations. To those willing to see, it was apparent from the very beginning that Modi's real intentions were never to obliterate kaala-dhan, but to use demonetisation as an exercise in personal image-building as an anti-corruption crusader ahead of assembly elections in Uttar Pradesh and other states.

It is hardly a secret that, like many strongmen leaders, Modi sees himself as invincible and beyond reproach. Such leaders tend to love doing things on a big scale to capture the public imagination, usually by touching on emotive subjects like corruption, nationalism or injustice. Demonetisation was Modi's attempt to position himself as a Rambo-meets-Robin Hood figure who would take from the corrupt elite and redistribute the seized goodies to the poor and needy. He was helped along by a largely pliant media, a toadying corporate India and 'independent' analysts who serenaded demonetisation. Of course, Modi's voodoo economics had the full endorsement of RSS ideologues, some of whom were on the board of the RBI. Demonetisation was a scripted show meant to augment Modi's cracking façade. For a while it worked; India's trusting population queued up for several hours to withdraw their own hard-earned savings. Modi won the Uttar Pradesh and Uttarakhand elections. That the BJP lost or trailed significantly in Punjab, Goa and Manipur did not seem to make it to the national narrative.

When the RBI officially announced that 99.3 per cent of the demonetised currency was back in the banking system, all hell broke loose.[243] Even Modi fans had to concede that the black-money plug was all smoke and mirrors. And another question remained unasked or unanswered: in the age of electronic banking, why did it take the RBI two years to make the reconciliation?

BJP rebel leader Arun Shourie called demonetisation the 'biggest money-laundering scam'[244] in history, given the fact that there appeared to have been a tip-off to favoured cronies who conveniently converted their black money to white before 8 November 2016.[245] A new government in 2019 (if it was a non-BJP, non-NDA one) would have launched a full-scale forensic investigation into the alleged fraud. Several skeletons could have rolled out of polished cupboards. Modi's other stated objectives of demonetisation also proved to be chimera, whether it was the successful elimination of Naxalism and terrorism, stone-pelting in Kashmir or fake notes. Simply put, the move was not just economically unsound (and oh, how unsound it was!) but also politically immoral. It was a great betrayal of trust. Yet, the move had somehow successfully repositioned Modi as the messiah of the poor.

Two outstanding economists had warned India of these outcomes: Nobel laureate Amartya Sen and former prime minister Manmohan Singh. The cost of printing fresh notes was higher (approximately Rs 11,000 crore) than the currency that was not returned. There is speculation that, by the time the monies locked in cooperative banks and the confiscated cash and currencies in Nepal and Bhutan got counted, the accounted-for cash may have crossed 100 per cent (this was never officially confirmed or denied by RBI). This begs the question: why did the anticipated minimum of 6 per cent black money not remain outside the banking system?

There were several befuddling developments that were never fully investigated, whether the purchase of large plots of land by the BJP, or the unusual growth in deposits in cooperative banks.[246] Demonetisation was not just a blunder but a calculated plunder of India's financial system to benefit crony capitalists and facilitate legitimisation of ill-gotten wealth.[247] The BJP, as is still its wont, dismissed these serious allegations as a slander campaign. And since it is unlikely to order an independent forensic investigation into the matter, it is safe to assume that the issue will be scrutinised in any depth only when a new government takes over.

The fallout of demonetisation was far from only political. It destroyed the informal economy—there was the loss of millions of jobs, a 1.5 per cent collapse of India's GDP, rise in bank frauds (Rs 41,000 crore and 5,835 cases in 2017–18), and an actual increase in currency as a percentage of GDP to nearly 10.9 per cent (closing in on pre-November 2016 levels), an escalation in terror attacks and enhanced stone-pelting and militancy in Kashmir. Both fake notes and counterfeit currency were in kinetic circulation. And 140 Indians died as a direct result of demonetisation, whether standing in the long queues or associated inconveniences.

Through all of this, Modi and the BJP said nothing about the big sharks, the true source of black money. They had not a word on the Panama Papers that exposed how tax havens concealed ill-gotten monies. Or the Paradise Papers, another master document of fraudulent off-shore investments. Many Indians were named in both lists. Forbes was trenchant in its criticism: demonetisation was 'sickening and politically immoral'.[248] The *Wall Street Journal* described the hard sell of a cashless society as creating economic devastation and termed it an usurpation of an individual's economic liberty.[249]

By end-December of 2016, Rs 14 lakh crore of the Rs 15.4 lakh crore worth of scrapped notes had returned to the system. Ultimately, 99.3 per cent of the demonetised Rs 500 and Rs 1,000 currency notes returned to the RBI (15.31 lakh crore of the 15.41 lakh crore that was nullified, which meant that a measly Rs 10,720 crore had remained unreturned (0.7 per cent of demonetised notes). Then, suddenly, the daily updates by the RBI on returned notes were halted. The RBI board was as good as a dummy board, rubber-stamping demonetisation (even though they got to know about it just a day before). Not a single big tax fraudster was handcuffed. The astonishing delay in the disclosure of final audited numbers was not questioned. The report finally came on 24 August 2018, nearly two years after the fatal exercise was announced. Expectedly, the cost of printing new notes doubled to Rs 7,965 crore in 2016–17, from Rs 3,421 crore. Demonetisation had been a dismal disruptor, an ill-conceived policy that had effectively jeopardised India's immediate economic trajectory.

Modi got the then finance minister Arun Jaitley to do some sandbagging on his behalf.[250] A past master at PR spin, Jaitley wove a tale about how the real intent of the government was digitisation and formalisation of the economy—a new story and a new goalpost. An increase in taxpayers and tax returns is logical progression in an expanding economy, but forced formalisation is bound to boomerang. This is especially true of a country that still has no robust technological infrastructure or technical literacy and where traditional norms of doing business involve substantial use of cash. As of 26 October 2018, the currency in circulation stood at 19.7 lakh crore (up by 9.5 per cent since November 2016), and cash withdrawals from ATMs were up by 8 per cent at 2.75 lakh crore. The currency to GDP ratio was back up at 10.9 per cent in the financial year 2017–18, after falling to 8.8 per cent. Evidently, Jaitley had done some cherry-picking to spin his cockamamie theory. The BJP, red-faced and thoroughly flustered, came up with another argument. This time they said that the investigating authorities had initiated proceedings for income-tax violations against 18 lakh entities who allegedly deposited more demonetised notes than was proportional to their tax profile. Five years later, no one knows what happened to that much-hyped inquiry.

By an extraordinary coincidence, the Centre for Monitoring Indian Economy released data on 8 November 2018 which showed that unemployment was at a two-year high at 6.9 per cent,[251] a clear indication of the economic ramifications that voodoo economics had wrought in India. The loss in GDP was conservatively calculated as Rs 300,000 crore. Small farmers, petty traders and MSMEs are still recovering from the lethal blow. The MSME sector comprises 6.3 crore units and employs about 11.1 crore Indians, contributing roughly 30 per cent to the GDP, and accounting for close to 43 per cent of manufacturing output and around 40 per cent of total exports.

Demonetisation and the ham-handed execution of GST were the 'terrible twins'. GST was of course a UPA brainchild, and its operating architecture had been ready for long. The GST Bill had been introduced in 2011, but the BJP opposed it, citing cooperative federalism. Modi felt it trampled upon state autonomy. But when it was finally passed on 1 July 2017, the Central Goods and Services Tax Act was nothing like the one the UPA had envisaged. The mechanism that was finally enacted had a flawed construct, with multiple rates, a cumbersome procedure, and a confused classification of goods and services. It was hastily executed, and thus, India's milestone moment in indirect-tax reform—instead of helping business and industry—ended up aggravating India's economic downturn. Combined with demonetisation, it knocked the steam out of India's MSMEs, small traders, shopkeepers, wage labourers and small farmers. At a conservative estimate, more than Rs 300,000 crore was cumulatively lost from India's GDP. Modi may have won the perception battle with big political gains, but India lost big time.

By the end of Modi's term, it was hard to find a silver lining amidst the gathering clouds. The poor integrity of India's official data came in for criticism; its GDP back-series data tampering was legendary. Opacity became a standard operating procedure under the NDA. Morgan Stanley economist and author Ruchir Sharma remarked that 'the dramatic upward revision of the GDP growth rate is a bad joke, smashing India's credibility and making its statistics bureau a laughing stock in global financial circles'.[252] Shockingly, the government passed the 2018 budget without any discussion. Even Arvind Subramanian, former chief economic advisor to the Ministry of Finance, concluded that the GDP was overestimated by 2.5 per cent. That was a severe indictment.

Leading up to the 2019 elections, Modi had, at best, scored a C–on the economy. The great Indian hope had flattered to deceive. But a crucial question still remained: would the economy be a deciding factor in the 2019 elections when the national buzz was aggressive deshbhakti nationalism, national security and, well, the supposedly appeased minorities? As India headed towards a bitterly contested Lok Sabha—with the BJP and the Indian National Congress as principal combatants, with powerful regional satraps in one or the other coalition—one expected substantial fireworks.

So, where did the government stand on economic performance over the last five years? Frankly, it was an unremarkable period, and the report card was far from flattering. Modi was in perpetual election mode, which left him little time to take care of the minutiae of running a country. Not surprisingly, his government must rank as one of the worst yet in governance standards. Its policies were ad hoc and ill planned, a medley of administrative bloopers: demonetisation, GST implementation, NPA recoveries,

Aadhaar execution, the destruction of institutions like the RBI and CBI. Both demonetisation and GST were tweaked several times (GST over 200 times[253]) through notifications and circulars. If the government did not have an oil bonanza (it is estimated that the Central and state governments collected Rs 15–16 lakh crore as tax revenue from petroleum products), it would have been a wreck. Institutional integrity was being degraded, compelling the deputy governor of the RBI, Viral Acharya, to say in October 2018 that: 'Governments that do not respect central bank independence will sooner or later incur the wrath of financial markets, ignite economic fire, and come to rue the day they undermined an important regulatory institution.'[254] Since then, both he and Urjit Patel have quit the RBI.

The electorate, however, chose to overlook all this. The lowest farm income in fourteen years (despite abundant food production) and a record unemployment level of 7.3 per cent, the highest in forty-five years, were not election issues, it would appear. Poverty increased to 22.8 per cent in 2017–18 under the NDA from 21.9 per cent in 2012 during the UPA tenure, a singular failure for a country where 350 million people already lived on the edge of survival. Agriculture growth in NDA-1 was a woebegone 2.9 per cent. Exports were dismal at 3.4 per cent (under UPA-1, they had reached 24 per cent per annum), and industrial growth was stagnating.

One day, however, all of this will come back to bite the NDA. For India is not just about the 1 per cent that follows the news from Davos. It is about that man who carried his dead wife on his shoulders for 12 km because he could not afford the transport expenses. Or the three little girls, aged eight, four and two, who died of starvation in Delhi while power brokers traded India's mining rights for attractive bribes. The three siblings had not eaten for eight days. Listening to the endless baloney of BJP ministers and spokespersons manipulating data and selling dreams of a US$ 5 trillion economy by 2024, one was reminded of what Prof. Jagdish Bhagwati (a Modi supporter) once said of the RSS/BJP leaders: 'If they are economists, then I am a Bharatanatyam dancer.'[255]

With economic data (GDP, employment, farmer suicides, demonetisation, and so on) being manipulated to suit the government's propaganda, political messaging assumed humongous significance. The Opposition rightly questioned duplicitous figures that were regularly dished out to prove that India's jobs crisis, for instance, was fictional. A confused public turned to its usual source to sort the truth from fiction: the Indian media. The fourth estate, as it is appropriately called, given its crucial role in a democracy, had its task cut out for it.

5

MEDIA

The Republic of Hate

I had watched Arnab Goswami on television, like the rest of the country perhaps, during the horrendous 26/11 terror attacks in Mumbai that played out live on our television screens. Ajmal Kasab walking furtively through Mumbai's Chhatrapati Shivaji railway terminus carrying an AK-47 is an image few Indians will forget. Times Now, the television channel from India's largest media conglomerate, Bennet, Coleman and Company Ltd, owner of brands such as the *Times of India* and the *Economic Times*, was launched in the year 2006. Initially, it appeared to be struggling—a poor cousin of the industry lodestar NDTV, started by Dr Prannoy Roy, India's original television entrepreneur. But 26/11 was the turning point. Times Now suddenly sprouted to life. Its principal anchor, Arnab Goswami, had introduced a unique style to hosting a show: aggressive, provocative, rambunctious and, honestly, quite entertaining. He was a former NDTV anchor, but at the time, little else was known about him. Content was not quite his forte, but he more than made up for it with his flamboyance and a shocking impertinence towards his guests.

My tryst with television began when my internet venture CricketNext.com[256] was absorbed in surviving the post-dotcom meltdown in the latter half of 2000. As internet companies collapsed left, right and centre, we were pushed overnight to the brink of bankruptcy. From being the revenue earner of the portal, I became its editorial face. NDTV's sports anchor Sonali Chander noticed my anti-establishment (read anti-BCCI, or Board of Control for Cricket in India) tirades. Soon, on her hugely popular weekend programme 'Cricket Controversies', Navjot Singh Sidhu, cricketer and later Congress leader, and I were having frequent and entertaining exchanges. This was how I became a regular feature in TV shows. It certainly helped that I was among the few who took on cricket administrators Jagmohan Dalmiya and Sharad Pawar, and former coach Greg Chappell.

I met Goswami around the time that the Lalit Modi-led Indian Premier League (IPL) Twenty20 cricket scam exploded. It was a lesson in graft management that the public sector would have been proud of. '*Is hamam mein sab nange hain*' (everyone is naked in this public bath) was the refrain in television debates around it. Lalit Modi was the IPL commissioner, an arrogant man, visibly contemptuous of the existing rules, and one who thought that the BCCI was a fuddy-duddy body that needed his chutzpah. Modi was cricket's Gordon Gekko. Arnab Goswami loved to chase moneybags who displayed hubris, and so Lalit Modi was exciting prey. His TRPs shot up sharply.

The Times Now office was in Mumbai's Kamala Mills compound, once home to textile mills, and now bustling with start-ups, snazzy restaurants, corporate offices, curio shops and the ill-organised buildings typical of cosmopolitan wildlife. I had imagined that Goswami would be a tall, hulky fellow with an intimidating presence. But television amplifies everything; Arnab was modestly built. He, however, possessed a manic energy that threatened to flow out of the small screen. Our introduction was, to put it mildly, terribly awkward. I had been critical of him in my blogs, aghast at his wanton attacks on my Congress colleague Shashi Tharoor, among others. In all fairness, he appeared at the time to have a general disdain towards politicians, even if Shashi appeared to elicit a particularly visceral disrespect, perhaps because he was not the conventional politician Goswami loved to lynch. He could give back in equal measure and do so with charm and the use of abstruse words that left both opponent and viewer equally befuddled. I suspected that I was looking at a mammoth and fragile ego here.

'I really liked you last evening on the NDTV Profit programme; you were terrific,' said Goswami, beaming warmly as we shook hands. 'I wanted you on our channel. Times Now is where the action is.' The thing is, in person, he is instantly likeable. He makes a conscious effort to be gentlemanly, as if to compensate for his boorish excesses on screen. At any rate, the fact that he reached out to me, a vocal critic of his brand of electronic journalism, impressed me. We clicked, because I found in him a strong voice for middle-class angst against political corruption and corporate malfeasance. A voice for India's silent majority, as he put it. During the IPL scam days, Goswami and I had become a formidable combination, given our collective pursuit of the frauds perpetrated in the administration of the game we both loved, including betting, pay-offs and match-fixing.

The format of Goswami's signature show, 'The Newshour', was to have a panel of talking heads who held seemingly opposing positions. I say 'seemingly' because, for him, the perception of impartiality, that holy grail of classic journalism, mattered. The views of his guests were pre-checked by his guest relations officers, who would junk a subject expert and replace him or her with a half-baked opinion-maker if that created the numerical balance. In any case, it was Arnab who decided the outcome of the debate—the balance was only a veneer. One way he drowned the other side of the argument was to give the speakers limited time, and then interrupt them until, exasperated, they gave up. Just as Michael Jackson's *Thriller* made it imperative in the 1980s that singers be actors and dancers as well, Goswami introduced a theatrical element to anchoring: melodrama. Anchors had to be actors too.

Since I lived quite near the Times Now office, I would go over to Goswami's studio rather than do the show from home through the OB van. Doing a show from a remote location causes an eight-to ten-second time-lag that invariably leads to everyone being either collectively silent or barking at each other in a chorus. Being in the studio gave me the advantage of instant response, and I could also sense which way Goswami was veering in a debate as I was privy to his off-camera conversations. Usually, Goswami led the charge: 'So, tell me, am I right or wrong? Didn't your cricketing franchise have a deal with Lalit Modi? Why are you dodging my question; answer me now! Don't evade!'

Soon, I was spending as much time with Arnab Goswami in his Lower Parel studio as I was with my wife, and trust me, that is no exaggeration. We became such a permanent fixture that, even after we parted ways acrimoniously in 2015, I met people, as late as 2019, who thought they had seen me on Times Now just a few weeks earlier. My daughter would jokingly tell me that Goswami and I were like Thomson and Thompson from the Tintin comics, an inseparable duo pulling in different directions. He and I often had long conversations after the show was over. Gone then was the haranguing, intemperate, impertinent anchor. He was instead the personification of humility, gentlemanliness and almost exasperating niceness. It was infuriating. I had contempt for his brand of journalism, but I could not dislike him. Yet, slowly but surely, I began to understand that Goswami was not just an enigmatic character but a complex one who was affecting the political conversation and the public mood. He was certainly making the Congress look limp and leaderless.

The Congress had won the 2009 Lok Sabha elections with 206 seats in the Lok Sabha, which was a significant accretion over its 145 seats in the 2004 general elections. Thus, the Congress-led UPA was expected to be a stable coalition cruising ahead to 2014, especially since the ideologically refractory Left was not needed to muster up the coalition. Then came the Commonwealth Games scam in 2010, involving Congress MP Suresh Kalmadi and the Delhi government led by the Congress party. The CAG reports on telecom spectrum and coal allocation, leaked to the media, created feverish headlines. The UPA's response was jaded and amateurish, and while there may have been procedural violations committed by the telecom ministry led by the DMK leader A. Raja,[257] there was a compelling public policy case for the decisions taken by the Manmohan Singh government. The media had a field day; every evening, the UPA was put on trial. It became a national obsession as people scratched their heads to understand the Amazonian scale of the corruption: according to CAG Vinod Rai's report, Rs 17,600,000,000 crore for 2G spectrum and Rs 18,600,000,000 crore for coal allocations. These 'presumptive losses'—pure mathematical fantasy—were the fodder that anchors live for. Goswami was willing to die for it.

In April 2011, Hazare and Kejriwal added the final nail to the UPA coffin by taking their well-organised public protests onto television screens. The India Against Corruption movement was, in the public eye, about 130 crore people against the UPA.

The Congress had just two spokespersons who could tackle the mess head-on, and try to distinguish fact from fiction: Abhishek Manu Singhvi and Manish Tewari. Occasionally, the spirited Renuka Chowdhury would also take the bull by the horns. But the monumental scale of the alleged fraud, the lopsided guest-lists and anchors who had smelt blood made their task unenviable. I became the other sacrificial lamb for this prime-time slaughter, although it was of my own volition. My friend Rajeev Gowda (former Rajya Sabha MP), then a professor at the Indian Institute of Management, Bangalore, and I had started a website called HamaraCongress.com to augment the party's abysmal internet presence. We posted blogs and articles that pushed the Congress's ideological and developmental agenda along with the regular political commentary. The media noticed this, and we soon started appearing on television shows, often labelled as 'Congress sympathisers'.

Manish Tewari, in fact, was instrumental in egging me on to do TV shows on behalf of the Congress. By 2012, some channels tagged me as a Congress spokesperson when I was not even a primary member of the party. Later, Digvijaya Singh coaxed me into becoming an official voice of the party. Digvijaya and I also started the Congress's social media department, with barely a few volunteers and little organisational support. The 'Feku' campaign against Modi was created by our team (it became a global trend) to counter the BJP's 'Pappu' attack against Rahul Gandhi. Eventually, Ajay Maken, Congress veteran and chief spokesperson of the party, recommended me as a national spokesperson. Earlier, I had been a media panellist (they cannot hold press conferences or give direct media sound bites, unlike spokespersons). One day, Maken told me to do a press conference while I was visiting Delhi. I was taken aback, and only truly realised the enormous responsibility this meant when I sat in the venerable AICC media office with several microphones clustered together on my desk. One slip and you could be breaking news. From being on the same side on the Lalit Modi and BCCI shenanigans, Goswami and I were now on opposite sides of the fence. The season of fireworks between us soon commenced in deadly earnest.

Goswami was a tough proposition: he had a ready list of questions that he would unyieldingly rattle off, while also slipping in snide remarks and unsubstantiated charges that prejudged the discussion. You were guilty before you said Vinod Rai. After that, the theatre of the fantastical took over. Everyone spoke at the same time, people screamed at each other, while Goswami conveniently disappeared from the screen. Since I was often in the studio with him on these occasions, I can share that these were moments he found uncontrollably funny, and he took these periodic breaks to get his breath back. No channel barring NDTV, and to some extent India Today and CNN-IBN, could lay claim to informed, level-headed discussions, so Goswami was not the only performer out there, but he was by far the most effective. Soon, the world was hooked on his nocturnal hell-raising entertainment shows.

As cable television grew more aggressive and competitive, Times Now was determined to maintain its market share, and Goswami's shows extended to 11 p.m. One had to admire his stamina as he held fort for two hours at a stretch. In between, he would sip tea and warm water; his throat certainly needed that. He dismissed former colleagues like Rajdeep Sardesai and Barkha Dutt as the 'Lutyens cabal', and took particular satisfaction in the fact that his was the most watched political show even though he was working out of Mumbai, thousands of miles from the capital. 'Distance makes you dispassionate,' he once said to me. Speaking of the Lutyens commentariat, he said, 'They are boring and traditional.' It may have been the most noisy and cantankerous show on earth, but outside the blue semicircle where Goswami performed his studio histrionics, an impenetrable, almost spiritual, silence prevailed. His research team and other anchors were clearly nervous in front of their mercurial boss. On a couple of occasions, Goswami had become furious, his choleric outrage visibly sending shivers down the spines of his team. Seconds later, he would be the personification of charm, enquiring whether our tea was okay.

Arnab was obsessed with TRPs. During commercial breaks, he would share with me interesting titbits on the audience viewership numbers that he received on his mobile, as well as adulatory messages from adoring fans. And there were many. There is an unsaid understanding that exists between journalists and politicians; the relationship is inherently antagonistic. So, despite the overt camaraderie, Goswami and I maintained a respectable distance.

He would often see me off at the elevator, a show of courtesy that felt genuine even if it was minutes after we had been at each other's throats. At the time, I do think there was genuine mutual respect. I believed he was a committed crusader for the urban middle class whose causes he espoused (he was not overly concerned with farmers, NGOs, environment or poverty and destitution). But on 17 April 2015, our equation changed irrevocably.

Rahul Gandhi had just returned from his sabbatical overseas, and there was a lot of curiosity about where had he gone for fifty-six days. Rahul had publicly announced that he was taking an extended break, and formally informed the Congress office as well. It was a smart move; his unannounced foreign visits had resulted in a lot of unflattering publicity. I understood the public curiosity about his whereabouts—it is not easy being a Gandhi. The family is under constant and minute media surveillance; one of them cannot so much as watch *Star Wars* at a multiplex without it becoming news. In our conversations, Goswami had been vocal about his belief that the Congress should back Rahul's sister Priyanka Gandhi

Vadra for the top job. He thought Rahul was too decent, too naïve for Indian politics. To outwit Modi, 'you need a Machiavelli, not a Mahatma', he once told me. But Priyanka, with her Indira Gandhi-looks and effortless communication, could upset the BJP apple cart, he advised me. On 17 April, Goswami looked intent on decimating Rahul.

The other guests that evening included Nalin Kohli, spokesperson of the BJP, and journalists Sankarshan Thakur, Pankaj Vohra, Arati Jerath and Shahid Siddiqui—all accomplished individuals and moderate liberals whom I liked and respected. Unlike so many from his party, Kohli too was a more reasonable adversary. The topic under discussion was, where had Rahul Gandhi gone to and why, and was he not accountable to the people of India when it came to his travel itinerary? Goswami and I greeted each other as usual. The tea served to me was nice and hot. It looked like just another day in the park.

It was a typical Newshour debate, and Goswami made no bones about the fact that he was going after Rahul. He jokingly told me before the programme, 'This is going to be tough for you, Sanjay.' Knowing that I had been forewarned so I would tense up with nervousness, I said with a smile, 'Bring it on!' I steeled myself.

I had a simple explanation for Rahul's absence; he had informed the party and the public before leaving, so he had been transparent. How many politicians actually do that? As to where he went and why, he was entitled to his fundamental right to privacy—a right that one does not lose by virtue of being a politician or a public figure. I also added that the Modi government must be aware of Gandhi's destination because he was under SPG security, which reported directly to the Central government. In my opinion, these were irrefutable arguments in Rahul's defence. And to put the BJP on the defensive, I posed an inconvenient question: how come no one was discussing why Modi had hidden his marital status till 2014, lied to the Election Commission and misled the public knowingly for years? He was the prime minister of the country, surely the burden of disclosure lies heavier on him? In the US, such a scandal would have tarnished a politician's reputation beyond repair. In India, everyone appeared tongue-tied. Why? Despite the fact that everyone was critical of Rahul's opacity, I thought I was on a strong wicket. Then things suddenly took an unexpected and dark turn.

At some point, Goswami referred to Rahul's 'mental fitness'—a remark I thought was in poor taste, and also disrespectful towards those who actually suffered from mental health issues. I told him so. He then pulled a fast one on me, saying that a Congress leader from Delhi, Sandeep Dikshit, had said so himself. Now, I knew Sandeep. Although he was one of the few Congressmen to call a spade a spade, Sandeep was far too civil and polite to say something so impertinent about anyone, let alone his own leader. More importantly, I had had a fleeting glimpse of Sandeep's video bite earlier, and he had said no such thing. So I called Goswami's bluff and challenged him to show the video right then, adding for good measure, 'And if you are proved wrong, you must issue a public apology right now.' The words were strong but we were both combative debaters, and occasionally, I can get stagey myself.

Goswami, however, was not used to being taken on aggressively; he was the insuperable showman of his turf, the unconquerable hero. I suspect he was very peeved with me for escalating the tension and issuing an ultimatum; that was his prerogative alone. He stunned me by saying that I was misbehaving and he would throw me out of the show if I didn't behave. Goswami rebuking anyone for poor conduct was rich. I realised just how cornered he felt. The others looked stunned too. At any rate, Goswami had no choice but to play the Sandeep Dikshit video. He took a deep breath and, in all fairness, let his panicky producer play it; it was obvious that Dikshit had said no such thing. I could have rubbed his face in it, but I let it go. Goswami had had a bad hair day.

When the programme ended, he turned to me, his face a contorted mess, and hissed, 'Why did you make it personal?' 'Personal? When did I get personal with you?' I asked, stupefied.

'You mentioned my son!'

For a while, I was too shell-shocked to respond. During the debate, to establish the fact that Rahul did not 'bunk' as Goswami kept saying, I had said, 'If your son—' (and I would have gone on to say, 'took permission from school for leave, how is that the same as bunking?'). But he never let me finish that statement on live television, and here he was, accusing me of dragging his son into the national debate. It was an asinine remark, and honestly, a lie. It was clear to me that Goswami was disconcerted by my aggressive salvo, and the video challenge had hurt his credibility. We had spent considerable time since 2008 on onscreen and offline conversations. I genuinely thought he was someone Indian politicians could not ignore, no matter how vehemently they disagreed with him. In fact, I had even endorsed him on a television commercial that Times Now had made for their principal protagonist. But after that night, we would never meet again.

To give the devil his due, Goswami had been able to hold urban English-speaking households in thrall even as he stayed away from the capital's power-brokering. Until 2014, this was true. There was this one time when he was upset with me for bracketing him with his former NDTV colleagues Barkha Dutt and Rajdeep Sardesai in an article. He railed against their professional competencies, poured scorn on the 'Delhi mafia' in journalism and declared the Lutyens gang a licentious bunch. Ultimately, this proved to be only grandstanding. For, when he launched his own television channel, Republic TV, one of its principal investors was ex-BPL CEO Rajeev Chandrasekhar—a former business entrepreneur close to Lutyens power brokers, who boasted of big contracts in his commercial ventures. He was also a member of the BJP. Goswami's halo had fallen right off.

Donald Trump loves Fox News for a reason: Fox News loves him. It is a symbiotic relationship based on transparent transactional impulses; they need each other. Rupert Murdoch's Fox News is the most watched television channel in conservative America. Goswami sensed the shifting social dynamics as Modi and the BJP gained rapid ascendancy. The Congress was struggling, and it was obvious that the electronic media was going to be a critical influencer of voter behaviour. At Times Now, he had to pretend to be ideologically agnostic and politically neutral. Clearly, Goswami sensed that if he could become the Indian version of Fox News, he would hit the jackpot. Then, he could be unambiguously right-wing and unambivalent about his antipathy for the secular-liberal crowd. And in a country that seemed to come to terms with mob lynchings and widespread Islamophobia, where the Hindu Hriday Samrat was the unopposed political chieftain, Republic TV could become the number one TV channel (in 2020, his channel would be accused of being a mastermind in an alleged TRP scam[258]). Needless to say, for a newbie business venture, nothing is more reassuring than guaranteed government ad revenues.

Goswami had found his business model; he would now escape the shackling pretensions of neutrality. For several years, he had cleverly camouflaged himself as the protector of middle-class interests while propagating the political agenda of the BJP. Now, Republic TV was to be his onscreen homecoming.

The timing could not have been better. It was early 2016; his broadcast licence had been cleared, and he was all set to recapture the airwaves. Clearly, the BJP too was in a hurry to have him up and running; the charade was so blatant, it was laughable. Modi still had three years to go until the next elections, and every available survey indicated that his popularity had barely waned, despite a declining economy and rising social strife. He would probably get re-elected, assuring Republic TV of a dream run. Goswami mounted his anchor's seat on Republic TV on 6 May 2017; the BJP's strategy of media capture had begun in deadly earnest.

In the years since, Republic TV has been accused of fake news, instigating religious tensions, attacking young students (JNU, Jamia, AMU being the preferred whipping boys) protesting against the government, haranguing supporters of local parties of J&K, spreading Islamophobia, provoking hate speeches and platforming bigoted fanatics.[259] Back in 2013, after a fiery debate on communal politics following the Muzaffarnagar riots, Arnab had looked at me and said, almost like he was trying to convince himself rather than me, 'I am secular, you know.' I was saddened to see him now. His channel was being called a disgrace to journalism, and he a mad monster. I knew he was better than that. Had he continued to be an anti-establishment journalist when Modi became prime minister, Goswami could have become a metric of fearless independent journalism. It did not pan out that way, but he did remain a master of his trade, his legions of right-leaning fans swelling every day.

By election time in May 2019, Goswami was doing a better job than most BJP spokespersons in amplifying the party's political messaging. His show was flagrantly anti-Congress, and venomous about Rahul Gandhi. It was as if Rahul was the prime minister and the Congress occupied the treasury benches. Fake news had become his staple tactic; his channel accused the Jama Masjid in New Delhi of non-payment of electricity bills, and skewered author Arundhati Roy for saying that 70 lakh Indian armymen could not stop the azadi gang (freedom fighters) of Kashmir. Both news items were malicious and fictitious. Once the poster boy of middle-class angst, Goswami had converted India into his own version of a republic of hate.[260]

While Goswami may have become the symbol of all that has gone wrong with Indian journalism, it would be unfair to prop him up as the stand-out villain. He was in august company. There were other channels that were such ardent cheerleaders of the Modi sarkar that they probably embarrassed Modi himself. The joke went that some of these anchors took a private briefing from the information and broadcasting ministry before starting their show; Arun Jaitley was jocularly called the 'bureau chief'. Joseph Goebbels, it would appear, was still alive and barking orders.

Since hyper-nationalism was the BJP's tactic for keeping India hooked, war-mongering fanatics (mostly retired army personnel) went on crazy rants after terror attacks in J&K and Punjab. One such 'defence expert' on a channel suggested that, even if 500 million Indians were to die, it would be worth it if Pakistan was annihilated. Some anchors even wore military uniforms to simulate the crossfire zones. By targeting the left-leaning activists in JNU or Jamia Millia Islamia, and calling them the 'tukde-tukde gang' (or break-up India gang), these channels helped amplify the saffron party's political narrative. Anyone who dared to criticise the government, and particularly Modi, was instantly branded anti-national. An anchor I know rather well sheepishly conceded that it was 'like a circus'.

What remained of the independent media were termed 'presstitutes' by no less a person than former army chief and BJP minister, Gen. V.K. Singh.[261] The BJP had an unalloyed revulsion for free media. Modi himself described journalists as news traders,[262] up for sale to the highest bidder. And so, for all the criticism they faced, media outlets gladly prostrated before the supreme commander, hawking their own conscience.

By 2019, the mainstream media was being mocked as 'lamestream media'. The late Dilip Padgaonkar (erstwhile editor of the *Times of India*) once famously stated that his job was the 'second most important job in India' (after the prime minister, presumably). That was neither hubris nor an exaggeration. But the Grand Old Lady of Bori Bunder can no longer claim a monopoly. Besides an expanded media scene, the dissemination and distribution of information has been democratised with the advent of social media. Facebook, Twitter, Instagram, YouTube and several independent online news portals and blogs have arrested the oligopoly of the big fish. Equally, they have led to the rise of fake news. The notorious BJP IT cell is a veritable fake-news factory.

In this age of news content directed by commercial imperatives, investigative journalism is dying out. When did the mainstream media last break a major scandal exposing big business? The pink papers blush crimson in the company of generous billionaires. B. Ramalingam Raju of Satyam Computers confessed to a Rs 7,000 crore fraud he committed on his own company. Sahara India's massive larceny on unsuspecting small investors was hardly covered by the electronic media. Dhirubhai Ambani's youngest son, Anil Ambani, alleged beneficiary of India's largest defence contract, actually threatened the media and Congress leaders with defamation suits for the Rafale kickbacks exposé. The *Hindu* newspaper had published a devastating exposé on Rafale which said that the PMO was running 'parallel investigations' that had undermined the position of the purchasing authority, the Ministry of Defence.[263] Normally, this damning revelation would have led to a media frenzy and further investigations. Instead, large sections of the mainstream media politely ignored it.

A 2010 report on 'paid news'[264] by the Press Council of India, the self-regulatory watchdog of the media, gathered dust. That there was evidence of newspapers selling space for press releases and fixed interviews, which were not clearly distinguishable from editorial content, ought to have caused a furore. While the report suggested guidelines, there was no mechanism to implement them, so it was easy to look past it. The Indian media believes self-regulation is the best way to maintain independence. But that is like expecting Harvey Weinstein to turn himself in. Paid coverage posing as dispassionate reporting is furtive advertising. It is unethical.

Since most media houses are corporate funded, they know who not to target and who to go after. During the Uttar Pradesh polls in 2017, *Dainik Jagran*, a high-circulation Hindi daily, was caught customising exit-poll surveys favouring the BJP.[265] Sting operations done by Cobrapost confirmed that eminent names from renowned media brands were not averse to pushing the Hindutva agenda for the right fee.[266]

The Birla-Sahara Papers[267]—a set of documents, emails, spreadsheets, diaries and notebooks seized during raids on the Aditya Birla Group and the Sahara Group, which involved powerful personalities, including Modi himself—briefly caused a flutter, but most TV channels averted their eyes when faced with this combustible material. This is the self-censorship ingredient of the 'undeclared Emergency'[268] prevailing in India. Once, a prominent journalist called me and requested me for a comment on Modi's communally tinted speech in Uttar Pradesh. His editors did not wish to pursue the story independently, scared of the political vindictiveness that could follow, but they were okay to cover a Congress kerfuffle over it.

I asked veteran journalist Karan Thapar what he felt about the daily ballyhoo in the TV studios. (Narendra Modi, then chief minister of Gujarat, had walked out of Thapar's show when questioned by his poker-faced host about his role in the Gujarat riots.) He said, 'TV debates have never been the forte of Indian television. So I do not believe the decline is recent. Of course it can be reversed, but that entirely depends on whether anchors and television bosses see the need to do so. So far, I do not think they do.'

Competitive journalism is a business, like investment banks and public firms. But they are also meant to play the role of society's watchdog—a difficult balance to maintain when the media business model is disproportionately dependent on government advertising and most media houses are owned by corporates that depend on government cooperation for their businesses. All political parties are guilty of this galling manipulation.

In a polarised polity, every institution becomes polarised too; the media is no exception. Thus, some channels, like Zee News, Republic TV, India TV, News X and certain select anchors were bracketed as pro-BJP, while NDTV, Rajdeep Sardesai, Barkha Dutt, Ravish Kumar and online portals such as the *Wire*, *Scroll* and *Quint* were deemed pro-Congress. The BJP IT cell often fuelled anti-minority sentiments, and working in tandem with the 'Godi Media' (lapdog media), weaponised it in their rampage against 'libtards' and 'sickulars'. Abhisar Sharma, Milind

Khandekar, Punya Prasun Vajpayee, Ravish Kumar (who went on to win the prestigious Ramon Magsaysay award), Karan Thapar, Rana Ayyub and others defied the trolls to doggedly do their job. The threat was not only psychological. When the *Wire* ran a detailed investigative story on how Amit Shah's son Jay Shah had seen a quantum jump in his business fortunes, a criminal defamation suit was filed against the editors. Many journalists were subjected to intense harassment, compelling compromised corporate bosses to sack them.

NDTV, unsurprisingly, felt the heat too. The garrulous BJP spokesperson Sambit Patra got a dressing down by NDTV's star anchor Nidhi Razdan. He looked miffed, unused to being called to order. Usually, friendly anchors allow BJP spokespersons uninterrupted soliloquies. Soon thereafter, Prannoy Roy had India's most powerful investigative agency, the CBI, at his door. The charges, even to tyro analysts, seemed facile.

Away from the world of the high-profile English-language press, the situation was even more grim: forty journalists were killed and over 195 seriously injured in attacks on them during the five years ending in 2019. It was hardly surprising that India's ranking in the World Press Freedom Index had deteriorated even further.

Meanwhile, flagrantly right-wing media titans have become establishment propagandists peddling BJP handouts. The loyalty miles billboard anchors earn are displayed on their Brooks Brothers suits. Guests opposing the ruling party are called names and treated uncivilly, Hindu–Muslim differences are their main fodder, and their guests include rabid rogues from all sides, Left, Right and centre, to maximise the pitch of the debate. The television studio influences hashtag trends, and social media trolls package fake news for shock value to confuse the average consumer of digital news. There is bedlam out there.

India has over 850 television channels, of which a staggering 389 are news channels, and they reach 197 million households. Indian democracy is thus being greatly shaped by a largely irresponsible media and its supersized influence. The news media has been a wilful accessory to the BJP's and Modi's narrative-setting moves. News television often degenerates into gladiatorial battles between binaries—Congress vs BJP and Hindu vs Muslim—that are sure-shot TRP generators. The anchor's job is to provide entertainment garbed as news. A well-known journalist, often accused of hectoring his guests, confessed to me: 'We are under continuous pressure from our owners to deliver high viewership numbers. What choice do we have? When we do regular shows, few watch. When there is an explosive communal subject, our audience numbers grow manifold.'

There have always been acrimonious exchanges between political rivals, sometimes degenerating into cheap slander, baseless allegations and defamatory abuse. But what we have been witnessing in India since May 2014 is a new and peculiar kind of viciousness. Mostly, the attacks are personal and savage, and they are amplified by right-wing social media trolls. Television shows are now like gladiatorial battles without any rules, where there must be only one man standing. A case in point is an audience-participation show hosted by a popular national Hindi channel, Aaj Tak. The BJP's ubiquitous chief spokesperson, Sambit Patra, was on the show. Now, Patra, as far as one can tell, has become a social media celebrity by making outlandish and obtuse statements. To all appearances, he revels in this notoriety. He is usually well prepared, like a movie actor who has mugged his lines. In this particular episode, he referred to Jawaharlal Nehru, India's first prime minister and a freedom fighter, as a 'Thug of Hindoostan', inspired by a mega-budget Bollywood release that had recently bombed. He referred to two martyred former prime ministers, Indira Gandhi and Rajiv Gandhi, by the same sobriquet, adding 'dakait' (dacoit) for good measure. Then he went on to vehemently abuse Sonia Gandhi and Rahul Gandhi.[269] His Congress counterpart, the late Rajiv Tyagi, was visibly stunned by the coarse outburst, and retaliated with the popular sneer of '*Chowkidar Chor Hai*'. By then, the audience had swarmed the makeshift stage to back their respective representatives. The moderator Anjana Om Kashyap watched helplessly as the show collapsed messily amidst this hooliganism. But Patra looked mighty pleased with himself.

Competitive journalism is not a bad thing in itself, but instead of quality coverage being the product differentiator, TRP-generation strategies have become the only focus. Republic, Zee and Sudarshan, all notoriously right-wing, have been leading the TRP race. Celebrities contribute liberally to the channels in an I-scratch-your-back-you-scratch-mine relationship. Former information and broadcasting minister Arun Shourie had coined the term 'North Korean TV channels' for the pro-government mouthpieces. These outlets wreak havoc with their coverage on burning issues that are liable to arouse sectarian emotions. Kashmir, Article 370, NRC, CAA, NPR, Ram Mandir, lynching, terrorist attacks, Pakistan-bashing, JNU, AMU, Jamia Millia, Kanhaiya Kumar and Umar Khalid—when the 'North Korean' anchors raise the temperature on these issues, a verbal bloodbath follows. Panellists are called terrorists, which in these days can pose actual danger to their lives, either at the hands of a lone wolf or a rogue mob. Through it all, the BJP spokespersons look smug, knowing the trajectory the debate will take.

As George Clooney's film on the Joseph McCarthy era in the US, *Good Night, and Good Luck*, showed, the media has the power to resist government-sponsored propaganda that is detrimental to society—if it chooses to. Most in India choose to remain silent or actively collaborate with the government.

Corporate benefactors of government policy have significant equity stakes spread across television channels and media groups, which makes the fourth estate unreliable at best, duplicitous at worst. Besides, quarterly pressures of EPS (earnings per share) for publicly listed media companies can add further to the pressure—editors cannot be both brand managers and crusaders for truth. Proximity to glib industrialists, political power brokers and the deep state comes at a price.

In the age of visual media, smartphone-based citizen journalism and the wide reach of social media, the BJP understands that large-scale communal riots can seriously boomerang on it (even though the Muzaffarnagar riots helped it win Uttar Pradesh in 2014). The BJP's political strategy, therefore, is decentralised social anarchy, distributed across India and flaring up intermittently. It is a low-intensity communal heat that is modulated to adapt to electoral schedules. The fringe has been folded into the mainstream. Now, violence against Muslims and Dalits is quotidian, the new normal as it were.[270] And social media is a helpful instrument in hand.

Maximising the impact of the media's pro-government coverage is the IT cell's social media strategy. The collective muscle power of its paid army is unmatched; no other party is as cash-rich as the BJP. In the run-up to the 2019 elections, a commercial for the washing powder Surf Excel had enraged the troll army—often called #ModiToadies, a term popularised by the writer Salman Rushdie. The storyboard of the ad showed a girl child voluntarily getting drenched in coloured water on Holi until the sprayers' supply of water and paint is exhausted. She thus makes sure that her young Muslim friend can go to the mosque for the namaaz in his pristine white kurta-pyjama.[271]

The advertisement was saccharine, sure, but it was innocuous. Only the BJP cyber-army could possibly find it unpalatable. They churlishly called for a boycott of the detergent.[272] A year later, Tanishq put out an advertisement showing an interfaith situation, with a Muslim woman organising a baby shower for her Hindu daughter-in-law. The troll army forced its withdrawal.[273]

The right-wing trolls are drawing on a deep ideological animus towards minorities, and a long history of directing hate at Muslims through slogans like 'Love Jihad' and 'Ghar Wapsi'.

The print, visual and social media, the troll army, are all part of a carefully programmed action plan to keep the communal cauldron boiling. They are backed on the ground by door-to-door campaigning and dissemination of literature by RSS foot soldiers. The rewriting of textbooks and distortion of history has already begun the process of re-programming young minds. So comprehensively have school textbooks been 'corrected' that the Mughal period has been reduced to a transient phenomenon.[274] One textbook hints that Gandhi had committed suicide.[275]

WhatsApp, Facebook's instant messaging platform has become a powerful personalised 'news' medium for influencing voters. At about 400 million users and rising exponentially, its penetration—aided by low telecom prices in India—is perhaps the largest in the world. The BJP IT cell, for instance, wilfully pushed distorted information that the Nehru–Gandhi family had Muslim antecedents,[276] or that the Congress was in secret parleys with Pakistan Prime Minister Imran Khan to subvert Hindu interests.[277] This sort of fake news quickly goes viral through an internet army that has apparently mobilised over a million volunteers. Apparently, the job of each volunteer is to create WhatsApp groups of 256 members each from various databases and then keep dumping saffron propaganda and fake news on these. Rumours planted on WhatsApp groups have led to lynchings in the real world. The BJP has kept fact-checking websites such as Alt News and Boom Fact Check busy, although other political parties too are guilty of similar shenanigans. Sadly, social media today threatens India's democratic future.

The general elections of 2024 will be fought as much on the digital battlefield as on India's dusty plains because the number of participants has risen to stratospheric levels—by 2019, Facebook had 320 million Indian users, Twitter had 12 million, Instagram had 80 million and YouTube had 31 million. With over 1,200 million mobile users and 560 million internet users, public outreach can be truly personalised now. The BJP is using every algorithmic tool it can to leverage its digital clout; the Congress is far behind in the game. A political party that turns a blind eye to this reality would be doing so at its own peril. And the country's, perhaps.

A buoyant democracy requires a strong opposition party that keeps the ruling dispensation from becoming autocratic. The BJP has reset the national narrative using its media and regulatory capture and its brute majority in Parliament, especially in the states where it receives the popular mandate. There is understandable apprehension that we have become an illiberal democracy, allowing for the rise of a dangerous authoritarian culture. If ever India needed a vigilant Opposition as vanguard against its fast-eroding liberal culture, it is now. And the political party that possesses the wherewithal, political experience and leadership potential to stop India's slide is its grand old party, the Indian National Congress.

6

CONGRESS

A Time for Renewal

One early morning in the last week of February 2014, I got a call from Kanishka Singh, Rahul Gandhi's private secretary. A Wharton business school postgraduate, Kanishka, called K by party insiders, is an unusually perceptive man. Besides managing Gandhi's appointments, he provides crucial inputs to his political thinking and works hard to nurse the Amethi constituency. When I saw his name flash on my mobile, I knew it would be something important.

'Tell me everything about Arnab Goswami. Everything; his career, family, friends, political ideology, what do his peers think about him, etc.'

'Why?' I asked, sensing that this would be something big. I had a hunch that Rahul Gandhi would be giving an exclusive interview to the man who had become the poster boy of anti-establishment journalism—a euphemism for whiplashing the Congress and its first family.

Although most Congress leaders avoided him like the plague, I had become a regular fixture in Goswami's signature show, The Newshour. But I knew nothing about his personal life.

The spokesperson–journalist equation leaves limited scope for genuine relationships to flourish. Both parties are guarded, fully aware of the high-risk public screens they operate on. There is no margin for error: you are as good or bad as your last show. Manish Tewari once told me, 'You can never become real friends with a journalist.' This is probably true. There are no 'off-the-record' conversations I can have with media persons; everything is of import, especially if it is off the record.

I told Kanishka what I could, based on my personal experience: 'He is a relentless interrogator who does his homework well, but only on issues that suit his political fancy of the day. If he decides to go after an issue or a person, he goes the whole nine yards. Goswami has to have the last word and the last laugh; he hates being cornered and can get vindictive when challenged. On the rest, he is predictable. He relies on his theatrical loudmouth style to manipulate debates. Besides his trademark interruptions, his standard operating procedure is to get guests to go at each other's throats and pepper his discussions with obscure anecdotes that take them by surprise. But he can be handled. A TV debate is like a community blood-fest, which is poles apart from a one-on-one interview. And to give the devil his due, he goes after each and every one equally, although the Congress is more often at the receiving end of his bombardment.'

Kanishka listened without interruption. Then he asked me what I had failed to clarify: 'Is he a hard-core pro-BJP guy?' I was expecting that question. Times Now had built its popularity on the lambasting of Congress governments, both at the Centre and in the states, while being somewhat restrained when it came to BJP wrongdoings. To be honest, he was unsparing in his criticism of the right-wing hardliners of the VHP and Bajrang Dal, but there is no doubt that he was ill at ease taking on the prime ministerial candidate Modi and his comrade Amit Shah.

'Well, he is anti-Congress for sure,' I told Kanishka. 'He plays to the urban middle-class constituency of English-speaking households, the aspirational class if you will. He knows that they would not like a kowtowing journalist. He wants to be seen as their barrister, providing a pro-bono service. They love him. If we are doing anything with him, I have just two suggestions to make: be very well prepared and don't be fooled by his affected civility.' Then I asked pointedly, 'By the way, who is talking to him?' Kanishka, master of the non-committal, let that one slide. But it was obvious to me that Rahul Gandhi was going to do an interview with Goswami. This was huge. And it worried me.

There is a reason why Narendra Modi does no television interviews, except a few 'fixed' ones. Unlike high-rise podiums during election campaigns, party forums and election rallies, where politicians can do and say as they wish, including reading from a prepared text or even regurgitating a mugged speech—or using a teleprompter, as Modi often does—television interviews demand instinctive and quick responses. TV hates pauses or pregnant silences. And even the best-prepared interviewee can be caught off guard by a tricky inquiry. Cameras are focused firmly on the face, and minute expressions can convey more than words might. It is not for everyone.

Rahul had not given a formal interview to any television channel thus far. He had given short sound bites infrequently, of course, but this was an entirely different proposition. I had been at the Talkatora stadium in Delhi when he delivered a superlative speech, bursting with unbridled aggression, with cool aplomb. He looked in command as the Congress bugled its war cry for the 2014 general elections at the well-attended and boisterous AICC general session. Expectations were running high, and the Congress needed a monumental perception shift to catch up with the BJP, which was galloping ahead, with Modi looking triumphant in the saddle. Times Now began to advertise Rahul's interview with Goswami a day in advance. A reticent, reluctant Rahul Gandhi, seen as a future prime minister of India, was to be in conversation with India's celebrity TV anchor, known to spare no one. It promised to be great television. Gandhi was biting the bullet. Would he suddenly seize the political story away from Modi and the BJP? The snippets promoting the programme made Rahul look thoughtful, cerebral and leader-like. But the film itself was nothing like the trailer.

The thumb rule for doing an interview well is to get your key messages out. It is important to prepare an FAQ list that assumes the most difficult, personal or unexpected questions possible, and be prepared with short, crisp answers to them. A lot of people asked me why the Congress or Rahul chose Goswami, and I had no answer to that. Goswami's show was easily the most popular at the time, even if it was insufferably noisy and intentionally cacophonic. But then again, Goswami was a maverick and not to be trusted, and besides, he was not an admirer of the Gandhi family. The decision to go with him for Rahul's interview debut left me nonplussed. There were better editors who conducted tough interviews with great élan, and would have been by far better options: Karan Thapar, Rajdeep Sardesai, Barkha Dutt, Dr Prannoy Roy, among them. I feverishly hoped that Rahul was sure about his ability to steer the interview. India would be watching with bated breath to hear Pandit Jawaharlal Nehru's great grandson articulate his vision for leading 16 per cent of the world's population to a better future. But by the time the interview reached the halfway stage, two things were clear—Rahul was unprepared on his biggest night out, and Goswami was directing the interview towards his predefined destination: Rahul's annihilation.

When I saw Goswami being uncharacteristically polite, I was immediately on alert; Rahul was in trouble. His advisers had utterly failed him. Did they not know that if things went badly—

and they did, horribly—it could seriously impact the public perception of both an untested leader as well as a party fighting on the backfoot? The first factor that established Congress's unpreparedness was the length of the interview. Any TV editor would have happily agreed to reasonable preconditions for an interview with an elusive high-profile interviewee in the midst of an intensely fought election. The interview should have been at most thirty minutes long, which would have given Times Now the flexibility to make a one-hour capsule using promotions and fillers. In the interview post-mortems that followed, Rahul was accused of repeating himself ad nauseam, looking distracted, not making enough eye contact and appearing generally unprepared; in a briefer interview, that would not have happened. Rahul would have looked good, sensitive, willing to take questions, giving priority to the issues that he felt India needed to grapple with, and biting the bullet on the dynasty and the 1984 riots. Instead, as the interview dragged on, exactly the opposite happened.

A well-meaning, sincere Rahul got ridiculed for sounding repetitive (RTI, women's empowerment, MNREGA, systemic failures, etc.) and appearing dodgy. Goswami showed characteristic gracelessness, of course. Soon after the interview, he invited guest speakers to mock the man who had given him, in good faith, a breakthrough interview. It was journalistic immorality, but only expected, and it begged a serious question: why did the think tank closest to the topmost leader of the Congress party take such a vacuous decision, imperilling his political stature?

The BJP went to town calling Rahul 'Pappu'—a tag that suddenly caught on and would end up destroying Rahul's personal brand, with a cataclysmic effect on the Congress. Even as I messaged Rahul, telling him that he had done okay,

I knew that would not be the overwhelming public verdict. Overnight, Modi had leapt a thousand miles closer to 7, Race Course Road.

The Congress is its own worst enemy, the saying goes. Infighting is in the party's DNA, and internecine feuds are exhausting. Scurvy wheeler-dealers forget that the real adversary is the BJP, the default beneficiary of the Congress's self-destruction. The party has been in power in a sustained fashion over decades, both at the Centre and in various states, and this has fashioned it into a gargantuan entity infected with lassitude and sloth. It also gave members a sense of invulnerability as they waited and watched for the BJP to fold in on itself—an attitude that betrayed not only colossal arrogance but also political myopia.

The magical Gandhi family charisma had made a national hero of many a substandard politician in the Congress. Many did not even have to campaign hard to triumph in the elections. And so they swore allegiance to India's unofficial first family in a show of cringe-worthy genuflection. Dynasty politics thus became integral political strategy, seen as divine compensation for the brutal tragedies that the Gandhis had encountered and, with prodigious strength, endured.

This faith is also what blinded Congress members to a harsh reality: the party had begun to wither away, its organisational muscle atrophying. A toxic combination of indolence and hubris during the UPA years had caused the rot to spread more rapidly. Poor internal communications, large and unwieldy committees that existed only to massage the egos of senior leaders, the absence of a clear direction for the future, opaque appointments and personal aggrandisement had become the party's core culture. The Congress was once a well-oiled machine that ran on daily contact with grassroots workers, took public feedback, delegated powers right up to the district level and fought for social justice. But it had now morphed into a giant bubble, divorced from its social environment and changing times. The top leadership of the party was being told that all was hunky-dory. It was not. All of this is also evidence of the truth that the party had indeed become hostage to the 'Delhi darbar politics' it was accused of, puffed with palace intrigues and shady conspirators.

The 2014 rout left the party shell-shocked. It was not until 2017 that it found the energy and focus to fight back, years in which there were several missed opportunities.

The Radia tapes controversy in 2013 had besmirched the Congress, but in 2015, the Essar tapes emerged—and it ought to have been more damaging to the BJP than the Radia tapes ever could have been to the Congress. If the BJP had been in the Opposition, they would have staged nationwide protests, sponsored civil society campaigns, held daily press conferences and unleashed their most bellicose spokespersons on television. The Congress, still sulking and in a torpor after the rout, did nothing. Manish Tewari, former minister, and one of the few combative voices within the party, held a press conference. But there was little follow-up, and the Essar tapes were soon forgotten.

It is deeply ironic that a much older Modi (he is over two decades older than Rahul)—a former RSS pracharak who believes in religious supremacy and lacks a scientific temper (and loves witchcraft-like medical solutions), who had looked away from the Gujarat pogrom and was clearly illiberal—was considered more of a youth icon than Gandhi. How was this possible? Rahul was considerably younger, tech-savvy, wore jeans and a T-shirt often, was a certified deep-sea diver and loved the occasional high of a motorbike. He also holds a black belt in aikido. Rahul is also genuinely progressive, speaking up for the LGBTQ+ community and creating democratic spaces within the party apparatus. He also spoke up on human rights and modern science. And yet, among the young, it was Modi who was the hero. At a BITS Pilani event in Goa, where I was addressing engineering students, every time I exposed the PM's weaknesses and spoke about his faults, a 'Modi! Modi!' chant would go up in protest. Nothing could shake his followers' faith in him: not his divisive agenda, not international condemnation, not even record levels of unemployment. It was baffling.

There are many more dynasts in the BJP than there are in the Congress,[278] but the post-Independence history of the grand old party is the storybook of the high-profile Gandhi family. Barring a few years, a member of the Gandhi family has been either prime minister of India or president of the Congress since 1947, and their contribution to India's storied milestones are legendary. Modi went after the Gandhi family like a man possessed. His '*kaamdaar aur naamdaar*' (worker vs grandee) jibe hit home because, as Modi knew, in damaging the Gandhi name, he was nuking Brand Congress. So closely was the party's history interwoven with India's own, it had once looked like the Congress was invincible. Many called it the natural party of governance. But Modi tore into its image, and thus its prospects, with precision. The Gandhi family was easy bait.

Although Rahul knew about the malicious campaign that the BJP IT cell was running—morphed videos, memes and fake attributions—both the Congress and he underestimated the damage it was causing. The fightback was insipid. The 'Pappu' tag caused near-irreparable damage. Rahul's sincere efforts, farsighted observations and emphatic analogies were twisted so they appeared foolish. By the time he finally joined social media and began engaging more actively with television reporters, and people began to see him as he really was, it was too late. The BJP had monopolised smartphone applications, blogs, podcasts and all digital platforms in a massive outreach programme. The Congress, on the other hand, was still struggling to activate online membership on its official website. This was a race between a BMW and a bullock cart.

It was senior leader Digvijaya Singh who, in 2012, in his relentless exploration of new platforms, had taken the initiative to set up a social media outfit. Perhaps his ongoing repartees with BJP leaders played a part in this. A bundle of energy, and never one to shy away from risks, Singh marshalled some of us and pushed for a formal organisational structure to drive social media strategy, even if it was principally manned by volunteers. Most leaders in the party those days thought of social media as only a frivolous distraction. Rahul Gandhi had refused to join Twitter—he thought it was just an 'urban fad', as he once told me. Eventually, Shashi Tharoor, perhaps India's first public figure with a global following, inspired the party to rethink its social media strategy. But, by then, the BJP's cyber-presence had burgeoned, and its ferocious internet army was practically executing liberals online. The Congress was a social media tyro taking on a defending champion.

L.K. Advani's old dig at the Congress, that it practised pseudo-secularism, continued to bother many within the party. Several Congresspersons felt that the Hindu vote would desert the party because of the Ram Janmabhoomi movement. They were more worried about their own seats than the party's secular philosophy. In the face of the BJP's nakedly Hindutva appeal, this was a big concern in 2014. The Congress never really introspected on the minority-appeasement charges that it has long faced, and the image had stuck in the public mind because the BJP was reminding them about it every day. I was dumbfounded by the party's lethargy and its unwillingness to bite the bullet.

At its core, the Congress was and remains secular, even if it has been guarded in its defence of minorities of late. In 2014, the party's clear political intent was hamstrung by confused articulation and a defensive posture that made it look unreliable and fishy in the eyes of the common person. The BJP entirely hijacked the religion debate, instating itself as the original custodian of the Hindu faith. The desecration of Babri Masjid in 1992 had set in motion a centrifugal force in Indian politics. For a party that had just two seats in 1984 to rise to a mammoth majority of 282 in 2014 was a singular success story.

After 2014, the senior Congress leadership stopped talking about the Gujarat genocide of 2002. This meant that millions of young Indian voters were not hearing about it. The BJP gathered that the Congress was uncomfortable about attacking Modi on Gujarat, risking further alienation of the 'Hindu vote'. So instead, it mounted a massive offensive on the 1984 Sikh massacres under the Congress watch. A horrendous blot on India's and the Congress's secular record, 1984 was indefensible. The fact that Rajiv Gandhi was prime minister then made the Gandhi family easy pickings for Modi, diverting attention from his own shameful conduct during the 2002 Gujarat pogrom. Soon Rahul Gandhi was being compelled to respond to 1984 (he was ten years old when it happened) and make a public apology for that gruesome period, while Modi, who was the chief minister of Gujarat when 2002 happened, was getting away scot-free. This travesty alone is proof of how clueless and muddled the Congress was. For India's young, the Congress had been tarnished as communal, while Modi played the hapless victim of a vicious conspiracy to malign his character over the riots. Hadn't the courts quashed the cases against him, asked the BJP in his defence.

In the 2017 Gujarat assembly elections, Rahul visited several temples, but he also went to mosques, synagogues and churches as he travelled across the country. Expectedly, he was accused of playing soft-Hindutva politics. And there was no denying that the Congress was playing the BJP on the latter's turf: religion. It was myopic and thoughtless. The A.K. Antony report, following the 2014 election defeat, had apparently concluded that the Congress was being perceived as a pro-Muslim party, and that it had to impress upon the Hindu voter that it was not anti-Hindu. (Barring a select cabal, no one else in the Congress has seen the report's findings and recommendations.)[279]

The BJP's unambiguous agenda of creating a Hindu Rashtra ought to have been the preoccupation of the Congress think tank (its Central Working Committee, or CWC) and the top leadership. Instead, the party responded to each BJP barb in an episodic manner, appearing more incoherent with each statement. In Gujarat, for instance, the Congress rejoinder was that Rahul is a janeudhari (sacred thread-wearing) Brahmin and needed no certificates from the BJP to establish his Hindu lineage. The implied casteism of the statement is staggering, more so when seen in the context of Gujarat's Una atrocity, where Dalits had been beaten up for skinning a cow.[280] The Congress played into the BJP's hands, showing itself up as the duplicitous, two-tongued party that it had been portrayed as. An ardent chest-thumping Hindu was, in any case, smitten by Modi; the Congress could never compete with that loyalty. This assertion of Brahminical Hinduism was a sore political miscalculation. While it is true that the Congress gave a close run to the BJP in the state election, it was largely on account of a demoralised business community and a sharp deterioration of living standards among the poor, following demonetisation and GST. The BJP was setting the agenda, the Congress was only reacting to it.

After the Congress party's rout in the Lok Sabha elections of 2014, Rahul Gandhi, then Congress vice-president and its star campaigner, came in for trenchant criticism. Although collective responsibility is a plausible defence in a parliamentary democracy, Modi had made 2014 into a presidential battle; NaMo vs RaGa. It was unfair to place the blame at Rahul's door, but as they say, the buck stops at the top. The Congress had experienced electoral washouts in rapid succession in the December 2013 state elections as well (Rajasthan, Madhya Pradesh, Chhatisgarh and Delhi). The general elections of 2014 were really the knock-out punch. The Congress was battling a massive anti-UPA sentiment, which Rahul was valiantly attempting to reverse. We know now that he did not succeed.

The truth is that, much before Arvind Kejriwal became the country's iconoclastic symbol, Rahul was the original outlier. He questioned the lack of inner-party democracy within the Congress, lamented the embedded culture of dynastic politics, expressed serious reservations about the growing chasm between a boisterous and buoyant India and a subsistence-seeking Bharat, reminiscent of his father's celebrated speech at the AICC session held in the Cricket Club of India, Mumbai, in 1985 (where Rajiv Gandhi talked about only 15 per cent of government resources reaching the needy). Rahul's trips to Bhatta Parsaul and the Niyamgiri hills in Odisha were not synthetic attempts at crowd-pleasing, but represented a genuine solicitude for the marginal farmer and tribal rights. He obsessed over the prevalent income inequality and unequal opportunities in India. The disproportionate imbalance in our society, Rahul recognised, would boomerang on those who had oversold the single-sided growth story, blindsided by mere GDP numbers. He encouraged lateral entry into the Congress from diverse occupations as early as 2004—the year this author, a corporate entrepreneur, started to engage with the complex political ecosystem. No one could fault his intentions. But after a great start, Rahul faltered.

Nothing reflects the mismatch of perception and reality better than the episode where Rahul Gandhi threatened to tear up the ordinance on the disqualification of convicted politicians. The cabinet had recently cleared an ordinance that would neutralise a Supreme Court judgement that sitting MPs and MLAs who had been convicted would have to resign their seats. Unsurprisingly, the media overplayed the fact that Rahul had abruptly interrupted a press conference to speak against this ordinance. It was unwise and a PR disaster, no doubt about it. People asked, quite reasonably: 'Why did Rahul not sort this out internally without embarrassing Prime Minister Manmohan Singh?' At that time, Dr Singh was in the US, in the midst of serious diplomatic engagements, including a meeting with President Barack Obama. He could have done without such an indiscretion on the part of Rahul and the resultant media hullabaloo. Why did Rahul not engage with his own party members in private? Hadn't Congress President Sonia Gandhi, his mother, concurred with the ordinance too? This shocking intervention prompted the genial Dr Singh to consider resignation in view of his government's public humiliation.

Yet, when all is said and done, there is this to consider: Rahul had helped change India's political contours; convicted politicians were now barred from contesting elections. It took a perceptive Supreme Court judge, Justice J. Chelameswar, to see this. 'A great man has intervened at the last minute and ensured the scrapping of the ordinance. That great man has done immense service to the nation through his timely intervention,' he said. This reaction was not like Kejriwal's dramatic dharnas before the camera. Rahul had publicly taken on his own government because he strongly disagreed with its viewpoint.

The fact that Prime Minister Narendra Modi's cabinet included 30 per cent ministers with criminal charges[281] made Rahul's stance on the ordinance even more significant. But he was ridiculed on social media as a spoilt and entitled princeling—the act of tearing up the ordinance was seen as the defiant act of a petulant young man who lacked political maturity. Both the Congress and Rahul himself underestimated the severe damage this character-assassination would do to his political reputation. We would pay for it dearly.

In his Jaipur address at the AICC general session in 2013, on becoming Congress vice-president, Rahul Gandhi made two significant statements with his usual candour. He jocularly said that sometimes the Congress itself did not know how it wins elections, thereby pointing to the need for greater organisational robustness that would have more predictive outcomes. He had indeed identified the problem correctly. The Congress still operated in the Jurassic age of politics, unable to reinvent itself for a world where sound bites, Twitter, WhatsApp and Facebook were the new vehicles of public outreach. He had correctly identified the problem, but he did not provide prescriptions for course correction.

Secondly, power is poison, he said, reminiscing about the personal tragedies that had bedevilled him. He did not shun responsibility, but for him, it was not about suzerainty. The work that was done to empower the citizens of this nation was what mattered, not titles and positions. Rahul appeared open to new ideas. *Newsweek* magazine, at the time, called him India's 'quiet revolutionary' in a piece full of adulation. But once again, besides the platitudes, nothing tangible was done at the ground level to strengthen a fast-depleting Congress.

After the 2014 defeat, most Congress workers were so demoralised, they somnambulated their way in and out of sparsely attended offices, where the only time anyone moved was to order tea and biscuits. Rahul's inability to motivate the cadres for the long haul would also affect the party at the hustings in several states. Organisation-building requires both exemplary management and experienced leadership. Rahul was steadily getting there, but the Congress, a lazy leviathan, only came awake sporadically before state elections. The party needed to attend to its bureaucratic maze and shake off this listlessness.

Getting the party battle-ready for several state elections before 2019, rejuvenating the cadre and ensuring greater organisational symmetry were Rahul Gandhi's priorities in 2014. The nearly 140-year-old Congress is no ordinary political organisation. It is byzantine, for one. Numerous committees and subcommittees exist, as everyone needs a title that will give them political heft. For another, there is a generation gap created by the entry of impatient millennials seeking instant gratification, chafing at the attitude of the veterans operating in their comfort zones, whose expertise in deal-making is quite enviable.

The party struggled because it remained indecisive on matters of critical import—for instance, the Communal Violence (Prevention Control and Rehabilitation of Victims) Bill. It had been tabled in 2005, but for nine years, the UPA laboured to build a political consensus around it. It would have been a watershed moment for India's secularism had it become a binding act. Among other things, it would have put the brakes on the institutional bias against minorities that prevails in the policing system. There were two reasons the bill was never passed: one, the BJP was already whipping up national hysteria at any mention of the bill, and secondly, many leaders in the Congress themselves were afraid of a majority-community backlash. This dillydallying brought into question the authenticity of the Congress's intent to build a syncretic India. Rahul was not able to shape the political narrative the way he would have liked to. And perhaps he did fight a lonely campaign, suddenly thrust into the role of the future prime minister of India. He had promised 'change like you have never seen before' post the Delhi assembly elections defeat, which marked Kejriwal's stunning political debut, but the Congress and its leader appeared to subsequently retreat into a languorous slumber.

Not all the decisions it was making in its waking hours were sound either. In early 2019, in the dead of a winter night, I got a call from Randeep Singh Surjewala, the head of the party's communication cell. Likeable and unflappable, he was in the hot seat as the Congress prepared for the impending general elections. I had met him for the first time in 2013, when Ajay Maken, then the chief spokesperson of the party, had asked me to hold a training session for future spokespersons as part of a talent hunt. Randeep stood out, and I remember telling Ajay so. I picked up the call expectantly.

'Would you be open to taking over as head of our party's social media department?' he asked. The general elections were less than four months away, and the Congress was proposing replacing a key person occupying a strategic role. It seemed bizarre to me. I declined instantly, because I thought Divya Spandana, a popular star in southern cinema and a former elected parliamentarian, was doing a tremendous job, giving the Congress much-needed traction on social media, even though she was starting from near scratch. Rahul's Twitter presence was generating positive word-of-mouth impact, and people were appreciating his cheeky humour, sarcastic jibes and carefree barracking of Modi. He was no longer the kurta-clad politician spouting the usual bromides; he was now cool, relaxed and friendly. The credit for Rahul's social media personality makeover must go to Divya. I knew her a bit and admired her feisty demeanour and no-nonsense attitude. If she disagreed with you, she would say so. I thought the party needed more workers like her. But she had many detractors within the Congress, people envious of her success and rising profile, and there was some disgruntlement around how she went about her job. It was true, perhaps, that she could have managed her team better, but her positives far outnumbered whatever quibbles there might have been against her. Once again, the party was shooting itself in the foot. She must have known that she was being pushed out, and I wondered how a demotivated asset could possibly be our trump card in the elections. Randeep asked me to sleep on it, but I firmly said no.

Change is not easy, but the Congress faces certain obsolescence if it cannot reinvent itself urgently. While it is not how he operates, Rahul recognises that power is the glue that keeps many Congress workers in the party, so sops are constantly on offer to vulnerable borderline supporters. Of late, even those have dried up. In an overhaul of the party, at a point where it is well removed from power, membership drives cannot be about statistics alone. There is need today for a reaffirmation of the party's core ideologies: inclusiveness, secularism, tolerance, the democratic spirit and progressiveness. Only a commitment to these values can override short-term electoral disappointments. If Congress MLAs and MPs happily jump ship when the BJP offers them a fat wad from the Operation Lotus treasury, the Congress is equally culpable. It is guilty of giving tickets to those who can mobilise muscle power and have the ability to fix underhand deals to recoup their original 'investments', political workers for whom ideology is like a third shoe. Over the years, questionable characters have come to dominate the Congress's political structure and organisation, leading to organisational fragility. Unfortunately, Rahul failed to stem the rot or chose to look the other way.

Behind his soft exterior and inherent decency, Rahul has a steely determination. I once asked him what it was like for him as a young boy, knowing that his father's life was constantly in danger. 'It changes you from within. You internalise and adapt to a harsh reality. You are not fearful thereafter. You become tough,' he said. Seven years after the assassination of their grandmother, Rahul and Priyanka lost their father to an assassin's attack. I think the losses have affected Rahul deeply and made him stronger, but they have also left deep scars. You find him talking often about the 'politics of love'; for him, it is always about reconciliation over revenge, remorse over retribution. He is a good man, unquestionably. But the Congress and he have struggled to find the perfect balance between good politics and smart politics that is required to reinvigorate a gradually weakening political organisation.

Rahul Gandhi is the proverbial long-distance runner and as all marathon men know, it is a lonely experience. India's destiny cannot be fulfilled through a series of epiphanies, short bursts of 100-metre sprints, but by a visionary, calibrated and determined targeting of the long-term finish line. The problem was that Rahul remained largely aloof and, to most people, almost inaccessible. Very few knew what grand strategy he had for a Congress comeback, if he had one at all. The party looked rudderless, but Rahul still sincerely believed that it would stage a comeback in 2019. He would be proven woefully wrong.

Rahul did have his moments in the sun, of course. His '*Suit-boot Ki Sarkar*' jibe became the rallying cry of the Congress's attack on NDA's crony capitalism. To counter this attack, the BJP worked very hard to shoehorn Rahul into an 'anti-growth' image. Indian industry was increasingly convinced that the Congress under Rahul was taking a diametrically opposite stance to Dr Manmohan Singh's liberalisation-driven regime. 'I think he is a closet communist, not even a socialist,' said the CEO of a bank to me. This was wrong, obviously. The Congress has always been a vocal advocate of 'inclusive growth'—including during UPA-1 and UPA-2—one that welcomes high private and foreign capital investment and regulatory reforms, but concomitantly encourages social-welfare allocations and pro-poor subsidies. India cannot ignore the Dalits, Adivasis and tribal communities, the migrant workers, and the millions of others who live below or dangerously close to the poverty line. But the perception that the Congress was moving to the 'extreme Left' was fast cementing, only hardening further when Rahul stood up for JNU students and tribal populations.

Since 2014, India has faced a severe threat to citizenly freedoms. It is to Rahul's credit that he has been consistently championing freedom of expression and individual liberty. His repeated assertions that the dangerous cocktail of hatred, anger and polarisation was destroying India's social fabric had, by 2019, become a reality. Religious extremism has been steadily mainstreamed since Prime Minister Narendra Modi assumed charge.[282]

There has also been a heavy crackdown on dissent. The government has been sending out the unambiguous message that criticism will be met with force. Threats of criminal defamation suits are casually delivered. In 2017, the *Wire* broke a story on Amit Shah's son Jay Shah's spectacular growth in business fortunes: 'Revenue from company owned by Amit Shah's son jumped from just Rs 50,000 to over Rs 80,00,00,000 in a single year.'[283] The entire government machinery was mounted against the online news and analysis website to prevent further public disclosures. In another instance, a Star Plus comedian's outstanding mimicry of Narendra Modi was met with online fury.[284] The programme was eventually edited out. *Mersal*, a Tamil film, was attacked because it showed GST as a Himalayan catastrophe, which it indisputably was. A Maharashtra constable critical of Modi was suspended.[285] India had become an Orwellian horror story. While the Congress did speak out against the oppression, it would appear frozen when reminded about the excesses of the Emergency. Whataboutery hurt an unprepared Congress considerably.

Just before the 2019 elections, I happened to be on popular stand-up artist Sorabh Pant's show, #TheRant. There was not a dog's chance that the BJP would attend. Pant did his usual fun stuff, and I enjoyed interacting with young people in an unrestrained, flippant, frivolous chat show that addressed core political issues. But I could feel my host's restraint. The stand-up industry appeared to be frightened of taking on the powers that be, when doing that is exactly what their job entails. To highlight this crisis, celebrity stand-up artist Vir Das posted a message asking what was kosher for comedy. The silence of the regime worked on both ends: citizens were silenced through threats, and the prime minister did not address press conferences. Indian democracy was in a limbo. In this environment, Rahul's Twitter presence had a breathtaking freshness about it.

In the corporate universe, it is often said that companies mimic the CEO's behaviour. It isn't so different for a country either. India had become like its leader: dictatorial, communal, aggressive and intolerant. Six years into his own term, Modi was still talking about the alleged Congress misrule that had derailed India. He continued to make uncharitable personal remarks against the Gandhi family. Once, he said 'RSVP' is the short form of corruption: Rahul, Sonia, Vadra and Priyanka.[286] Rahul's allegation that there existed a powerful machine that drove the divisive agenda of the BJP was no exaggeration. Modi follows some of these online stormtroopers, who are constantly peddling incendiary content and threatening 'sickulars', 'libtards' and 'Khangressis' on social media. The Congress media strategy of not naming Modi directly (right until 2014) was preposterous, but I honestly felt that communication was never taken seriously in the party. We were like headless chickens, running from one TV debate to another.

After the wretched defeat of the Congress in the 2013 Delhi assembly elections (after fifteen years of then chief minister Sheila Dikshit's rule, the Congress scraped together just eight seats), Rahul had promised big changes. But there was no evidence of this spirit of renewal. The Congress was riddled with a torpor that seemed incomprehensible in a party that was in a dogfight to win a third consecutive term in 2014.

To be honest, Rahul had flattered to deceive through much of 2014–19. He did have a golden period, though. It lasted a full calendar year, from the time he became Congress president in December 2017. Under his leadership, the party showed a spectacular fightback in Gujarat, overcame the attempted poaching of elected legislators in Karnataka by forming a coalition government with the Janata Dal (Secular), and comprehensively subjugated the BJP in the three crucial states of Rajasthan, Madhya Pradesh and Chhattisgarh in December 2018—the latter two after fifteen long years of being out of power in those states. The script seemed like it was racing ahead to a surprise denouement in May 2019, but that never happened.

His sudden resignation after the 2019 debacle and his obdurate resistance to assuming charge damaged Rahul's political brand, one that had been rehabilitated over the preceding two years. While his acceptance of moral responsibility for the defeat was a noble move, it was political suicide: he was drawing attention to his leadership failure. Even more importantly, he had failed to ensure a smooth transition to a new leader.

Also, in what was otherwise an introspective and insightful resignation letter, Rahul faltered when he talked about fighting the Lok Sabha battle 'alone'. For one, leaders are expected to do the heavy lifting. The Congress president is nearly a demigod in our party, make no mistake about it. The high command's diktat is sacrosanct. One call from New Delhi, and most Congress leaders would be on the next flight out even if they had serious prior commitments. Secondly, Rahul was very definitely not alone. He had an A-list of leaders to work with and assist him: seniors like P. Chidambaram, Anand Sharma, Kapil Sibal, Salman Khurshid, Ashok Gehlot, Capt. Amarinder Singh, Shashi Tharoor, B.S. Hooda, Ghulam Nabi Azad, and outstanding young ones like Sachin Pilot, Manish Tewari, Jyotiraditya Scindia, Milind Deora, Sushmita Dev, Deepender Hooda and Jitin Prasada. It was a fabulous team, especially when compared to the relatively new entrant to the national stage, Narendra Modi, with his mostly untested colleagues.

For Rahul to say that he almost single-handedly took on the RSS or Modi belittles the humongous contribution of several leaders, regional satraps and Congress workers. All of us gave the battle our all. As spokespersons, we bore the brunt of the bad news, but my colleagues were like Teflon, refusing to surrender. In any case, isn't it the leader's job to ensure that the entire team is collectively fired up for a do-or-die winner-takes-all battle? Or get a buy-in from those resisting his ideas? Perhaps the allegation was made in haste, or perhaps it was not entirely thought through, or written in a moment of despair.

There were reports of Rahul's deep disquietude about the Congress's unwillingness to join in his refrain of '*Chowkidar Chor Hai*.' At a CWC meeting, Rahul expressed his disgruntlement. He believed he was the only one who took on Modi on the Rafale corruption charges. It is true that many Congressmen felt that a slanderous attack on the prime minister would not bushwhack him. But, equally, the Congress had incorporated the Rafale allegations—which Rahul had a big part in bringing to the national attention—in its election manifesto, explicitly stating that if it came to power, the government would launch a criminal investigation against Prime Minister Modi.[287] No further corroboration was needed that the party had heeded its leader's clarion call. I feel that there was disillusionment within the Congress because of Rahul's scapegoating of his own team. Many were unhappy, and understandably so.

Speaking of team management, another Gandhi is an ace at it: Priyanka Gandhi Vadra. A significant differentiator between Rahul and Priyanka is her sharp emotional intelligence relative to her brother. I remember giving a talk to Priyanka's newly appointed Uttar Pradesh Congress office-bearers in Rae Bareli, in the latter part of 2019, wherein I contextualised selflessness and sacrifice by explaining the tragic assassination of Rajiv Gandhi in 1991. Priyanka was sitting at the back of the auditorium, but I could see that she had become visibly tearful. At other moments too, I had noticed her translucent vulnerability. She builds a rapport instantly with almost everyone, and has a genuine concern for the well-being of her team.

During the AICC meet in Delhi in 2018, unbeknownst to anyone, Priyanka had taken care of all the backroom logistics, operational planning, and the minutest nitty-gritties of the programmes. Late at 3 a.m. in the morning, we were even doing a dress rehearsal for event flows the next day. It is easy to understand the fantasy of devout Congressmen: that Priyanka Gandhi might one day become the Durga avatar of Indira Gandhi. There are indeed many startling similarities between them. Priyanka is made of sterner stuff than she is given credit for, and her powerful brand has not been used effectively. Her launch pad in Uttar Pradesh was a desperate gambit, thoughtlessly planned, unimaginatively conceived. It was always going to be an uphill task, given the short time in which to prepare to reclaim Uttar Pradesh during the highly polarised 2019 Lok Sabha elections. Anyone would have been doomed to certain failure, given the Congress's track record in the state. Unfortunately, charisma is not enough to create a grassroots organisational base, and voters tend to choose parties they believe are likely to win. To her credit, Priyanka was ready to be a sacrificial lamb for the party.

Compared to his sister, Rahul is more left-brained; he prefers analytics, number-crunching data, facts and figures, and logical assessment in PowerPoint presentations. Frankly, a party that had once even shunned social media has come a long way under Rahul's ambitious programme to leverage big data to understand India's political calculus. But politics in India is complex and intricate, and there is no straightforward formula that can help make sense of it. Priyanka's people-first approach is backed by the modern leadership theory that a successful leader must have a high emotional quotient.

Surprising as this may seem to many, it is a quality that Mrs Sonia Gandhi possesses abundantly. Jairam Ramesh was the one to introduce me to Mrs Gandhi and the Congress party in 2004. Both Jairam and Salman Khurshid were the personification of manic energy in their war-room as the Lok Sabha campaign was heating up, busy conceptualising the campaign theme, formulating media strategy as well as distributing publicity literature. Their brio was infectious. When I met Mrs Gandhi, she was warm, friendly and fun—a far cry from the complicated, cunning and condescending leader she was made out to be in the media and by the BJP. During my assignment with her, she came across as down-to-earth, resilient, and ready to burn the candle at both ends whenever required. In the three days I spent working with her at 10, Janpath that year, what struck me most was how trusting she was. I had been warned that, in politics, people do not even trust their own shadow. The Gandhis had been victims of several betrayals (party faithfuls named Jagjivan Ram, V.P. Singh, Arun Nehru, Sharad Pawar, P.V. Narasimha Rao, in particular), and if they were distrustful of strangers, who could blame them? I was in for a pleasant surprise.

One instance is especially worth recounting. We did a series of video shoots where Mrs Gandhi spoke about her life thus far, from being charmed by Rajiv Gandhi during their fairy-tale romance in Cambridge, the dark night of 21 May 1991, assuming the responsibility of a struggling Congress in 1998, the mischievous snub by Mulayam Singh Yadav and the forthcoming battle against the India Shining front runners, the Atal Behari Vajpayee-led BJP. She was at her candid best and, I dare say, in a new avatar. There was in the shoot a hilarious take on Opposition leaders that would be inconceivable for those who imagine a cold, calculating, coterie-creating matriarch. Equally, she was an emotional mess when she spoke of Rajiv, even thirteen years after his assassination.

As I was preparing to leave, I suddenly realised that these videos, several hours long, ought to be destroyed so the media or some unscrupulous person would not get their hands on it. So I returned them to her and asked her to destroy the tapes. But it had not struck the Gandhis at all that an unethical person with an ulterior motive could exploit the outstanding material. What I saw at 10, Janpath was a gossamer world, at once susceptible and fragile. My personal takeaway was that the Gandhis are essentially trusting people who are constantly manipulated by a few fawning members of a selfish cabal that fosters insecurity in them. I think they know this too.

The Congress is now seen as a risk-averse, conservative party in slow motion. But Mrs Gandhi was once a gutsy experimenter. I suggested to her that she should challenge then prime minister Vajpayee to an open television debate in the run-up to the 2004 Lok Sabha elections. The opinion polls had already written off the Congress (90+ seats), and the NDA was expected to make a hurricane sweep of over 330 seats. The late BJP leader Pramod Mahajan, huffing and puffing on a five-star treadmill, had dismissed any talk of getting less than 350. India was shining, and BJP was the brightest star on its horizon. Our proposition was to heat up the battleground stakes and make Mrs Gandhi appear like a confident, robust challenger. She was fully aware that if Vajpayee accepted the duel, he would make mincemeat of her—wisely, she had no illusions whatsoever about the likely outcome of a verbal TV contest with a man who effortlessly commanded prose and poetry and was one of the country's best public speakers. But she also knew that Vajpayee would not bite the bullet, as that would distract from the BJP's compelling campaign that everything was hunky-dory and all that remained was a ceremonial closure through election formalities. I was completely bowled over by Mrs Gandhi's chutzpah. We almost pulled her public challenge off, but some cautious Congress minds shot the idea down, pessimistic of its outcome. I remember Priyanka backed us, but Rahul apparently wasn't so excited about it.

During the go-go years of UPA-1 and UPA-2, India's industrial growth had begun to mirror the American Gilded Age of the late nineteenth century, when robber barons influenced factor pricing to monopolise scarce natural resources to emerge as business behemoths, thanks to dubious government largesse. As India galloped at close to 8–9 per cent GDP growth during UPA, crony capitalism came to be deeply entrenched, especially when it came to natural resources allocations. Under Modi, this became all the more brazen. The beneficiaries of the Gilded Age—John D. Rockefeller, Andrew Carnegie, J.P. Morgan, Henry Ford, Cornelius Vanderbilt—are famous; their Indian counterparts less so. Both the Congress and the BJP are guilty of having given big business a free run in pilfering public assets. Rahul consciously distanced himself from India's industry captains because he believed that they were solely responsible for the 2G-and coal-scam allegations that destroyed UPA-2. He also felt that they influenced the behaviour of the mainstream media, which was mostly corporate-owned. But the strategy of no communication with industry was, in retrospect, a mistake.

In 2014, the Congress believed that, with Rahul leading the charge, it would help mobilise crucial youth votes. Many first-time voters then were not just Gen Y, but 'post-1991 children'—born in or after the year that changed India forever. I remember the trepidation with which India had reacted in 1991 to then finance minister Manmohan Singh's bold step on partial convertibility of the capital account. The Gulf War had created a gigantic crisis, and NRI remittances into India grew manifold as panicky Indians in the Gulf moved their savings and personal assets back home. Desi industrialists—the famous 'Bombay Club'—loudly protested the economic liberalisation policies. They wanted to protect their deeply entrenched interests and the domestic industry; anything remotely foreign evoked a kind of xenophobia. Local companies clamoured for a 'level playing field'. But Manmohan Singh had other ideas.

At that time, India had foreign-exchange reserves to finance only two weeks of import bills, and a severe crisis loomed. But with the licence raj dismantled, export–import curbs and quotas abolished, and with the creation of a market economy that permitted transnational capital, India found the entrepreneurial adrenaline it was looking for. Everything changed. Incredibly, the Congress itself failed to make political capital of its remarkable reformative measures. It refused to take full credit for rebooting India.

Subsequent governments have further unshackled the economy, growing it further. The global technology revolution accelerated the traction India's economy had received. Today, India is the biggest market for Mark Zuckerberg's Facebook, WhatsApp and Instagram, for Reid Hoffman's LinkedIn, and other tech czars and wizards. It is also one of the most hyper-connected countries in the world, even if prime-time television debates have reduced its conversations to a cacophonous mess. Yet, the Congress did not read the straws in the wind. Neither did Rahul. A changing India had become more aspirational and ambitious, and it needed the Congress to proudly claim its role as the path-breaking torchbearer of growth. However, a centrist party that had veered towards the left, the Congress appeared unsure about holding aloft that badge.

Most political commentators observed that the Congress left the middle class disenchanted. This was a paradox; the Great Indian Middle Class was actually a Congress creation—from the open economy to foreign investments and the entrepreneurial boom, from satellite TV to IT investments that led India to becoming the back-office of the tech world and to the burgeoning BPOs/call centres. The Congress supported FDI in multi-brand retail, which could have changed the core nature of the Indian and farm economy; it was the BJP that opposed it.

Passport services, online railway bookings, vehicle registrations, driving licences, the registration of property transactions on websites to increase transparency—these were all well-lauded moves aimed at the middle class. Several cities, like Delhi, Bangalore, Hyderabad and Mumbai, saw improved infrastructure in the form of monorails, metros, flyovers, national and state highways and snazzy airports with fast-moving conveyor belts. The Eastern Freeway in Mumbai, for instance, cut the commute from Churchgate to Chembur from one hour to twenty minutes.

All of this work was undone by the Congress's ham-handed handling of the politically motivated Hazare–Kejriwal agitation. It led to middle-class disillusionment, and the shine began to wear off. Guilt-ridden over the corruption scandals that had marked UPA-2, the Congress failed to market its accomplishments. And, tragically, it lacked the political intelligence to understand the shifting urban dynamics of the time. For instance, during the 2014 general elections, the party had content-heavy MNREGA billboards in Breach Candy, Mumbai, an affluent downtown locality that sniggered at subsidies. It was an ill-conceived communication strategy that lacked scientific planning. 2019 was only slightly better.

Although the last few years of UPA-2 are widely believed to have been characterised by policy paralysis, it was, in fact, a parliamentary gridlock that had caused immobility.[288] An obstructive Opposition, led by the BJP, distanced itself from all debate, and chaos reigned. It prevented several transformative bills from being passed, among them, the Prevention of Communal Violence Bill, the Women's Reservation Bill and the much-talked-about Goods and Services Tax Bill. India lost 35 per cent of parliament time to mindless disruptions during 2009–14, when Jaitley famously quipped, 'Parliamentary obstruction is not undemocratic. It is BJP's political strategy.'[289] Instead of being collegial, Parliament was combative even on issues that demanded consensus, like the Food Security Bill. The BJP's confrontationist politics damaged a panicky Congress that struggled to respond speedily. The resultant policy paralysis caused humongous damage to the party's reputational capital among the business community, the middle class, foreign investors and India's young. The writing was on the wall in 2014. The Congress had not read it even by 2019.

Rahul candidly admitted that the Congress, in UPA-2, allowed a false sense of invulnerability to lead to political hubris. It was a refreshingly honest assessment. He was aware of his dynastic baggage, a matter on which he is persistently questioned. But a head start is no guarantee of assured triumphs (Gandhi would lose in the family-dominated constituency of Amethi in 2019).

The problem was that Rahul's plans were dismissed as hollow pontification by impatient voters who saw the Congress as a lumbering organisation that was slow to fight a determined adversary. Many thought of Rahul as a good and decent man, but one lacking the wiliness necessary to succeed on the treacherous turf of Indian politics.

Modi had won over industry and business, right-leaning liberals, the media and the middle class on his assurance of creating a market economy, boosting exports, reducing red-tape and working towards a free-market capitalism model. On all of this, he backtracked early in his tenure. By the time 2019 came around, he had transformed into a champion of the poor, a complete 360-degree image makeover. Rahul's announcement, that the Congress would ensure a Minimum Income Guarantee (MIG)[290] for the poor when it formed the government, gave Modi's pro-poor image a severe jolt. A rattled BJP retorted with the predictable accusation that it was a jumla—a word that is Modi's legacy to the political lexicon of India.

At the annual World Economic Forum in Davos, 2017, the big question was whether capitalism itself was in peril. A year earlier, there had been deep anxiety about the rising threat of income inequalities in the Western world and the popular backlash that followed. 'Responsible capitalism' was on everyone's mind in the snow-capped El Dorado of the rich and famous. There were echoes of it in India too. In Parliament, Modi had once mocked MNREGA. Four years later, his government was boasting about increasing government outlays on the same scheme.[291] 'Slowbalisation'[292] is what the *Economist* calls the downside of flawed capitalism—trade wars and protectionist barriers. The fact is that hyper-globalisation is facing a backlash, leading to the rise of nationalistic authoritarian leaders all over the world. Modi is one such leader, who rode to power mocking the cosmopolitan elite of Lutyens Delhi, while actually canoodling with them when it suited him (in the matter of election funding, for example).

In spite of a crumbling economy and a fractured society, the Congress and Rahul were not able to dent Modi's personal popularity; his individual charisma compensated for his abject underperformance and outrageous failures, like demonetisation or GST. The 2019 results were testimony to that reality.

It was not any one factor that caused the near-decimation of a leviathan like the Congress. Some of our mistakes were evident as they were unfolding, some are clear only in hindsight. But those who write off the Congress underestimate its capacity for regeneration. It may have an uncertain future in the prevalent political environment, but its magnificent history is an exposition of what it is capable of.

The Congress party was born in Mumbai at the Tejpal Hall in Gamdevi. The famous August Kranti Maidan, from where Gandhi announced the Quit India Movement of 1942, is just a stone's throw away. Gandhi's Mani Bhavan was close by too and was usually thronged by foreign visitors. The birthplace of the Congress—India's oldest political party, which successfully fought for the country's freedom, and has governed it for fifty-five years—is these days a near relic. Nobody even invokes the independence struggle anymore. The Congress itself seems sundered from its glorious history.

It also seems distanced from Mumbai today. Since 2014, its performance in the Mumbai elections, whether for Parliament, the assembly or the municipality (Asia's largest civic corporation), has been dismal. But not so long ago, when leaders like Rajni Patel and Murli Deora were in charge, the Congress was the city's default choice.

The Maximum City (as Mumbai is often called, thanks to Suketu Mehta's book by that name) is India's commercial and entertainment capital. And it shapes conversations on the state of the country. Whether it was a conscious decision or an oversight, the Congress had been ignoring policy discussions with India Inc.—which the party had once empowered—on capital markets, job creation, corporate transparency and foreign investments. Undoubtedly, this hurt its prospects with the business community. In its enthusiasm for the creation of rights-based legislations, which were undoubtedly crucial initiatives, the Congress had alienated India's booming private sector.

It also seemed divorced from its own internal needs. During the five years of UPA-2, there was not a single spokespersons' meeting to discuss forward strategy, tactical manoeuvring, retraining, handling of media relationships, sound-bite creation or inducting new talent. It was, to put it mildly, a case of monumental laziness. Surprisingly, political communication had become the Congress's Achilles heel. Its senior-most political figures were either taciturn or disdainful and dismissive of the media. At a time when Modi and Arun Jaitley were firing on all cylinders, the Congress was dependent on only a few spokespersons and the regular press briefings that remained Delhi-centric. This would soon result in lopsided media coverage, and while the Congress alleged bias, the fact was that it had begun to cede valuable television real estate to the BJP.

Ajay Maken, the congenial face of the Congress in Delhi, should be credited with giving the party's communication department a much-needed technological overhaul. I had met his predecessor, Congress veteran Janardhan Dwivedi, a heavyweight in inter-and intra-party politics and the party's revered authority on Hindi. As we were closing in on the 2014 election dates, he told me that the Congress party should strongly shun social media as it was a colossal waste of time. 'Let Modi do what he wants to do. This is all nonsense,' Dwivedi told me dismissively. It was clear he thought I was an urban intrusion into the sacrosanct territory of kurta-pyjama-clad wheeler-dealers. The BJP's prime ministerial aspirant, who loved single-sided messaging, was having a field day, unchallenged, unmonitored.

The Congress is also home to intellectuals who deal in abstract ideals. One such member (this person is part of the CWC) said to me, 'Congress has become controlled by a corrupt mafia that is hell-bent on destroying its Gandhian ideals and Nehruvian socialism by selling the party to the highest big daddy from the stock markets. The only way to stop this carcinogenic atrophy is to lose the 2014 elections and sit in the Opposition. Then, minus the perks of power, the Congress can purge the party of its criminal crooks, ideological compromisers and corrupt merchants.'

Unconvinced, I probed further: 'Agreed, there are a lot of opportunistic, self-serving people around, but why can't a restructuring take place when the party is in power? Is it not easier to change things when you command both leadership and resources?'

'No,' he said emphatically. 'When you are out of power, it is easier. There is time. It is a gigantic task.'

This conversation reveals another facet of the Congress mindset: a strong institutional belief that an electoral recession can effect a renewal, or, at least, that the latter is bound to follow the former. The party was certainly accustomed to the ups and downs of elections over seven decades of contesting them. Yet, instead of being chastised and therefore re-energised by a defeat, it only became further enervated, slipping into a deeper morass. Power is a glue; the Congress had forgotten the elementary wisdom necessary for a political resuscitation. The 2014 and 2019 elections would prove that many of the thinking heads of the Congress were off the mark, and were not the interlocutors that the party needed. Without power, the Congress seemed bewildered, baffled at its once dominant presence having gradually withered away.

While few in the party believed that this was a terminal crisis, most were hopeful that Modi would make a massive mess of governance, and anti-incumbency would kick in. It was a suicidal mix of arrogance and complacency. Between 2014 and 2019, there were just two AICC general sessions, and both were held in Delhi. These were missed opportunities to make regional pitches, to appeal to an India that yearned for solutions to bread-and-butter issues.

The Congress's ideological ambiguity too hurt its image—and its prospects. That it was soft-pedalling the BJP's Hindutva politics was evident from the manner in which it dropped the Gujarat pogrom issue from its agenda. For twelve years, Gujarat 2002 was the party's electoral salvo against the BJP and Modi; that was no longer the case. The new wisdom, it would appear, was that Modi's win in 2014 had made the 2002 riots a non-issue—India had overlooked a gory past to vote Modi in, after all, the think tank appeared to reason. In briefings sent to spokespersons, Gujarat rarely featured, if at all. But then, what was former Congressman Ehsan Jafri's widow, the eighty-five-year-old Zakia Jafri, fighting for in the courts? He had been murdered by the mob, with the chief minister's own residence ignoring his plea for help, according to Rupa Mody, who lost her eight-year-old son in the Gulberg massacre.[293]

Could the Congress also claim that, because it won a huge mandate in 1984, the largest in India's parliamentary history of 404 seats, its own stigma of the killings of Sikhs in India's capital had been washed away? Does the ballot box verdict overturn pending criminal investigations or a jail term? And yet, Congress leaders took a strategic decision to abstain from being drawn into Hindu–Muslim debates. It was a tacit acceptance of the BJP's communal narrative. It had been up to the Congress to push back against this onslaught of bigotry. Instead, the party unwisely and, worse, unethically chose to avoid the battlefield. Pandit Nehru had once said to India's majority community, 'If you harm one single hair on the head of one Muslim, I will send in a tank and blast you to bits.' Years later, his party had decided to abandon Muslims on the calculation that their electoral significance had been neutralised by Modi's Hindu-vote consolidation. The Opposition, barring the Left parties, who consistently pushed back, as did the Congress sporadically, rarely stood up for Indian citizens who were butchered in cold blood.

I will cite another example to explain the ideological vacuum that afflicts the Congress today. Former spokesperson C.R. Kesavan, C. Rajagopalachari's grandson, is a gritty fighter and a rising star in Tamil Nadu politics. On an election-counting day in one of India's northern states, the party told Kesavan to stay off television channels. Stunned, he queried: why? One of the AICC media guest coordinators replied that his south Indian accent would not be comprehensible to the cow-belt audience. A miffed Kesavan took up the matter with his seniors who could not convince him that this peculiar regional embargo was the party's media strategy. Needless to say, Kesavan refused to return to the small screen, and the Congress lost a forceful young voice.

It also infuriated me that, on communally sensitive issues, Muslim spokespersons were deliberately asked to absent themselves. The party's secular bloodline should have prompted the exact opposite position. Similarly, when incidents of gender violence were reported, male spokespersons were off the air, when, in fact, the offending gender should have been held to account.

I am not sure the party leadership was even aware of these fatal errors in its communication tactics. Once, I wrote to Rahul, telling him that no matter how mammoth his cynicism towards the mainstream media, he should watch the 9 p.m. bulletins in order to gauge public sentiment; after all, television producers choose topics that cater to popular appetite. I do know that Priyanka Gandhi Vadra follows the daily cacophony with avid interest, which perhaps explains her astute reading of political undercurrents. During my eight years as a spokesperson, she would revert to me with feedback, one of the few senior Congress leaders to do so, and appeared to correctly gauge the severity of the windstorms we faced.

Another aspect of the Congress leadership culture needs urgent rewiring. The party must minimise the influence of insecure courtiers who mislead the top leadership and run their own mini-kingdoms within the Congress. When the Yes Bank scam exploded into the national consciousness, former finance minister P. Chidambaram requested me to hold a press conference in Mumbai. He wanted to corner the BJP government in India's commercial capital, where bank depositors were already reeling under the PMC bank scam. I hastily began coordinating arrangements for a media interaction at Gandhi

Bhavan, the Congress headquarters in Mumbai. Imagine my shock when a senior member of the AICC asked me to cancel it because Chidambaram was already holding a presser in Delhi. It was bizarre—one did not rule out the other. The party frequently launches a nationwide offensive on burning issues that have caught the public imagination. Riled and ruffled, I called this gentleman to ask why I should not go ahead, only to be told that it was his final decision. No reasons were given. It is the Congress that lost out in its effort to bludgeon the BJP, because of an individual's capricious decision. Unknown to the party, there are several such seemingly minor events that are imperceptibly pushing it down a rabbit hole.

Loyalty (or at least the demonstration of it) is the sine qua non of success in the Congress; performance can wait in the elevator. Thus, the Congress has developed a non-performance work culture, where the password to political eminence is 'access'. It is an open secret. Everyone talks about 'when they last met RG' or received a message from a bigwig. This is why the Congress has gradually deteriorated in several states, as regional leaders spend too much time in Delhi 'oiling networks' instead of managing their teams back home. I was often asked why I did not visit Delhi more often. 'What am I going to achieve there?' I responded. But, in the Congress, if one is not seen hobnobbing in Delhi, and showing the expected obsequiousness to the immediate bosses in the food chain, chances are that one will quickly become obsolete.

So many Congress leaders complain about how difficult it is to meet Rahul Gandhi. Based on my own experience since 2014, this is absolutely true. After that defeat, Rahul withdrew into a cocoon; before then, he was reserved but not unreceptive. In early 2017, I prepared a comprehensive political strategy report for the Congress, and was extremely excited about sharing it with him. I informed Rahul and flew to Delhi. I spent two full days in the city and sent several messages to his office (Rahul changed his phone number frequently, and I was clearly no longer on his updated contact list). All I received was a perfunctory 'We will revert.' Ultimately, Kanishka Singh and I had a marathon post-dinner conversation, wherein I briefed him on the report in detail. Kanishka said he found several recommendations radical and many tactically brilliant, but expressed helplessness until Rahul saw it and took a call on it. He promised to talk to Kaushal Vidyarthee, Rahul's private secretary, to ensure that Rahul saw the presentation at the earliest. Vidyarthee did not even acknowledge my frantic messages. And I was never asked to come back to discuss my ideas further.

In the Delhi darbar politics of the Congress (although this is probably the prevalent culture in other parties as well), one indulges in the luxury of honest heart-to-heart conversations with colleagues at one's own peril. I do believe that the culture trickles down from the top. Everyone is on tenterhooks, looking over their shoulder. For a free-spirited individual, this can quickly get claustrophobic.

Behind the hugs and handshakes, politics is a ruthless enterprise. It is not meant for the thin-skinned or the hypersensitive; one needs to be power-obsessed, Machiavellian and merciless. The Congress leadership, if you remember, had refused to allow former prime minister P.V. Narasimha Rao's funeral procession to stop at the AICC headquarters at 24, Akbar Road. Former Congress president Sitaram Kesri was locked up in a room as the transfer of power was effected in 1998, when Sonia Gandhi became Congress president. Pranab Mukherjee was the ideal candidate for prime minister in 2004 according to many, but conspiracy theorists had been whispering in the ears of the high command. They spoke about his secret ambition of becoming prime minister, expressed during an Indian Airlines flight from Kolkata to Delhi, even as Mrs Indira Gandhi lay dead at AIIMS, New Delhi.

In making the apolitical Dr Manmohan Singh prime minister—even though he is one of the most distinguished, erudite and upright people in public life—the party suffered organisationally. Its various public-facing units, including the principal body the AICC, became fossilised. Internecine feuds were rampant, and few heeded the prime minister. The National Advisory Council (NAC) may have had good intentions in proposing itself as an adjunct to the Union cabinet, but in terms of perception, it was the government that came to be seen as the appendage. Mrs Gandhi had taken a calculated risk in creating twin power centres, but by 2011, it was obvious that the experiment was floundering. The ten years of UPA, between 2004 and 2014, resulted in a deep structural fault line within the party—even if it was, ironically, a significant decade in terms of policy achievements. The Congress that Rahul Gandhi inherited from his mother in 2018 was fairly incapacitated and fundamentally frail. The grand old party could not fathom the fervent passion for power that Modi–Shah had unleashed: *saam, daam, dand, bhed* (persuade, purchase, punish, exploit divisions). Chanakya Shah was on a roll. Unchallenged.

NYAY could have been a game-changer for the Congress in 2019. It was India's first attempt at creating a social security net. The proposal was also evidence that the party was thinking smart; India needed inclusive growth. Income inequalities had worsened, and the Congress needed an outlier blueprint. The problem was the timing. For one, it came too late in the campaign phase. While Rahul had talked about

NYAY during an election campaign meeting, it became part of the party's formal documentation only on 2 April 2019, which is also when the manifesto—another first-rate document—was announced. The elections were only a few days away. The Congress's communications chain is slumberous and slow, and so the message of its revolutionary policy never truly percolated to villages and small towns and non-English-speaking households. Television news debates in English cannot reach 170 million households nationwide.

The Congress focused its entire marketing campaign on NYAY; that was an obvious miscalculation too. Like in 2014, the campaign was solely targeted on the disadvantaged poor who needed state subsidies. There is no doubt that, between 2014 and 2019, the condition of farmers, the rural poor and urban migrants had sharply deteriorated. They must be a critical focus in any party's plans. But India has a vast neo middle-class population living in tier-2 and tier-3 cities. Even the older middle class had been battered on account of job losses, stagnant incomes and rising living costs. The industry sector had been on a downswing and was under pressure too.

Although the Congress tried to convey in its TV commercial that NYAY was about all injustices—social, gender, economic—in an overt wordplay, that subtlety went unnoticed. Every Congress leader, Rahul Gandhi downwards, spoke only about adding Rs 72,000 per year to the bank accounts of the poor; NYAY had translated in the popular imagination into a 'minimum guarantee of income' scheme alone. One angry CEO asked me: 'After five awful years of Modi, this is your only response, NYAY?' It had limited appeal across large sections of India. The Congress had put all its eggs in just one basket. Worse still, even the intended beneficiaries were sceptical about NYAY working out—if they had heard about it at all. To get the message out through the party apparatus and then to voter constituencies, in a coherent and precise manner, requires scientific planning. The humiliating drubbing of 2014 had not taught the Congress anything.

The Congress manifesto for the 2019 elections, a brilliant document, had been crowdsourced. It covered practically every challenge that India faced with impeccable clarity: national security, job crisis, farmer distress, corruption, foreign policy, Jammu and Kashmir, education and health, infrastructure, assurances on freedom of expression and freedom of the press, among other issues. But the party think tank had concluded that NYAY was going to be its game-changing USP, therefore, messaging about the party's other promises never quite made it through.

NYAY did not hit home as it should have because it had a strong appeal only for Left-liberal analysts. The manifesto, on the other hand, had a host of governance solutions to difficult and crucial problems, such as the right to housing, abolishing the Agriculture Produce Marketing Committee, giving full freedom to media houses, creating jobs, reviewing the Armed Forces (Special Powers) Act, etc. A lot of hard work had gone into creating a truly democratic document aggregated through public participation. Unfortunately, even some Congress members did not agree with their own manifesto. Ideally, the party should have sold its grand plans internally first and built a cohesive army willing to fight for the big picture. In not doing so (the majority would hear of the manifesto along with the rest of the world), it failed to win a unanimous buy-in, and so, trouble was brewing. One example will suffice.

A path-breaking, progressive commitment in the manifesto was the promise to remove the outdated and dangerous sedition law, Section 124 of the IPC, which the British had used to arrest Mahatma Gandhi and other freedom fighters. In modern times, and particularly under Modi, it had become a diabolical tool for State intimidation, both to prevent dissent and terrorise people. Kanhaiya Kumar, former president of the JNU Students' Union, along with fellow students Umar Khalid and Anirban Bhattacharya, was arrested by the government on dubious charges using this law.

Even if belatedly, the Congress was proposing corrective action. But as soon as the BJP pounced on this 'anti-national stance' of the Congress, and spoke of how the party was encouraging separatist forces—the 'tukde-tukde gang', as they called it—many in the Congress choked with fear. As the BJP mounted its muscular nationalism narrative, Congressmen began calculating what impact this would have on the majority-community voters in their constituencies. Instead of taking on the BJP's insidious campaign, the Congress abruptly went soft. Removing Section 124 was a call for a change from the strong-arm tactics that an authoritarian regime had unleashed on the country's citizens. Once again, the Congress appeared to be operating in an ideological vacuum, where every decision was negotiable at the altar of political profitability. As for the BJP, it was setting the agenda. And those who set the agenda usually win.

In December 2019, I anchored an event for the All India Professionals' Congress (AIPC) in Mumbai that featured the journalist Rajdeep Sardesai. He was launching his latest book, *How Modi Won 2019*, in various literary hotspots across town, and AIPC, of which I was the president in Maharashtra, had offered to host an interactive session for its members. The turnout was fabulous, and the interaction was both forthright and entertaining. Sardesai, while being a vociferous critic of the BJP, was also critical of the Congress's inability to square up to the BJP's elephantine electoral factory.

Imagine my surprise when, a few days later, I received a series of WhatsApp messages from a Congress social media member questioning my decision to invite Sardesai for the AIPC event. Among other things, this gentleman was bothered by the fact that Sardesai had been critical of Rahul Gandhi's close network of personal advisers, many of whom were urban hipsters with zero political experience. He was also concerned that Sardesai had given Rahul a mixed performance appraisal. Had the Congress become so thin-skinned that it could not take dispassionate criticism from a respected editor—one who had been harangued and harassed by BJP trolls for being soft on the Congress? Were we so divorced from ground realities that we had begun to believe that we were faultless, a storehouse of political purity and intellectual genius?

Post the May 2019 defeat, the Congress, in what is becoming a familiar pattern, withdrew into a dark shell. This inscrutable hibernation is mystifying. A political party must subject itself to the highest public scrutiny. The Congress had won 20 per cent of the vote share, the second largest after the BJP's whopping 38 per cent. A good 12 crore people still had faith in the party—despite its brand annihilation. They had to be the die-hard secular liberals that the BJP so hoarsely decried and feared. The Congress owed it to those voters to pick up the baton and run another marathon. But once Rahul Gandhi quit as the Congress president, the party became comatose. Rahul's assertion that no Gandhi would assume charge must have taken immense courage; it was clearly targeted at those who believed that the party could not think beyond dynastic politics. He was correcting that perception. Unfortunately, the Congress fumbled in its search for a replacement and frittered away an opportunity to start afresh, with a new set of leaders.

The party has a surfeit of outstanding talent, but inner-party squabbles keep forcing it into stasis or chaos. Eventually, a reluctant Sonia Gandhi had to take interim charge as Congress president as the core think tank was unable to choose a consensus candidate. The party was so embroiled in its internal politics that, right under its nose, the Karnataka government changed hands, undoing its remarkable achievement of just a year earlier. The government it had formed in alliance with Janata Dal (Secular) had led to new hopes of a mega political alliance as, in a show of camaraderie, leaders from various parties had congregated in Bangalore for a photo-op. That hope too was now in tatters. And the Congress appeared not to care. One was strongly reminded of the indolence that allowed the BJP to form governments in Goa and Manipur in 2017, even though the Congress had been tantalisingly close to the halfway mark and the BJP was trailing well behind.

The true character of any organisation is revealed in how it responds to a serious challenge or an existential crisis. The Congress has been out of power in Gujarat, Uttar Pradesh, Tamil Nadu, Bihar and West Bengal for several decades, and there has been little effort to revive the party. It took the party fifteen years to make a sterling comeback in Chhattisgarh and a modest recovery in Madhya Pradesh. Evidently, in defeat, the Congress mopes instead of hitting the road with a vengeance, the mark of a resolute warrior. By March 2020, the Congress had magnanimously handed over Madhya Pradesh to the BJP, courtesy fractious political machinations within the party.

In early March 2020, my friend and colleague Salman Soz, deputy chairperson of the AIPC, and I wrote an opinion piece in the *Times of India*. We were dismayed at the way the once-great party seemed rudderless and adrift. The unedited piece is reproduced here:[294]

INDIA NEEDS A RESURGENT CONGRESS; THE TIME IS NOW

By Sanjay Jha and Salman Soz

'There are moments in your life when you must act, even though you cannot carry your best friends with you. The "still small voice" within you must always be the final arbiter when there is a conflict of duty.'

–Mahatma Gandhi

In the aftermath of the devastating defeat in the recently concluded assembly elections in Delhi, that old phantom has inevitably surfaced; is the Indian National Congress party facing an existential crisis? The answer to that is, tragically, yes, which is why this unprecedented piece, co-authored by us die-hard Congressmen who want nothing more than a robust comeback. A dramatic turnaround is needed, because the Congress is the only bulwark (or the crucial lynchpin) against the authoritarian juggernaut that is the current Bharatiya Janata Party (BJP)-led regime, which is decimating institutions, polarising society, marginalising disadvantaged sections and destroying the core foundations of Indian democracy itself. The recent Delhi riots are a manifestation of the BJP's insidious political agenda, and the pernicious consequences are for all to see. India needs a reawakened and revitalised Congress party, ready to win the second freedom struggle against dark, oppressive forces. We must do the heavy-lifting.

This article is not provoked by a panic reaction to the dismal Delhi results; after all, we surprised political pundits by posting better-than-expected performances in Haryana, Maharashtra and Jharkhand. But the hard truth is that serious seminal fault-lines remain; a large complex internal structure that has resulted in organisational immobility, absence of speedy response times to compelling political challenges, factional infighting over petty issues and the absence of a clear roadmap. The leadership vacuum is the elephant in the room; almost two months shy of a year since Mr Rahul Gandhi resigned as Congress president, we are riddled with internal inertia and have not found a permanent replacement. This has aggravated despondency across the rank and file of the party. It is time for a bold makeover, as mere synthetic tinkering will only prove counterproductive. It will be like boiling an ocean. There is a silver lining; in our worst performance ever (2014), the party still garnered nearly 20% of the popular vote.

In the 1984 general elections, the Congress stood at 414 Lok Sabha seats, while in the last two general elections, of 2014 & 2019, aggregated together, we could muster only 96 seats. We need to acknowledge that either we have failed in doing a rigorous introspection of where we went wrong or adopted the wrong prescriptions. Either way, we have ourselves to blame for BJP's extraordinary triumphs. What is particularly intriguing is that the BJP won handsomely despite a ravaged economy, record joblessness, raging rural distress, abysmal governance, marginalisation of Dalits, brutalisation of minorities (particularly Muslims), corruption and regulatory and media capture. If the people of India still did not see an alternative in the Congress to a failed government led by the BJP, it means we have become disconnected from ground realities. Also, a challenger party needs that critical intangible element called the 'hunger to win'. Frankly, that is conspicuous by its absence.

The Congress party must have a thriving internal democracy and be a model for exemplary meritocracy. The old-fashioned forced representation model and large over-sized committees that merely pleases all need to be dumped. Instead, we should have outcome-driven groups; perform or perish. In a lighter vein, perhaps we are taking the Grand old party tag a tad too seriously; to many, we appear fossilised. We have drifted afar, because the most powerful decision-making body, the Congress Working Committee (CWC), which needs a continuous inflow of fresh ideas and creative energy, has been bogged down by transactional political imperatives. The serious brainstorming that must follow alarming electoral losses has just not happened. We suggest that there should be elections to the post of Congress President and the CWC, as which must be held under an independent bipartisan body of eminent citizens to ensure a fool-proof process: sunlight as they say is the best disinfectant. And this must happen within the next three to six months. Secondly, the AICC needs an organisational restructuring and greater decentralisation; the Congress must consider appointment of four regional Vice-Presidents to cover the 29 states and Union Territories of India. Thirdly, given the abundant talent we have, the Congress can appoint a formal shadow cabinet to keep the government in constant check. The Congress party has outstanding talent, but their collective brilliance remains untapped; we need a surfeit of independent state leaders. Fourthly, our ability to market ourselves remains amateurish. There is a laundry-list of things to do.

Our response to the BJP's playbook of majoritarian nationalism and segregationist politics has been either tepid or confused; whether it was the Pulwama terror attack, Article 370, Veer Savarkar, Ram Mandir, or being taunted for being pro-Pakistan (which is ridiculous). It is astonishing that the party that has a legendary contribution to India's historic freedom struggle and which won successive wars against Pakistan should be so inarticulate and mealy-mouthed in counterattacking the BJP's hyper-populist nationalism. Our categorical stand on CAA, NPR and NRC is a refreshing change. Ideological clarity helps.

We have to stop our slide forthwith before we slip into a freefall. The people of India have voted for us in 10 of the 17 general elections held so far, and we have governed for 55 of the 73 years of post-Independent India. Only the Congress party can thwart the torpedoing of the dreams of our great founding fathers, such as Mahatma Gandhi, Pandit Nehru, Sardar Patel, Dr Ambedkar, Netaji Bose, Maulana Azad and several others.

India's destiny is inextricably intertwined with that of the Congress party. In saving ourselves, we will have saved a country that deserves better, one which is being currently manipulated with dazzling lies and a vicious propaganda. No one can predict the future with certitude, but a rejuvenated, resurgent Congress party is the need of the hour. This op-ed is our commitment to push the Congress post-haste to realise its full potential. It is an urgent need. And that process needs to start now. The clock is ticking.

Many Congress leaders called to say that we had echoed their private sentiments even if they could not publicly endorse the article. It was obvious that we had hit the right buttons, and that most Congress workers were as disheartened as we were about the party not putting up a robust fight. Yet others were upset with us for airing our opinions publicly, in the country's highest-circulation newspaper. According to them, there were internal forums where we should have spoken up. Salman and I were warned that we would become persona non grata for our blasphemous overreach. We laughed the admonishments away. The truth is that those so-called internal platforms were phantoms. Inner-party democracy in the Congress had been radically eroded, and no one listened anymore.

Our article put to paper a chronic disorder in the Congress of late: an entirely ad hoc style of political management and a lack of open discussion on the way forward. For instance, there has been no election to the CWC since 1997, and a member of the Gandhi family has been president for thirty-five of the last forty-two years. This is the collective failing of the party as well as its collective responsibility to restore internal democracy. The principal challenges are:

* organisational resuscitation through transparent elections to the posts of Congress president, the CWC, and even to the district levels;
* a calibrated attempt to regroup with erstwhile Congress leaders, such as Sharad Pawar (Nationalist Congress Party, NCP), Jaganmohan Reddy (Yuvajana Sramika Rythu Congress Party, YSRCP), Mamata Banerjee (All India Trinamool Congress, TMC);
* and, crucially, the creation of a transparent work culture, where people can express their views frankly, without fearing political retribution.

The 3 March 2020 article created quite a flutter within the party. That was understandable. According to someone fairly senior, we had 'crossed the Rubicon', as it were, in boldly asking for organisational transformation. Honestly, we were not surprised that so many leaders expressed agreement with the article, but we were acutely disappointed that so few of them were willing to publicly endorse its contents. And therein lies the Congress's problem.

A few days after the article was published, a senior colleague descended upon me like a ton of bricks in our informal WhatsApp group. I was sarcastically told that I should be grateful that the party permitted the airing of my views in a leading newspaper when it would have been more appropriate for me to have shared them in 'internal platforms'. He had missed the wood for the trees; if there had been a forum for frank exchange of ideas and counter-ideas, why would we risk unwarranted disaffection from the senior leadership? If there had been open debate on how to get the Congress back on its feet, I don't think the party would have struggled for nearly a decade (since the anti-UPA-2 political whirlwind commenced).

Many in the Congress have not yet fathomed the consequences of being at the receiving end of dreadful negativity for so long or of its inability to set the agenda and seize the narrative. The party deserves better. It is just not true that there exists a robust internal democratic process that listens to individual voices, and more importantly, is continuously focused on party renewal, political strategy, tactical warfare, leadership development and resuscitation. As I've noted, most of us have only heard about the much-celebrated A.K. Antony report.

If a publicly listed company has even one bad quarter in corporate earnings, it is subjected to a brutal analytical examination. No one is spared, certainly not the CEO and the board. The company itself redraws its short-term revival plans, medium-term strategies and long-term goals to synchronise with business potential and market expectations. The Congress's lackadaisical attitude towards its own political obsolescence is baffling to say the least. Many well-wishers tell me that the Congress is giving the BJP a walkover. For someone like me, wedded as I am to Gandhian philosophy and the Nehruvian outlook that defines the Congress, it is dismaying to see the party's painful disintegration. It is particularly confounding, given that the current regime is patently clueless about even elementary governance.

The pandemic has, in the past year, shown up the Modi government's ineffectiveness at every level of governance: whether it is blindness to the needs of urban migrants and daily wage labour, or cluelessness about the medical and scientific response to the crisis, or an inability to work towards cushioning the shock to the economy. There are hard days ahead, but the Congress has not created an alternate white paper on governance for India, restricting itself to a few constructive suggestions. This is the time to step up and work for the national interest, put to use the party's immense experience in policymaking and governance, instead of waging a social media hashtag war.

Congressmen fondly remember our distinguished statesman-leader Pandit Jawaharlal Nehru on his death anniversary. I wish to remind us that Nehru once wrote a scathing advisory to himself, under a pseudonym, recommending distrust of centralisation of power. He was a true democrat who led by example. Instead of superficial gestures on 27 May, the Congress needs to internalise the best of Nehruvian ideals. Charity, after all, begins at home. I thus began to question my party in tweets on social media, personal chats, WhatsApp groups and in op-ed articles. The BJP cavalcade had to be stopped on the highway, but the Congress was still fixing its punctured tyres six miles off the road. Someone had to alert it.

I had just finished a TV debate on 14 July 2020 on NDTV when the channel broadcasted my immediate suspension from the Congress. I was stunned by the abruptness of it; the Congress had similarly dumped me as the national spokesperson about a month earlier with a brusque one-line dispatch. Apparently, I had indulged in 'anti-party activities'. If writing two op-eds in the

Times of India and raising red flags on serious fault line within the party was an act of treachery, I am guilty of it. If advocating a measured response to the cross-border military tensions with China was deemed apostasy, I must apologise. If supporting the case of Sachin Pilot for Rajasthan chief minister made me a BJP accessory, I humbly crave forgiveness.

The Congress, legitimately, accuses the BJP of a lack of democratic culture, but encourages similar imperiousness internally. More importantly, the Congress suffers from delusions of grandeur that prevent it from seeing the need for immediate course correction. There are five factors that signal a blockbuster washout for my party (and with it, the Idea of India). In an article in the *Times of India*,[295] I listed these worrying signals.

* DECLINING VOTE SHARE: The Congress traditionally aggregated an average vote share of 45 per cent, which peaked at 48.1 per cent in 1984 (a black swan election because Mrs Indira Gandhi was assassinated just a few months earlier). Since then, there has been a precipitous decline. Just a decade later in 1998, the Congress had slumped to 25.8 per cent, nearly 50 per cent of its supporters had vaporised. The party did not seem alarmed. The UPA years saw a minor bump to 28.5 per cent in 2009 (lifted by Manmohan Singh's brief romance with the middle class), before the catastrophic fall to 19.52 per cent, a fall of 59.5 per cent from 1984. Worryingly, the trend has been negative for decades and there is no strategy in place to arrest the fall.
* LOST STATES: The Congress has virtually surrendered political space in key large states of India. Its inability to launch a counter-attack after a defeat is clear now. The party has not formed governments in the following

states for decades: Uttar Pradesh (1989), Bihar (1990), West Bengal (1977), Tamil Nadu (1967), Gujarat (1985) and Odisha (2000). These states add up to 247 Lok Sabha seats. Worse, the Congress can at best piggyback on a regional contestant, its own units in complete disarray. While national and state elections do have different factors affecting outcomes, it is clear that the Congress is on a slippery slope here. Who is accountable for the sustained underperformance and near extinction of the party in vote-rich states? The BJP sarcastically dismisses the Congress as a 'super regional party'. The once formidable bastion of Andhra Pradesh of forty seats can now be added to the casualty list. The Congress recaptured Madhya Pradesh (since magnanimously gifted back to the BJP) and Chhattisgarh after fifteen long years.

* NUMBER OF VOTERS STATIC: This statistic is probably the knock-out punch. Between 2004 (10.3 crore voters) and 2019 (11.9 crore voters), the Congress added a miserable growth of 15 per cent in actual number of voters. Compare that to the BJP's performance; during that period, it grew from 8.6 crore to 22.9 crore voters, a staggering 166 per cent increase. Hidden in these numbers are India's large base of millennials—the Congress has lost the youth vote, one of the reasons for its electoral losses of late. In 2014 and 2019, India added 195 million young voters and they backed Narendra Modi's vision of India.
* POST-2019 SURRENDER: Following the devastating defeat of 2019, the Congress has withdrawn into a cocoon again, allowing the BJP to get back into Karnataka. But it was the political naivety in Madhya

Pradesh that took the cake, besides also seeing the defection of a huge political asset in Jyotiraditya Scindia. Gujarat, which in December 2017 was being hailed as the bearding of the lions (Narendra Modi and Amit Shah) in their own den, has since haemorrhaged as well. Rajasthan is the final nail in the coffin, a cavalier misadventure by the leadership has backfired. The Congress's playbook is titled: Self-Destruction Assured in Ten Easy Steps!

* LEADERSHIP VACUUM: Any organisation needs a continuous churn across hierarchies to remain fit. In the last twenty years, the Congress has had just two presidents and there have been no elections to the powerful Congress Working Committee since 1997. Since May 2019, it has not had a permanent president. Organisational atrophy is inevitable. The state of the Congress in Mumbai (the party was born here in 1885) reflects an apathy towards India's investment capital, industrial hub and entertainment industry, three significant constituencies in the political calculus. The old-fogey manner of working, with a high command taking decisions from a Delhi darbar, is no longer workable. A cunning cabal now runs the party. The Congress needs reinvention, and it needs to be hungry for a win.

The Congress was decimated in 2019, a defeat that was hard to understand despite the continuing 'Modi wave'. Understandably, regional parties that have usurped traditional Congress strongholds now see it as an effete partner, weakened at the centre. TMC President Mamata Banerjee, who was Youth Congress president in West Bengal during Rajiv Gandhi's time, finds it hard to negotiate terms with Rahul. She prefers the baronial worldly wisdom of Sonia Gandhi. NCP's Sharad Pawar probably has a similar predicament.

The Congress can yet be a serious competitor in 2024, but it does not have a moment to lose. It needs to take a bold call to signal its political intent: transparent internal elections and appointing a non-Gandhi Congress president, as Rahul has indicated his unwillingness to return. If the Congress is to make a strong comeback, it will need to solidify relationships with former Congress leaders-turned-regional-satraps, while going it alone in some states where it has been thoroughly marginalised for decades (Bihar, Uttar Pradesh and Jharkhand, to begin with). That said, unless the Congress wins a minimum 100/195 Lok Sabha seats in a head-on contest with the BJP, the grand old party of India will be a peripheral contestant at best. In the last thirty-one years (eight Lok Sabha elections), the Congress has crossed 200 seats just once, peaking at 206 seats in 2009. Right now, it is struggling to emerge from what feels like a bottomless pit. The party needs more than an adrenaline booster, it needs an electric shock.

That's just what a letter attempted to do—termed the G-23 letter, because it was written by a group of twenty-three Congress leaders, expressing dissent and calling for change. The G-23 is the inescapable consequence of the mindless drift within the party. The new political disruptor in town is a motley group, including veteran leaders (Ghulam Nabi Azad, Anand Sharma, Mukul Wasnik, Kapil Sibal), a global intellectual brand (Shashi Tharoor) and young Turks (Manish Tewari, Milind Deora, Jitin Prasada). It is a miscellany of Congresspersons deeply perturbed by the shiftlessness in the party that led to two consecutive Lok Sabha election routs, among other defeats. The Congress has been living in denial, but there is no time to waste anymore. The

G-23 wrote a forthright letter to the interim Congress president Mrs Sonia Gandhi, urging her and the party to face up to an existential crisis. It was about time.

The leadership vacuum since May 2019 has aggravated an already bleak situation. Abjectly surrendering Karnataka and Madhya Pradesh to the BJP, the Congress came close to losing Rajasthan. Jyotiraditya Scindia in Madhya Pradesh has joined the BJP, its nemesis, and the party almost lost the popular and dynamic Sachin Pilot as well. Its national vote share now hovers at about 19.5 per cent. The Congress has created modern India—from its multicultural society to its prosperous middle class, from the country's rising clout in global commerce to its stable foreign policy, from establishing India as the world's IT backbone to its strong democratic institutions. It still has the talent, experience and capacity to govern India, to take a long view on matters of progress and policy. The G-23 wants a transmogrification, nothing less. The group that calls for this internal restructuring comprises committed Congress leaders, each deeply concerned about the party's future.

Unsurprisingly, the media has been speculating about a potential split in the Congress—a repeat of 1969 and 1978, when the party split was engineered by former prime minister Mrs Indira Gandhi. By an uncanny coincidence, Mrs Gandhi had masterminded the splits citing 'drift' and lack of 'internal democracy'. These are the two principal factors causing uneasiness to the G-23 as well. Another being that the party is frittering away the crucial youth vote, which needs to be harnessed. But apprehensions about a split are entirely misplaced.

It is hugely regrettable that a senior leader like Kumari Selja should call the G-23 'BJP agents'. There was an organised attack on rebel leader Jitin Prasada in Uttar Pradesh by the so-called loyalists. Truly, the Congress's biggest political adversary is not the BJP but itself.

The Gandhi family's contribution, both to India's extraordinary success story as well as the Congress party's fortunes, is undisputed—it is a fact that the G-23 restates as well. Pandit Nehru was a statesman par excellence and a world leader. Indira Gandhi's role in the creation of Bangladesh demonstrated exceptional boldness of leadership. Rajiv Gandhi ushered in India's telecom and computer revolution that continues to be the fulcrum of our services economy even today. Sonia Gandhi stepped in at a crucial time to pull the party together. And Rahul Gandhi took on the RSS with unalloyed focus. Undoubtedly, the Gandhis will have a crucial role to play in the party's future moves on the political chessboard. But they have now publicly relinquished political leadership. It is imperative that someone else steps up to lead the party. The Congress has an incredible talent pool, with a wealth of experience in administration, political statecraft and grassroots connect. The prophets of doom who declare that the party will disintegrate without the Gandhis are only fortifying their own vested interests. Those who are committed to the party ideology will not desert it for short-term personal gains. A changed, aspirational India wants to see the emergence of a meritocratic political organisation that inspires the masses, as the Congress once did through mass agitations and huge public rallies.

Not unexpectedly, the fundamental issues raised in the letter, concerning organisational renewal and restoring vibrant internal democracy, have been overwhelmed by the debate on the Gandhi family's future political relevance. The Congress is one of India's most powerful brands, but the biggest of brands needs to go through periodic reinvention. Can the 135-year-old party survive without the illustrious Gandhi family at its helm? The answer to that is an unequivocal *yes*!

Two names that were once regularly invoked for party leadership were Jyotiraditya Scindia (when he was still part of the Congress) and Sachin Pilot. Both are young, self-driven, ambitious, great communicators, and deeply entrenched in politics. There are, of course, seniors aplenty whose names carry substantial currency, including Shashi Tharoor, Mukul Wasnik, Manish Tewari, P. Chidambaram and Captain Amarinder Singh, to name a few. Frankly, given responsibility, individuals tend to rise to the occasion. Within the G-23, there are several stalwarts who could assume the mantle of leadership. Unless the Gandhis change their mind, a non-Gandhi president is a fait accompli.

It is ludicrous to suggest that the Congress has no leader who can take the party forward. Unlike the BJP, there is no talent deficit in the party. Two non-Gandhi prime ministers, P.V. Narasimha Rao and Dr Manmohan Singh, remodelled India's economy and foreign policy. Besides, a non-Gandhi at the helm will also defang the BJP's incessant dynasty-bashing of the Congress. More importantly, the doomsayers who predict that the Congress will disintegrate without the Gandhis are forgetting their history. Morarji Desai, Jagjivan Ram (Congress for Democracy, CFD), Sharad Pawar, Jagan Mohan Reddy and several others left when a Gandhi was stewarding the party. Splits happen on account of organisational drift, ideological flip-flops, frail egos, personality clashes and political ambitions. That can happen under anyone. Lastly, until a new leader has a clear opportunity and is backed unanimously (including by the Gandhis, who want a Congress resurrection as much as anyone else does), it is premature to write off what they could potentially do.

The Congress needs a leader who is passionate and inspirational, a savvy communicator, hungry to win, and unrelenting in the pursuit of political goals. A leader who believes in the Idea of India: a liberal, democratic, socialist society that protects our secular diversity and creates equal opportunities for all. I know many who fit the bill. But first we need to go back to the drawing board. The BJP can be defeated, but we must begin by understanding why we lost.

It is galling that, despite two consecutive knockout blows in the Lok Sabha elections and in several states, there has been no effort at a thorough review of what went wrong, a brutally honest thrashing out of a roadmap for the future. The political-speak cliché used to describe situational assessment is 'introspection'—and there was none in the Congress until the G-23 forced it on the party. Barring the A.K. Antony report, there has been no effort at a performance audit. How is the Congress to start winning elections consistently if it does not know its past mistakes? It is an attitude that smacks of both indifference and cockiness, perhaps because the Congress has made several miraculous recoveries in the past (the 1980 and 2004 Lok Sabha elections, for instance). This may be wishful thinking, however, because this time, we are dealing with a formidable machine that takes no prisoners. This time we are dealing with a whole new paradigm in politics—Modi and Shah, the two BJP leaders from Gujarat, are unlike any adversary we have known. And the Congress appears completely unprepared for the fight ahead. At peril is the future of the country itself.

The G-23 has triggered a powerful movement within the party. Only a resurgent Congress can defeat the powerful election machine of the BJP and its dangerously bigoted politics. They say a week is a long time in politics. There are three and a half years to the next general elections in 2024. Calculate the number of weeks there.

Epilogue

My friend, a silver-haired doctor with a majestic moustache, was visibly seething. He is a Kashmiri Pandit, and he had just performed a major surgery on a fellow Kashmiri, a teenaged Muslim boy. 'He is recuperating well, and desperate to reassure his paranoid parents that he is fine. But he cannot reach them. No mobile or landline phones are working. There is no internet access. And he is convinced that a courier will never get there either. He is very disturbed. Now just imagine the plight of his poor parents back home. They must be worried as hell. I am trying to use my government contacts to get the message through to them.'

This conversation took place a few days after Home Minister Amit Shah made a stunning announcement in the Rajya Sabha on 5 August 2019: Article 370 and Article 35A, which accorded a special status under the Indian Constitution to the state of Jammu and Kashmir since 1947, stood abrogated. The erstwhile state would now be divided into two separate union territories (and thus be under New Delhi's supervision): J&K and Ladakh. Ever since, barring fleeting curfew relaxations, when a nervous government appeared to be testing the troubled waters by selectively opening schools, shops, clinics and banks, the state has been under an oppressive lockdown, particularly the sensitive Kashmir Valley. The government has bent its formidable propaganda machines to the task of signalling that all is well. But no one is buying the carefully chosen photos and video bites. National Security Adviser Ajit Doval was filmed having a lively chat with poker-faced locals, but it looked so stagey, it backfired.

Although the constitutional validity of the abrogation of Article 370 and Article 35A was upheld by the Supreme Court in December 2023, it remained obfuscated in raging contentiousness, with several eminent legal jurists disagreeing with its seminal arguments.

Be that as it may, every Indian needs to be worried by the move, whether or not they live in J&K. Why did the government lie to the people of India and particularly the people of J&K that its massive deployment of troops (estimated to be 40,000, in addition to the existing contingent of 700,000) was a counter-terrorism measure against a potential cross-border jihadi plot to massacre the Amarnath yatra pilgrims? The large-scale army movement had caused great consternation, and there was much speculation about the real reasons for it. One of the theories was that Article 370 was to be annulled—a plan that has featured repeatedly in the BJP's election manifesto (even if it was anti-Constitutional without the state assembly's acquiescence, which would have been impossible to get). Several BJP leaders had declared that Article 370 was 'sacrilegious', an impediment to 'national integration'. But the question remains: why indulge in the psychological manipulation of a fearful populace?

It is not an incidental matter that J&K was India's only Muslim-majority state. Its people had chosen mainstream politics to a separatist leadership's goal of independence, with its pro-Pakistan tilt. But the BJP had lost every last drop of that goodwill—perhaps it never wanted that goodwill. The opportunistic alliance between the PDP and BJP was, at its core, ideologically incompatible, and so they were constantly indulging in mutual recriminations. This only aggravated local disenchantment in the Kashmir Valley with the state political leadership, and had dire consequences. 8 July 2016 would prove to be a turning point in the Kashmir crisis. Burhan Wani, a twenty-two-year-old commander of the terrorist organisation Hizbul Mujahideen, who had become the poster boy of Kashmiri angst and spiralling militancy, was killed in a swift security operation. Wani had captured the public imagination through online entrapment, invigorating the restless unemployed youth to take to arms. The tinder-box exploded. A reported half a million grieving Kashmiris attended Wani's funeral prayers. The summer of 2016 soon became an interminable nightmare, as daily stone-pelting protests mounted despite a fifty-day-long curfew. The government, of course, treated it as a 'mere law and order problem'. By 31 August 2016, the end of the curfew, ninety-one people were killed, 12,000 injured and over 1,100 were either partially or fully blinded by pellet guns. Kashmir would not be the same again for a long while. The Indian state's predisposition to a muscular solution to the emotional distrust in the Valley was never going to work. The abrogation of Article 370, which happened three years later, was the last straw.

The principal stakeholders in Kashmir's politics were reduced to being prisoners in their own backyard. Former J&K chief minister Omar Abdullah met Governor Satyapal Malik to understand what was going on. Months later, along with his father Farooq Abdullah and Mehbooba Mufti (all three are former chief ministers of the state of J&K), he was still in detention and his Twitter timeline eerily silent (the Abdullahs have since been released). The draconian J&K Public Safety Act had been deployed to keep them prisoners. Common citizens were also picked up and detained in preventive custody.[296] Even local inspirational hero and IAS topper Shah Faesal was put under detention. Some BJP politicians expressed delight at the prospect of marrying 'beautiful, fair Kashmiri girls'—the discourse had turned perverse and misogynistic. Large sections of Indians even celebrated the brutal blockade.

Anyone with even a minor following in Kashmir appears to have been incarcerated. Serious political analysts have been relying on foreign media rather than local journalists to understand the public mood in Kashmir, which is at a new low, even given the long history of mishandling that the region has known.

Prime Minister Modi had initially raised hopes that he would do better than the UPA did by reiterating Vajpayee's healing-touch politics of '*Insaniyat, Jamhooriyat, Kashmiriyat*' (humanity, democracy and Kashmiri identity). As history shows, he did not follow through. J&K is bubbling with a simmering anger that is both unprecedented and unreported. The government may gradually restore landlines, mobile telephony, internet access and satellite television. Curfew will be eased. But there are many people in the newly instituted union territory who no longer trust India. The damage may well be irreversible.

While life in Kashmir was brought to a standstill, Modi lined up a repeat of his razzle-dazzle Madison Square Garden show of 2015. In Houston, USA, the cleverly hashtagged #HowdyModi was an even bigger success. US President Donald Trump turned up, giving it the American imprimatur (and Trump had the Indian American vote bank rooting for him). #HowdyModi trended globally, even as 7 million Indians continued to be locked down in Kashmir, forced to remain indoors out of fear and cut off from communication with the world outside.

The second term of the NDA has been relentless. Emboldened by an aggressive win at the hustings, the Hindu Rashtra plan had been on fast forward. Following the annulment of Article 370, Modi and Shah next introduced the Citizenship Amendment Act (CAA). This blatantly anti-Muslim law saw the largest and most sustained protests ever in the last six years. India's multicultural diversity, its religious pluralism was being effectively destroyed, and it appeared that its citizens had finally shaken off the shock-induced stupor that had beset them. The CAA fast-tracked citizenship for illegal immigrants and cross-border refugees who were Hindus, Christians, Buddhists, Parsees, Jains and Sikhs (residing in India before 2015), but it excluded Muslims fleeing religious persecution on the grounds that they belonged to Muslim-majority countries. It was a specious argument, and legally untenable (the matter is pending in the Supreme Court). Firstly, there are Muslims facing extreme prejudice in several neighbouring countries (Rohingya Muslims in Myanmar; Shias, Baluchistanis and Ahmadis in Pakistan; Hazaras in Afghanistan; Uyghur Muslims in China). The law also overlooked Tamil refugees by expressly leaving Sri Lanka out of its ambit. Secondly, by introducing a religious criterion into the law, the CAA challenged India's secularism as enshrined in the Constitution.

Amit Shah called illegal immigrants 'termites' that ought to be thrown into the Bay of Bengal, clearly alluding to Bangladeshi Muslims—a key propaganda factor in the ethnic politics of Assam and the communal hotbed of West Bengal, two key states in BJP's blueprint of electoral politics. With the National Register of Citizens (NRC) being implemented in Assam, the state was already faced with the prospect of almost 2 million people being rendered stateless, of families being sundered on account of insubstantial documents.[297] The NRC is a government process mandated by the Supreme Court to identify infiltrators who must be either deported or kept in detention centres in Assam. Amit Shah then announced that the NRC project would be implemented all over India to flush out 'illegal immigrants'. '*Aap chronology samajhiye*' (Understand the chronology), he said. CAA will define who can be a citizen if they do not have documents (not Muslims), and then the National Population Register (NPR) will flush out people who do not have documents—a transparent method to exclude Muslims from assumed citizenship of India as well as to reassure non-Muslim citizens that they have nothing to fear. So naked was the phrase in its intent that it set off scores of memes.[298] The fear among the Muslims was legitimate. The wife of a celebrity Muslim social commentator told me, 'We are scared like never before.'

In real terms, Indian Muslim citizens, even those who had voted in several national elections, could find themselves disenfranchised if they did not have the right documents to establish their residence in India before the stipulated cut-off dates. There was panic all around. The communal mercury in India was rising rapidly. The prime minister added fuel to the fire. Modi said that those who had taken to the streets in protest 'could be identified by their clothes', alluding to the fact that Muslims were being marked. The BJP, of course, claimed that the CAA was in accordance with their 2019 manifesto.

Even as civil society organised large-scale protests across the country—and Muslims finally poured out into the streets—prominent Muslim voices fell silent. Every household, one assumes, has a hardcore Bollywood Khan junkie. But Shah Rukh Khan, Aamir Khan, Salman Khan and Saif Ali Khan were quiet. These men have, between them, played Asoka, Bhuvan, Bajrangi Bhaijaan and Langda Tyagi, their raging popularity making them a symbol of India's secular tapestry. Then again, it has not been easy to live with a Muslim surname in post-2014 India, and why should the burden always be on the Khans to speak up? They have, in the past, been subjected to hate campaigns that have targeted their commercial releases and brand endorsements.

In response to the new threat, India's campuses came alive. Faiz Ahmad Faiz's revolutionary poem (against military dictatorship in Pakistan) *Hum Dekhenge* rang out loud among students across the nation. They have been threatened and brutalised intermittently, but have not been silenced. Yet.

Since May 2014, the psychological ghettoisation of Muslims in India has begun in right earnest. This othering will soon have a physical infrastructure in the form of detention centres (in Assam[299] and those already under construction in other states[300]). All those who fail the dual NRC/CAA test will be prisoners in that barricaded compound. Too many of us had foolishly believed that the brutal murder of Mohammad Akhlaq in Dadri, Uttar Pradesh, in 2015 was an isolated example of mob savagery. It proved to be nothing of the sort, spiralling into serial killing triggered by rumours of beef-eating, cattle-trading, child-kidnapping or random theft. Bloodthirsty revanchists posted videos on social media of their hapless victims. When a popular television-friendly face of the BJP, Jayant Sinha, garlanded a lynching accused, the crime finally had official sanction. He was not punished or reprimanded in any manner. Presumably, the Khans were reading the writing on the wall in choosing to be mum.

If Bollywood is the popular culture hub of India, corporate India is the heart of wealth-creation in the country: no government, whether left-leaning or free-market advocate, can afford to be dismissive of them. But post 2014, India's billionaire club has become, by and large, a bunch of supine cheerleaders. When veteran India Inc. captain Rahul Bajaj castigated the government for shoehorning India by creating fear, the BJP's response was a vicious troll-back. I saw a puny BJP spokesperson irascibly talk down to one of India's most respected entrepreneurs, Kiran Mazumdar-Shaw.

India Inc. is not alone. Authors, intellectuals, artistes, activists: they are all being subjected to flagrant threats by an unsparing, intolerant State.

The Delhi assembly election results in January 2020 assumed humongous import in the public mind in the context of the anti-CAA agitation. Modi invoked his perpetual obsession, Pakistan, and Uttar Pradesh Chief Minister Yogi Adityanath sniffed anti-Hindu conspiracies all around. Clearly, these macho men of the Right had been rattled by the fearless defiance of the daadis (grandmothers) of Shaheen Bagh, who had been stubbornly protesting the CAA for months. A tiny patch of the city near Okhla occupied the national consciousness. Sympathetic protest sites came up across the country. The public show of dissent made headlines across the world. Bilkis Bano, the eighty-two-year-old protestor who was the face of Shaheen Bagh, made *Time* magazine's '100 most influential people of 2020' list.[301] The grandmothers so rattled Amit Shah, BJP's chief strategist, that he urged Delhi voters to transmit an electric current so strong through the EVMs that it would reach Shaheen Bagh directly and incinerate it. It was a chilling threat, and from the country's home minister, no less.

But then, the country had been marching to this point for a while. In June 2014, IT executive Mohsin Shaikh was lynched in Pune on the suspicion that he had posted a morphed photo on Facebook.[302] Pune, that tranquil city of aspirational middle-class residents and retired pensioners. I grew up there, and remember it as a place of social harmony and genteel hospitality.

Shaikh's lynching received little attention from a media that was doing the salsa with the BJP. His murder was part of a pattern of hate and violence that had been growing since 2014, and should have constantly occupied the media's attention. By the end of Modi's first tenure, there had been roughly thirty-three lynchings, several of them videotaped for social media consumption. Through it all, India's prime minister said nothing, other than an occasional homily. The mainstream media, with a few honourable exceptions, played it down. And India simply 'moved on'.

In June 2019, exactly five years after Shaikh's murder in Pune, and just a few weeks after the BJP's second triumph, a young man was brutally thrashed in Jharkhand.[303] A hysterical mob shot a video of it, to the sound of laugher and abuse and a call to chant 'Jai Shri Ram'. Tabrez Ansari died a few days later. The pattern was familiar by now. In cosmopolitan Mumbai, a Muslim taxi driver was similarly harassed—'Jai Shri Ram' had been converted by venomous bigots into a slogan of hate.[304] Sometime later, a retired army captain, who fought for his country, was mercilessly beaten to death in Amethi, following an altercation with local thugs.[305] His name was Amanullah. In another instance of the raging anti-Muslim narrative, a man demanded that his Zomato food delivery be brought only by a Hindu scooterist.[306] The company refused to back down and a gobsmacked social media community fought back, but the hate confetti found a large, willing audience. An aggressive majoritarian strain has begun to see Muslims as intruders in their own homeland.

Vigilante mobs now patrol India's streets in search of cattle traders and beef sellers, or even just bearded men going about their lives. They are subjected to humiliating interrogation and frequent harm. These mobs are the new extra-legal institution, and have abundant political support from the BJP.[307] The communal tension they stir up helps the right-wing party's electoral prospects, while being explained away as sporadic violence with no direct connection to the party.[308] The lynchings attract only transitory media attention and public scrutiny, but the local distrust and animosities they engender endure.

The ghettoisation of Muslims in Juhapura locality in Ahmedabad is part of the much-lionised Gujarat model. As author Christophe Jaffrelot writes, 'Like most other areas of Ahmedabad, Juhapura accommodated Hindus and Muslims when it was established in 1973 as a colony for Sabarmati river flood victims. Riot after riot, Hindus left and more Muslims fled for safety to Juhapura and could not return to their original homes, a process fuelled by the Disturbed Areas Act. Currently, it is home to more than 3 lakh Muslims and Ahmedabad has more Muslims at its periphery than in the old city, their traditional home.'[309] What we are seeing now is psychological apartheid on a pan-India scale.

As India celebrated its seventy-third Independence Day in 2020, it had slipped into a dark abyss.[310] The idea of a secular India, enshrined in the Indian Constitution, is being trashed as a construct of the liberal elite, which Modi caricatures as the 'Khan Market gang'. Nothing could be sadder for one of the most diverse countries in the world. Socialism, liberalism, tolerance and progressiveness are all on the recess. India is seeing the beginnings of a regressive era that could well be irreversible.

To ensure that we do not become a tinpot dictatorship or a quasi-religious theocracy, the Congress will have to galvanise the people of India into believing in the country's founding vision: a dynamic, modern, inclusive and democratic society. It won't be easy. In a post-truth age, reality has become hazy, and history has been the casualty. As also the Indian economy.

After six successive quarterly declines, former chief economic adviser Arvind Subramanian warned that India was in the midst of a 'Great Slowdown'. And yet, an arrogant BJP believed that India could do without Amazon founder Jeff Bezos's US$ 1 billion investment in his e-commerce venture, and snubbed him on his India visit. Political hubris coupled with myopic vision is usually the perfect recipe for an economic catastrophe.

A well-to-do South Mumbai entrepreneur, once a fervid advocate of Modinomics, who had voted BJP in both 2014 and 2019, told me, 'I just closed my seventy-four-year-old family business formally. The most painful part was telling my workers of several years to leave. Thanks to Mr Modi, I had to give them azaadi.' I nodded sympathetically, biting back a 'you asked for it.'

Senior industry leaders like Rahul Bajaj and Kiran Mazumdar-Shaw, who warned of the impending cataclysm and the 'atmosphere of fear' that choked open discussion, were told that they were damaging India's global brand. The fact is that global headwinds were gathering ferocity, the US-China tariff war was hotting up, the political trouble in the Middle East could escalate oil prices, Brexit would certainly impact the sluggish European Union and, in general, the world economy forecast was bearish. India was in serious trouble. In the midst of this gathering storm, one of Modi's celebrity supporters and Dalal Street mogul Rakesh Jhunjhunwala declared that India's growth story was being hindered by its democracy. Once upon a time in India, this would have led to a major showdown. But not now.

The government seems to have misread the problem confronting the economy, which was actually a demand contraction created by demonetisation and GST execution. Instead, it was fixing the supply side; it was like giving someone a foot massage as a cure for migraine. By appropriating Rs

1.76 lakh crore from the RBI and giving it as a tax bonanza to the corporate sector, the government missed an opportunity to boost public expenditure, increase MNREGA outlay and help the MSME sector, all of which would have augmented demand. Instead, most likely, industry absorbed the higher earnings as retained profits, given the fact that capacity utilisation was at a mere 75 per cent. The economy was adrift, but showmanship was on a roll, as was the communal agenda.

It was an odd image: US President Donald Trump was at Mahatma Gandhi's Sabarmati Ashram in Ahmedabad, Gujarat, during his maiden India visit. At that time, Delhi was rocked by communal violence. People were killing each other, but both Trump and Modi had more urgent things to attend to: Namaste Trump, a massive public assembly at the inauguration of the giant cricket stadium in Ahmedabad that could house 100,000 spectators. This was Modi's return gift to Trump for the bedazzling Howdy Modi promotional in Houston just five months earlier. Both leaders were using taxpayers' monies to indulge in political campaigning. Both pretended not to have noticed the country's burning capital.

The algorithm of religious divisiveness has been delivering electoral windfalls for the BJP. The Muslim vote of 14 per cent, once considered the Congress's catchment area, had been rendered irrelevant by a massive consolidation of the majority vote. It was a consolidation that required constant fodder.

In January 2020, the BJP had suffered an ignominious rout in the Delhi elections (winning just eight seats in the seventy-seat assembly). One of their defeated candidates was Kapil Mishra, a new entrant who outshouted the BJP's most venomous loudmouths. Mishra swore revenge on the protesting members of the Muslim community who were standing up against the

CAA, NPR and NRC.[311] What followed on 23 February 2020 was not a spontaneous communal riot but an orchestrated splintering of an area.[312] It was political retribution. At least fifty-three people died, seventy suffered gunshot wounds and over 200 were injured.

Initially, it was hard to believe that a riot could happen in Delhi in this age. Some thought fake inflammatory videos were being posted by rogues floating about on Twitter and WhatsApp. Soon, however, the horror unravelled, including the horrendous footage of bruised and battered young men being forced to sing the national anthem by menacing policemen. In the age of social media and instant communication, videos of unspeakable ugliness began to surface. The police, supposed guardians of the city, were either disinterested spectators or willing accessories to the riots.

The ruling party was undoubtedly complicit. Parvesh Verma, its MP, had said, 'The people from Shaheen Bagh will enter homes and kill daughters and sisters.' At an election rally in January 2020, Union Minister Anurag Thakur had exhorted BJP supporters, '*Desh ke gaddaron ko*' (traitors to this country), and they had filled in, '*Goli maaro saalon ko*' (shoot those traitors). That clarion call was being executed by some.

Journalists were attacked and threatened, and some had to prove they were Hindu to survive. A police constable was murdered, even as religious shrines were ransacked. Both communities rioted, but it is apparent that Muslims were disproportionately impacted. Amit Shah, responsible for internal security as the home minister, had nothing to say: no public denunciation, no call for peace, not even a banal Twitter post with a bromide condemnation.

The prime minister, of course, was busy ensuring that broccoli samosas were palatable to Trump's Anglo-Saxon taste buds. By the time the president of the world's oldest democracy boarded his Air Force One return flight, the capital of the world's largest democracy was making headlines globally for the riots and for the State complicity or impotency in controlling them.[313]

That India has mainstreamed violence as an instant remedy for political grievances in the last six years must worry its 138 crore citizens. A dangerous subversion of civil liberties is gathering pace. The media has buckled. Even the judiciary, always the last bulwark against executive overreach, has not been effective in controlling these blatant human rights violations. Meanwhile, the industrialisation of hate puts some political careers on the fast track to success. That is India's tragedy.

But even as India was reeling from the Delhi riots and its aftermath, a diabolical vector had quietly entered her shores. The novel coronavirus, SARS-Cov-2 or COVID-19, was in India.

Most outlier events have a visual symbol. The end of World War II had the US Navy sailor George Mendonsa swooping up a nurse in his arms at Times Square, New York, while the Vietnam War had the nightmare picture of a young Vietnamese child, crying, naked, running for her life, even as dark clouds of toxic smoke, an aftermath of American fighter jets bombing her village, mushroomed into the sky. Similarly, the COVID-19 pandemic has created two indelible images in India. The first, of an inconsolable woman carrying her inanimate three-year-old son in her arms, breaking down, unable to find a single ambulance to take her child to a hospital in Bihar. The second representation, a little later.

The first COVID-19 case in India was registered on 30 January 2020 in Kerala. The Central government had been extraordinarily disinterested in the unfolding epidemic in China, a country with which India shares a contentious and amorphous 4,000 km border. It was a monumental error. And inexplicable. China is India's second-largest trading partner. Even as the death toll in the Chinese city of Wuhan was burgeoning, Modi was hosting Trump at a crowded mega-event in Ahmedabad. When the World Health Organisation (WHO) finally began admitting that the threat was serious, the BJP was casually looking the other way. Uttar Pradesh Chief Minister Yogi Adityanath prescribed yoga as a sure-shot remedy, while the even less scientifically tempered prescribed cow urine. Within two weeks, a hundred countries were infected.

A somnolent WHO, still smitten by Chinese red-carpet hospitality, declared a global pandemic only on 11 March, and India's first COVID-19-related death was recorded a day later. By that time, Europe and America had already become global hotspots. Epidemiologists made grim forecasts based on their mathematical models. But the Ministry of Health, evidently in Alice-in-Wonderland mode, said on 13 March that there was no medical emergency in India. Eleven days later, on 24 March, Modi declared a national lockdown that matched those in repressive societies like Syria and Rwanda. At that time, perhaps out of relief that the government had recognised India's precarious position, the move was lauded. There were about 500 cases recorded then; as of 17 October, at 7,432,680 infections, the figure looked set to cross that of the US, which held the No. 1 position, and 112,998 people had been officially declared as having died of COVID-19 in India.

To be fair, no government could have been prepared for this unprecedented global health emergency. But the NDA did not take a holistic view of the matter or act quickly. A few statistics reveal India's risks: it has just one hospital bed for 2,000 people, 350 million live below the poverty line, 42 million migrant workers struggle to eke out a subsistence living and the country's public health systems are frail. But Prime Minister Modi seemed oblivious to these facts when he ordered 1.35 billon people into self-quarantine with a four-hour notice. Within days, frantic migrant workers were on a mass exodus. Without their daily income, hungry and homeless, the migrants took to the national highways, heading for their villages. According to researchers, nearly a 1000 people died[314] during what came to be called the 'migrant crisis'. A road safety NGO collected data, which showed that 198 migrant workers had died due to road accidents while they were walking back home.[315] It was the largest migration of human beings since India's partition.[316]

This crisis was a stark reminder that the trickle-down growth model had failed. The disadvantaged had no social security safety nets. The government did nothing to help them—an apathy that stunned even its most trenchant critics. And once the lockdown was lifted, the government just washed its hands of the whole thing. It was India's moment of greatest shame.

The government's attention was focused on entirely different things. The missionary group Tablighi Jamaat had congregated in Nizamuddin, Delhi, for a religious gathering. They had been given travel visas despite the fact that, in a Malaysian mosque that many had visited earlier, there had been a dramatic spread of the virus. The Jamaat displayed great irresponsibility, it is true. But the BJP's barefaced exploitation of the Markaz incident to increase the communal temperature against the Muslims was repugnant.[317] It is even more appalling when you consider that, while the Jamaat event was held between 1 and 15 March, on 13 March, government health officials had stated that the novel coronavirus was not a health emergency in the country. There were a number of Hindu religious events of equal and greater magnitude that were not questioned,[318] nor were the attendees tested. The Jamaat congregation proved to be a virus hotspot, but this was also because they were at the time the only group that was being actively traced and tested. None of this excuses a large gathering during a pandemic, but it is important to record the communal propaganda that was spun around a health emergency.

The Hindutva project refused to pause even during humanity's gravest crisis. Muslims were accused of waging #CoronaJihad against Indians. A BJP MLA posted a video cautioning people not to buy vegetables from Muslim vendors. Soon after, some sections of the mainstream media, propagandists of the government, went berserk when two Hindu monks were lynched in Palghar, Maharashtra. They claimed it was a religious murder by a Muslim mob—this was untrue. The BJP was applying social distancing with 180 million people.

The government was flummoxed by the human lives versus livelihood binary; they have been able to handle neither. India's GDP collapsed by a massive 23 per cent between April and June 2020, with the year likely to end at 9 per cent negative GDP according to the RBI. The county's pre-COVID-19 GDP was already in a funk at 4.5 per cent. Coming after the demonetisation and GST disasters, the lockdown was a huge blow to the economy. The human cost of this economic devastation may ultimately outnumber the fatalities caused by the virus. Many of those who survive death will live in wretched poverty. The Great Depression of 1931 eviscerated societies, and India is headed in that direction now.

Meanwhile, the hugely hyped PM's Citizen Assistance and Relief in Emergency Situations Fund (PM CARES Fund) was launched on 28 March 2020, as soon as India went into its first long lockdown. The fund was cleverly named to spotlight India's CEO, as has been the wont since 2014. It is obvious that this had been on the drawing board for a while. Suddenly, high-profile CEOs, Bollywood personalities, celebrities and big industrialists were making sizeable contributions to the fund and tweeting about it. The prime minister was thanking them prodigiously too. Public sector firms were coerced into making contributions. Now, India already has the Prime Minister's National Relief Fund for meeting such contingencies. What was the need for another fund—especially one that was not subject to either RTI or a CAG audit? It appeared very odd. But this was not a government the public could hold to account.

Which brings us to the second image of the COVID-19 pandemic in India. Safoora Zargar, a twenty-seven-year-old doctorate student at Jamia Millia Islamia, was arrested under the oppressive Unlawful Activities (Prevention) Act (UAPA) for sedition and sabotaging national interests. She had been at the forefront of the anti-CAA campaign. Zargar was in the second trimester of her pregnancy. A young, pregnant woman was jailed during a pandemic, endangering her life and that of the unborn child, only because she disagreed with the government in power.

COVID-19 has speeded up, not slowed down, the government's attack on its ideological adversaries. The young firebrand and former JNU student leader Umar Khalid has been arrested under the UAPA for being a key conspirator in the riots. It is on record that he was appealing for social tranquillity and togetherness during the anti-CAA protests. Ironically, he is a member of a group called United Against Hate. Needless to say, BJP leaders such as Mishra, Thakur and Verma, who screamed out incendiary hate speeches were not on the chargesheet. So flagrant is the farce, it would have been laughable had it not been so chilling. Among those who find themselves being mentioned (although not yet accused, at the time of going to press) as accessory to the mob violence are Swaraj Abhiyan leader Yogendra Yadav, Delhi University professor Apoorvanand, respected economist Jayati Ghosh and CPM leader Sitaram

Yechury. Left-leaning activists are clearly a target—a glaring political prejudice that no one is bothering to hide.

Even as China's credibility as a responsible superpower was taking a battering for its reckless export of COVID-19 to an unsuspecting world, the Asian giant was barefaced about its expansionist intentions. Besides Taiwan, Hong Kong and the South China Sea, where it was flexing its muscles, China had amassed massive troops along the Line of Actual Control at eastern Ladakh in India in May 2020. It had wantonly violated the status quo on border agreements reached between the two countries in 1993. On 15 June 2020, the stand-off took a violent turn at Galwan valley, and twenty Indian soldiers were killed in hand-to-hand combat (India claimed forty-three Chinese casualties, which was denied by Beijing). As national outrage escalated, Prime Minister Modi called an all-party meeting to assure Indians that all was under control. Then, instead of delicately handling a diplomatic conflict, he played to the gallery with characteristic braggadocio: 'No Chinese troops entered India or occupied any of its posts.' While TV channels went berserk promoting this muscular aggression, the Chinese saw a big political dividend in the PM's tactless and frivolous machismo. China happily staked claim to the Galwan valley, forcing an embarrassed PMO to hastily issue a clarification. Governance is Modi's Achilles heel, as evidenced in the difficult summer of 2020.

The pandemic has brought on a number of difficult confrontations. It has taken a heavy toll on those with anxiety or other mental health problems. One of India's brightest young actors, Sushant Singh Rajput, a self-made star in the cut-throat universe of Bollywood, committed suicide on 14 June 2020. The loss felt especially poignant in a world changed by a virus. Then, in a series of grotesque twists, which included drugs, former girlfriends, Rajput's family in Bihar, two camps at war in the film industry, television anchors pushing conspiracy theories of murder and black magic, Sushant's death became India's national fixation. It dwarfed the rising pandemic figures, a crumbling economy and a broken system. A young girl and her family were subjected to a vicious campaign of vilification. Private WhatsApp messages were broadcast on prime-time news. State investigative agencies deliberately leaked selective information to keep the sordid saga alive.[319] With his death eventually confirmed as suicide, all these theories were proven wrong. As it turned out, with state elections due in the state of Bihar in November, Rajput's death had been reduced to a sorry tool.[320]

In other news, the offices of the human rights organisation Amnesty International were forced to close down, causing global outrage and sealing India's new image as a democracy on the brink of collapse. Amnesty India's bank accounts were frozen, forcing it to lay off 140 employees. From the situation in Kashmir to the Delhi riots, the organisation had been steadily holding up a mirror to India, which is probably what led to a backlash from the government. Its former executive director Aakaar Patel, a bitter critic of PM Modi, was arrested.[321]

But human rights, of course, were not on the government's agenda. That might explain the bizarre case of my friend Salman Soz's father, Saifuddin Soz, a former Union minister, who was under arrest in Kashmir. Soz's wife had filed a habeas corpus petition challenging his detention. In an absolutely stunning disclosure in the Supreme Court, the J&K government said in a written affidavit that it had never arrested him. They were actually claiming that Soz remained home-bound out of choice for one year! This, in spite of the fact that there were videos on national television showing armed guards preventing him from stepping out of his house.

In what has come to be called the 'New India', a government could do such a thing and then lie about it to India's highest court.[322] In fact, the Supreme Court itself made national headlines for demanding a formal apology from lawyer Prashant Bhushan for criticising it in a series of tweets. Everyone is now easily offended. Ultimately, the contempt of court case saw closure with Bhushan paying a token one-rupee fine for his supposed indiscretion.

Earlier, on 9 November 2019, in its historic, if wildly criticised, judgement on the disputed Babri Masjid–Ram Janmabhoomi site in Ayodhya, the Supreme Court had observed that there was 'unlawful destruction' of the mosque. It called the 6 December 1992 demolition an egregious wrong. Less than a year later, on 30 September 2020, in the criminal conspiracy case of the mosque's demolition, where the accused were high-profile BJP veterans such as L.K. Advani, Uma Bharati and Murli Manohar Joshi (among thirty-two others), the special CBI court acquitted everyone. It stated that the mayhem and madness were spontaneous; it was not a planned decimation of the sixteenth-century monument, which had been razed to the ground with stones, hammers and pitchforks. The communal riots that followed killed 2,000 people. The CBI's investigation and prosecution of the case was, to put it mildly, disastrous. India's criminal justice system was now an appalling burlesque of broken procedures. This, then, is the New India.

The *Washington Post* masthead famously says 'Democracy dies in darkness'; in India it dies in the daylight too.

Then Hathras happened. And it felt like a point of no return. A young nineteen-year-old Dalit girl was allegedly gang-raped and murdered by upper-caste men. She had provided details about the criminals who had raped her, cut her tongue and fractured her spinal cord. But demonstrating a callousness and crudeness that was stupefying even in this changed world, the Uttar Pradesh police cremated her body late at night despite her grieving family's pleas. They did not get an opportunity to say goodbye. The young woman died probably because she was born into the wrong caste. Her ugly death proves India is facing a civilisational crisis, no less.

On a more practical level, it is also facing a crisis of governance. In his national address only a few months earlier, Modi had sounded triumphant about India's handling of the virus. Yet, here we are at the end of October 2020 with nearly the highest number of cases in the world. The government has failed India.

And to add to my personal heartbreak, the Congress is failing India as well.

My journey with the Indian National Congress had formally begun sixteen years ago. In the last week of February 2004, my heart pounding with breathless excitement, I drove to 10, Janpath to meet the Congress president, Mrs Sonia Gandhi. Just a day earlier, I was playing tennis at the Willingdon Club, Mumbai, when a phone call interrupted my topspin forehand with the information that Sonia Gandhi was keen to listen to new ideas from non-political communication professionals. I was thrilled beyond imagination at the thought of meeting Mrs Gandhi. The security guards frisked me several times, but I did not mind. I had driven past the famous address a thousand times when I worked in Delhi in the mid-1980s, and often wondered what its occupants were all about. I admired their valiant sacrifice, dignified disposition and several contributions to our country. I was a Rajiv Gandhi fan; the night he was assassinated on 21 May 1991 had left me broken. I was a Congress supporter for its incredible history, illustrious stalwarts, its fight for

India's freedom and its liberal, inclusive ideology. At the time, the opinion polls were fairly unanimous that the Atal Bihari Vajpayee-led NDA, with its India Shining marketing, would have an easy victory. The forecast was a double-digit embarrassment for the Congress-led UPA. These were the circumstances in which I was ushered into the drawing room of 10, Janpath. A few moments later, Mrs Gandhi entered.

'It is very tough, this election,' she said looking genuinely worried.

But I was an eternal optimist. Because ultimately humanity lives by hope. Or maybe I was too overwhelmed by the moment to add to her hopelessness.

'I think you are going to win,' I said.

Acknowledgements

I love writing, and if you have reached the end of the book, you will probably agree that I am terribly opinionated. Sitting on the fence, playing safe and pussyfooting around, is never an option, especially when a lot of edifices around you are disintegrating. If you are in politics, and more so in Indian politics, the middle-ground is non-existent. Any attempt at being reasonable, candid and opening oneself to an alternative viewpoint is considered sacrilegious. In television debates, it is called committing political hara-kiri. Thus, I am delighted that, in Westland, I have had an amazing publisher who, more than anything else, invigorated my spirits by asking me *not* to temper my outrageousness. Karthika V.K., despite the awful lockdown and several deadline compulsions, read my book at one go and gave it a big thumbs up. Coming from probably one of India's finest editors, I was both overwhelmed and as pleased as a puppy with two tails. Then the meticulous Ajitha G.S. took over, and I understood what minutiae meant. Her constructive suggestions, circumspect eye for detail and extraordinary promptness was mind-boggling. If this book captures facts and figures that cannot be challenged, and a seamless flow in narrative, then it is Ajitha who deserves the accolades. I remain humbled. My gratitude also to the entire Westland team, as well as the book's typesetter, Rajinder Ganju, for his promptness. And how can I forget the matchless genius who generously introduced me to Karthika! He is a versatile writer who I believe could be the next Einstein of modern journalism, the inimitable Kapil S. Komireddi. He made this relationship possible.

I acknowledge the following publications, where I have written articles occasionally, for the use of content from those pieces wherever relevant in the book: the *Times of India*, the *Indian Express*, *National Herald*, *Huffington Post* and *Yahoo*. I also referenced Dr Montek Singh Ahluwalia's book *Backstage: The Story Behind India's High Growth Years*, Yashwant Sinha's *India Unmade: How the Narendra Modi Government Broke the Economy*, written with Aditya Sinha, and Pooja Mehra's *The Lost Decade (2008-18): How India's Growth Story Devolved into Growth Without a Story*, while writing the chapter on the Indian economy.

While I was gathering my thoughts about the book and had commenced structuring it, India went into a national lockdown in March 2020 following the global outbreak of the novel coronavirus. That made working from home the only option, sans distractions. Only, I neutralised the sudden windfall that had emerged considerably by getting infected with the coronavirus in the month of May 2020. But once I healed, I got down to the task of writing the book, like a man possessed. During that time, it is my wife Pallavi who, besides enduring my insufferable presence 24x7, gave me her ideas and thoughts, quite different from giving me a piece of her mind. It has helped. I rarely win an argument with her, and it has been three decades of democracy. My daughters Maithili and Mohini kept reminding me that deadlines are not meant to be broken. I adhered to their advisory like a rare obedient child.

My executive assistant Kamini Bangera slogged away without an iota of complaint when I made irrational demands of her time. In fact, she told me that I was a great boss. Following that adulation, I promised her I would mention her in the acknowledgements. As you can see, I am quite reliable (albeit the Congress party does not think so). Shachi Nelli, a fiery millennial with a mind of her own, has helped me with some data and research, which are thankfully not her own but from original sources. And finally, thank you, my very dear altruistic readers for the great unravelling of your purse. Your magnanimous gesture is good for the soul of India.

Notes

Scan this QR code to access the notes.

About the Author

Sanjay Jha is a former national spokesperson of the Indian National Congress party. A former banker and an internet entrepreneur, he began his political innings in 2004. He is the author of *My Illegitimate Son: A True Story* (2023) and *2024: India in Free Fall* (2024), and co-author of *The Superstar Syndrome: The Making of a Champion* (2013).

As a former managing editor and co-founder of CricketNext.com, Jha was at the forefront of those who warned about the looming Indian Premier League scam. He has been a frequent contributor to mainstream media publications such as *The Times of India*, *Deccan Herald* and *The Indian Express*. He appears regularly on television panels as a political analyst.

Jha lives in Mumbai with his wife, two daughters and a few dogs.

HarperCollins *Publishers* India

At HarperCollins India, we believe in telling the best stories and finding the widest readership for our books in every format possible. We started publishing in 1992; a great deal has changed since then, but what has remained constant is the passion with which our authors write their books, the love with which readers receive them, and the sheer joy and excitement that we as publishers feel in being a part of the publishing process.

Over the years, we've had the pleasure of publishing some of the finest writing from the subcontinent and around the world, including several award-winning titles and some of the biggest bestsellers in India's publishing history. But nothing has meant more to us than the fact that millions of people have read the books we published, and that somewhere, a book of ours might have made a difference.

As we look to the future, we go back to that one word—a word which has been a driving force for us all these years.

Read.

Harper Collins

HARPER PERENNIAL

HARPER BUSINESS

HARPER BLACK

हार्पर हिन्दी

HarperCollins *Children's Books*

HARPER DESIGN

Harper Sport